AF802677

Communities and Courts

The entanglement of law and religion is reiterated on a daily basis in India. and groups turn to the courts to seek positive recognition of their religiou sentiments, as well as a validation of their practices. Equally, courts have bec potent site of the play of conflicts and contradictions between religious group power thus not only arbiters conflicts but also defines what constitutes the ' demarcates its limits.

This volume argues that the relationship between law and religion is not competing sovereignties – as rational law moulding religion in its reformist v ligion defending its turf against secular incursions– but needs to be underst wider social and political canvas. The essays here demonstrate how questior pluralism, secularism, law and order, are all central to understanding how the the legal remain imbricated within each other in modern India. It will be of ir demics, researchers, and advanced students of Sociology, History, Political Scie

The chapters in this book were originally published as a special issue of *History and Culture.*

Manisha Sethi teaches at NALSAR University of Law, Hyderabad. She is t *Kafkaland: Law, Prejudice and Counterterrorism in India* (2014) and *Escapin Women Renouncers among Jains* (Routledge, 2012).

Communities and Courts

Religion and Law in Modern India

Edited by
Manisha Sethi

Routledge
Taylor & Francis Group
LONDON AND NEW YORK

First published 2022
by Routledge
2 Park Square, Milton Park, Abingdon, Oxon, OX14 4RN

and by Routledge
605 Third Avenue, New York, NY 10158

Routledge is an imprint of the Taylor & Francis Group, an informa business

© 2022 Taylor & Francis

All rights reserved. No part of this book may be reprinted or reproduced or utilised in any form or by any electronic, mechanical, or other means, now known or hereafter invented, including photocopying and recording, or in any information storage or retrieval system, without permission in writing from the publishers.

Trademark notice: Product or corporate names may be trademarks or registered trademarks, and are used only for identification and explanation without intent to infringe.

British Library Cataloguing-in-Publication Data
A catalogue record for this book is available from the British Library

ISBN13: 978-1-032-19558-2 (hbk)
ISBN13: 978-1-032-19559-9 (pbk)
ISBN13: 978-1-003-25977-0 (ebk)

DOI: 10.4324/9781003259770

Typeset in Minion Pro
by codeMantra

Publisher's Note
The publisher accepts responsibility for any inconsistencies that may have arisen during the conversion of this book from journal articles to book chapters, namely the inclusion of journal terminology.

Disclaimer
Every effort has been made to contact copyright holders for their permission to reprint material in this book. The publishers would be grateful to hear from any copyright holder who is not here acknowledged and will undertake to rectify any errors or omissions in future editions of this book.

Contents

Citation Information

The following chapters were originally published in *South Asian History and Culture*, volume 10, issue 2 (2019). When citing this material, please use the original page numbering for each article, as follows:

Chapter 1
Introduction – Communities and courts: religion and law in modern India
Manisha Sethi
South Asian History and Culture, volume 10 issue 2 (2019), pp. 109-123

Chapter 2
Framing religion in constitutional politics: a view from Indian Constitutional Law
Mathew John
South Asian History and Culture, volume 10, issue 2 (2019) pp. 124–135

Chapter 3
Ritual death in a secular state: the Jain practice of Sallekhana
Manisha Sethi
South Asian History and Culture, volume 10, issue 2 (2019) pp. 136–151

Chapter 4
Codification of Islamic Law in South Asia, or how not to do comparative law
Abhik Majumdar
South Asian History and Culture, volume 10, issue 2 (2019) pp. 152–166

Chapter 5
Shari'a politics, 'ulamā and Laity Ijtihād: fields of normativity and conviviality
Neshat Quaiser
South Asian History and Culture, volume 10, issue 2 (2019) pp. 167–186

Chapter 6
Religion, law and state policing: accusations, inquests and arbitration of religious conflicts in colonial India
M. Raisur Rahman
South Asian History and Culture, volume 10, issue 2 (2019) pp. 187–198

Chapter 7

The mosque as juristic person: law, public order and inter-religious disputes in India
Tanweer Fazal
South Asian History and Culture, volume 10, issue 2 (2019) pp. 199–211

Chapter 8

Art, law and the violence of offence taking
Malvika Maheshwari
South Asian History and Culture, volume 10, issue 2 (2019) pp. 212–225

Chapter 9

Secular moral/legal commitments revisited: an interlude by way of afterword
Sasheej Hegde
South Asian History and Culture, volume 10, issue 2 (2019) pp. 226–237

For any permission-related enquiries please visit:
http://www.tandfonline.com/page/help/permissions

Notes on Contributors

Tanweer Fazal Department of Sociology, University of Hyderabad, India.

Sasheej Hegde Department of Sociology, University of Hyderabad, India.

Mathew John Jindal Global Law School, Sonipat, India.

Malvika Maheshwari Department of Political Science, Ashoka University, Kundli, India.

Abhik Majumdar National Law University Odisha (NLUO), Cuttack, India.

Neshat Quaiser Department of Sociology, Jamia Millia Islamia, Delhi, India.

M. Raisur Rahman Department of History, Wake Forest University, Winston-Salem, USA.

Manisha Sethi NALSAR University of Law, Hyderabad, India.

Introduction – Communities and courts: religion and law in modern India

Manisha Sethi

One of the key characteristics of the modern condition is an increasing fetishization of law, whereby it has come to be the hegemonic framework for asserting one's claims and rights in an ever-increasing spectrum of everyday matters. Law becomes the vehicle by which religion is to be reformed and made consistent with modern values, and the mode too by which faith asserts its autonomy over its domain repels attempts to regulate and control it, and cast the world in its own image. This essay explores the imbrication of law and religion by examining the stream of cases in India and elsewhere – the hectic turning towards courts by communities and groups seeking positive recognition of their religious identities as well as validation of their practices. But it also argues that this relationship is not merely one of competing sovereignties, nor can it be understood by focussing on courts alone, and asks instead to place this relationship in the wider social and political canvas.

Defining religion through law

Definitional battles over religion have bedevilled sociology and anthropology for a long time.[1] Many foundational debates in the discipline congregated around the concept and field of what was marked off as Religion. Nonetheless, from the time Tylor proposed the belief in souls and spirit as a minimalist definition, no people were thought to inhabit so arid a moral universe as to be devoid of higher guiding light. One effect of this was the widespread understanding generally, and in the social sciences in particular that religion was analytically isolatable and bounded off from other sorts of experiences – the legal, the political, business, the aesthetic and so on. The former was attuned to the sacred, the holy, the transcendent – the latter to the quotidian. The classic proponent of such an understanding was Clifford Geertz who defined religion as that system of symbols that formulated general conceptions of a general order of existence.[2]

There have been calls such as W.C. Smith's persuasive, if rhetorical, appeal for scholars to abandon the category of religion altogether. Whilst Smith's was a plea to turn to the interior, almost unreachable experiences which he characterised as 'faith' over its external observable features he termed 'cumulative tradition',[3] Jonathan Z. Smith proclaimed that Religion was an "anthropological not a theological category".[4]

It was Talal Asad who insisted on religion's imbrication in the practices of power. Neither a system of symbols linked to the cosmic order nor the innermost convictions of the believers – religion for Asad is always contingent and created through authorising discourses which in the first place grant meaning to symbols. It is in post enlightenment juncture when the right to individual belief remains "the only legitimate space allowed to Christianity"[5] that the illusion of separation between religion and power takes hold.

Lawfare and religion

If religion is not an ahistorical abstraction comprehensible only through symbols but created and forged in the furnace of power, the law can be seen playing a key role in tempering it. It is one of the key discourses through which religion is constituted. Though the imbrication of law and religion is a feature as much of modern states with an avowed commitment to the separation of church and the state, as of 'sacred monarchies',[6] the heightened Juridification of religion and lawfare over rights, entitlements and identities designated as religious has been a distinctive feature of modern nation-states.[7] Indeed, one of the key characteristics of the modern condition has been identified by scholars as an increasing fetishization of law, whereby it becomes the hegemonic framework for asserting one's claims and rights in an ever-increasing spectrum of everyday matters, ranging from bodily intimacies to consumer and trade disputes. Law becomes too the vehicle by which religions are sought to be made consistent with "basic standards of human dignity and integrity",[8] and ironically the mode too by which faith asserts its autonomy over its domain, repels attempts to regulate and control it, and to cast the world in its own image.[9]

One's claims to belonging, and even the claim that what once belonged to was religious, the argument that one could live one's life by the rules of that group, and marking it off from other such groupings, are in the main today, legal claims, and not simply religious assertions. These bundled religio-legal subjectivities are produced in and through multiple modes of governance and law. The demand to be recognized by groups as a body of believers, or adherents of an independent religious collective, not merely a sect, constantly turns people in the direction of courts. Religious freedom – whose legal enshrinement seems to be the preeminent hallmark of modern nationstates – first of all, makes demands upon the state for recognition as a corporate body. American people of faith, notes one commentator, turn to the Supreme Court "rather than to God" in their search for legitimation: "They do not seem to be confident that if their religion is not recognized as such by the Supreme Court that it will still be a religion."[10]

So while religion seeks suzerainty and validation from courts, the latter are forced to respond to a range of questions, from whether Wicca or Rastafarianism are faiths to whether smoking cannabis qualifies as a Rastafarian religious ritual.[11] All of this not only requires the courts to determine whether 'rights' of religious peoples have been violated – 'Rights' being an essential corollary to spread of legalization and the rise of legal consciousness – but also simultaneously, to define what is properly religious, and what are the limits of religious freedom, the justifications for state intervention and so on. This means that a variety of social phenomena – and even individual predilections or 'beliefs' – are constantly measured against a legal understanding of what constitutes a religion. To take only one example, the European Court of Human Rights has become one of the most significant instruments of producing international legal discourse around religion, and rights that are seen to cluster around that category outlined in the Convention's articles 9 (freedom of religion) and 14 (prohibition of discrimination). While both are at the centre of the robust case law on the subject, it is in Article 9 that we can glean an understanding of Strasbourg's definition of religion. Clause 1 pertains to "the right to freedom of thought, conscience and religion" and clause 2 to the "freedom to manifest one's religion or beliefs". Only the first is absolute freedom, because according to the ECHR, "deeply held ideas and convictions that are forged in a person's individual conscience and cannot therefore in themselves prejudice public order".[12] Such a dichotomous conception of religion, locating the personal, inner faith as worthy of protection on the one hand, and external manifestations, somehow not really religion and thus amenable to restrictions on the other hand mirrors the anthropological commonsense – itself derived from Protestant ideas, as Asad would say – and is bound to produce a cultural hierarchy whereby privatized forms of religiosity are privileged over tangible, public expressions, more likely to be viewed as recalcitrant and in need of disciplining.[13]

In the US though a different trajectory has been charted. Sullivan has noted how, following the judgments in *Smith* (commonly called Peyote case) and *Hosanna-Tabor*, large coalitions of religious advocacy groups have demanded not only as integral to religious freedom, exemptions from laws which burden their religious practices, but also greater and greater "corporate jurisdictional autonomy from the state for religion". This turn away from the idea of "sincerely formed consciences" (or beliefs) towards Establishment (or support to sectarian religious institutions) has emerged alongside a new and muscular religious politics in the US which thrives on raising the "specter of unreligion".[14] According to Sullivan it has also transformed the (very American) idea of churches as voluntary and private to public incorporated institutions recognized and supported by the state.[15]

Whether fixated on privatised belief as in Europe, or the increasing public support to religion by the state, the law can be understood as one of the key discourses through which religion is constituted in our times. This gives rise to several distinct but interrelated questions: first, in this time of increasing juridifcation of religion, who can approach the courts for redress, on whose behalf and to what end?; second, what happens when faith and law confront each other, and relatedly, do we see faith and law as contested sovereignties;[16] and finally, what does secular law do when one faith confronts another.

Emerging from different disciplinary locations – history, sociology as well as constitutional law – the essays in this collection cohere around these issues. This collection is not meant to be encyclopaedic – in the sense that Baird's edited volume is, covering a wide gamut of legal themes pertaining to religion in contemporary India, nor focussed on one theme, such as the one on personal laws and secularism edited by Larson.[17] Instead it shines the spotlight on specific moments – chosen serendipitously rather than by elaborate design, but in their entirety raise a range of questions that have assumed paramountcy today.

Religion and law in India

In the altogether brief career of the making of this collection of essays, hardly a day went by without the courts being called upon to intervene in the 'religious'. A group of women appealed to the courts to ensure their access into the sanctum sanctorum of the Haji Ali dargah;[18] another, speaking for women in the menstruating age, sought the courts' intercession to enforce their 'right' to enter Sabrimala shrine.[19] The highest court of the country mulled over whether Muslims in the defence forces could be allowed to grow a beard as a right to religious freedom;[20] and in yet instance, whether an exception could be made to the rules for the medical entrance exam to allow Muslim female students to wear hijab.[21] A high court ruled the Jain practice of self-killing to be criminal, while the Supreme Court stayed it. A municipal corporation in Maharashtra banned the sale (and not simply slaughter) of meat during the Jain holy days of Paryusan.[22] The issue of instant triple talaq dominated national headlines as the Constitution Bench heard a rash of petitions challenging this provision of the Muslim Personal Law, finally declaring it invalid.[23] Marriage between a Muslim boy and a Hindu girl who had converted to Islam was annulled by the Kerala High Court, and then spurred the apex court to institute an enquiry by the National Investigative Agency, which usually investigates terror cases.[24]

Then there were legislations too. The government of Haryana enacted a law ostensibly for the conservation and protection of indigenous varieties of cow – but it was difficult to divorce the new law from the spate of targeted attacks on Muslims and the high decibel stereotyping of the community as the killers of the animal sacred to Hindus.[25] Jharkhand became the latest state in India to propose the misnamed Freedom of Religion Bill that curtails proselytization and conversion.[26]

Feverish arguments on all sides invoked sometimes related, sometimes conflicting ideas of religious freedom, individual rights, and religious sentiments. In brief, the entanglement of law and religion was reiterated on a daily basis. This surfeit of litigation and judicial and legislative pronouncements was however hardly a unique moment in the country's recent history.

Legal historians working on South Asia have shown how the imperatives of colonial rule triggered codification of law – a process that has been understood variously as Janus-faced (the splitting of the modern notion of contract on the one hand, and the centrality of status on the other,[27] and one of expropriation and displacement of traditional law[28] – but which nonetheless assembled identities, hitherto fuzzy or localized, under signages of religious communities. Where exemptions were made, as in Hindu and Muslim personal law, the ambit of the 'personal' was much reduced and the British unwavering quest for fixed and uniform laws even in this domain produced a corpus of authoritative texts[29] which were seen as the sources of law; creation of schools of law of inheritance and succession, which some thought was artificially implanted on Hindu law[30] and for the Muslims a law which could only be termed 'Anglo Muslim'. The custom was parsed from law, and all peoples were pigeon holed into the sharply demarcated boundaries to be governed by the personal laws applicable to that group.

Simultaneously, the colonial courts unleashed a barrage of litigation, which "would never have arisen without the availability of official courts".[31] While on the one hand, it freed an individual from the tyranny of local traditional tribunals and the attendant social opinion and prescription, state law also offered a new theatre for individuals and groups to put forward claims, against others, and against the state as well. Often these claims were made on behalf of communities (as in disputes over pilgrim sites or places of worship), or invoked communal affiliations (such as on questions of inheritance for widows, legal status after conversion, restitution of conjugal rights). It was a dynamic process, with the state law reifying religions and communities, and communities seeking a law to clarify their own place in the social order.

The post-colonial state was an heir to variegated legacies: colonial legal structures and their jurisprudential categories, and socio-religious reform movements and anti-caste struggles of the previous century which powered the newly decolonised state's ambition to create a just and equal society. Derrett writes how the competence of the Constitution makers and courts to make such definitions and intervene in religious practices seen to be abhorrent to modern constitutional values (such as untouchability etc) could thus not be circumscribed by religious doctrine.[32] The strident communal polarization, violence and finally, the partition of the country also produced contradictory results: the formal disavowing of a state religion, commitment to the protection of minorities and guarantees to all to freely profess their religion was accompanied nonetheless by a barely repressed majoritarian anxiety. In the debates, for example, on the ban on cow slaughter in the Constituent Assembly, and its final inclusion in the Directive Principles of State Policy (Article 48) – the animal's agrarian utility served as a poor alibi for the caste Hindu religious sentiment.[33]

Courts became the most potent site of the play of these conflicts and contradictions. Some faithful complained that the promulgation of a range of articles promising a social revolution, such as Article 17 that abolished untouchability, collided with their religious right to determine who could be allowed entry into their temples. If such legislative mechanisms were necessary to reform Hinduism's caste practices, surely it applied only to those who called themselves Hindus? Could the Satsangis or the followers of Ramakrishna Mission claim to be outside the purview of Hinduism, and hence plead freedom from these reform measures? Explanation II of Article 25 that defined Jains, Buddhists and Sikhs as Hindus for the purposes of law also drew them into the circle of reform. Were Jains obliged to abide by the Bombay Harijan Temple Entry Act? Besides, the slew of regulations in the field of management of religious institutions also provoked legal challenges on grounds that religious rights had been infringed upon by the state. Legislations were challenged, petitions were filed seeking the enforcement of their multifarious religious rights under articles 25–28, or to exercise their rights as minorities delineated under articles 29–30.

These challenges and litigation required the courts to sift religious from non-religious (i.e., that what is protected from that which can be reformed and changed – or as in the case of Representation of Peoples' Act, which banned the use of religious appeals for votes, to determine if a specific appeal was religious or not), to separate obligatory and essential practices from superfluous ones, and to carefully balance the competing values enshrined in constitutional principles. The courts were also expected to apprehend, recognise and name religion when they saw it and were thought to be endowed with insight and ability to distinguish religious groupings from the categories of sect or denomination etc. (see John in this collection).

Diversity, difference and neutrality

But should we be seeing this unending stream of court cases as only a clash between competing sovereignties – as religion defending its turf against secular incursions and as a struggle for the place of faith in society?[34] In a country like India – but also elsewhere as ECHR case law shows – this fraught relationship between religion and law cannot be understood by focusing on the courts alone without placing each of these cases in a wider social and political canvas. Even a case such as Santhara, which has appeared to many to be a question of competing sovereignties of religion and state over life and death, is framed in reference to the Hindu practice of Sati, and even when liberal jurisprudence is mobilized by the defendants, it is not only in terms of the right of the faithful ("rights and rites", as Comaroff would say) to practice their faith but their rights as a minority in a Hindu-dominated nation-state (see Sethi). In fact, almost all essays in this collection attest to this (See Rais, Fazal). This is also consistent with the recent developments in the anthropology of religion that insist that increasingly religious subjectivities are forged not in isolation, in one religious tradition singly – but in the background of religious pluralism. Religious diversity is our normal condition.[35] Religious diversity however does not automatically transform into religious tolerance – even as nation-states acknowledge, albeit pragmatically and reluctantly, this heterogeneity.[36] It should therefore not come to us as any surprise that diversity and difference is the lynchpin on which many of the disputes in contemporary India turn, and it also returns us to the question of law's neutrality.

Take for example, 'vegetarianism', which has been elevated to a moral principle in contemporary public discourse. It is not difficult to see why this should be so. It allows for easy communal encryption, triggering a series of codes and associations. Anecdotal evidence suggests that vegetarianism is the most common – and the most respectable – mode of asserting one's caste and communal prejudices. Denial of housing to those belonging to specific communities (namely, Muslims and Dalits) on the pretext of their non-vegetarian diet – regardless of individual preferences – is rampant.[37]

But it also serves as an excellent instance of how a religiously neutral state acknowledges religion/s through many 'positive' ways.[38] We are speaking here of vegetarianism imposed by local government bodies through municipal bylaws prohibiting the sale of poultry, meat and fish in deference to religious sentiments in a complex of towns – comprising Haridwar, Muni ki Reti and Rishikesh. The amendment in the bylaws by the Rishikesh local authorities to include the trade-in eggs in the list of prohibited items in the late 1990s was challenged on grounds that it was not a reasonable restriction and that it hit the petitioner's right to practice the profession or occupation of his choice. The challenge was rebuffed in the High Court, and the Supreme Court too upheld the municipality's right to enforce such a ban. The Supreme Court in its endorsement of the amended bylaws chose to test the reasonableness of the complete restriction on the trade of non-vegetarian food items on the touchstone of "cultural and religious background of the three municipal towns".[39] The court then provides us a catalogue: these towns are the site of the Kumbh Mela, and as gateways to the pilgrimage to Badrinath and Kedarnath, they are host to "several communities" about whom there was "common knowledge" that they "are strictly vegetarians and shun meat, fish and eggs." It points to the large number of individuals and religious organisations who, desirous of a "vegetarian atmosphere" had demanded an absolute ban on meat items and products. The change in law and the broadening of the ban is a response to these petitions. Having approved of the municipality's reciprocation to these demands, the court then reminds those who deal in non vegetarian items to follow the Fundamental Duties enshrined in DSPS, namely, Article 51 A which enjoins on citizens to respect the faith of each other and thereby 'promote harmony and spirit of common brotherhood'. [40] Indeed, for the Supreme Court, these are sound grounds upon which to base "the legislative and executive actions of elected or non-elected institutions and organizations of the citizens including the municipal bodies".[41]

But when the court calls for respecting the faith of others, whom exactly is it speaking to since the petitioner is one Om Prakash Singh, most likely a Hindu. This oversight can probably be explained as the court's blindness to the dietary diversities within Hinduism, and also an attempt to address a wider constituency than the specific petitioner.

Similarly, through the 1990s, municipal slaughter houses in Ahmedabad were closed down for the period of Paryusan "having regard for the citizens of the Jain religion" by the local corporation. (Since the Digambars and Shvetamabars observe paryusan on different dates which follow closely, the closure was effected for nearly 18 days though the Jain appellants and the state maintained it was only for nine days). These closures were challenged as arbitrary and violative of the rights of butchers as well non-vegetarians who were deprived of their choice of diet during these days.[42] The Ahmedabad Municipal Corporation's stand was interesting. It claimed through this ban to be promoting respect between communities and a "more tolerant society where people of different religions can live together happily". The court cheerfully concurred with both the corporation's goal and the means:

> What the Corporation is attempting to do is to see that the religious beliefs of all communities and classes of society are respected placing as little restriction or curb on the other community so that all can live harmoniously and peacefully.

The court then upholds as the basis of the closure of abattoirs the beliefs and feelings of the Jains', of which there is "a large population in Rajasthan and Gujarat". "Out of respect, for their sentiments surely the non-vegetarians can remain vegetarians for 9 days in a year."

Clearly, certain religious groups have called upon the state to positively recognise their 'sentiments', and the state, in turn, responds to this call by framing laws guaranteed to assuage those feelings. Equally clearly, however, it is difficult to understand these judgments as merely Religion (with a capital R) staking its claim over the domain of the secular. They need to be mapped within a range of ideas: tolerance, diversity, accommodation, respect – all of which get curiously twisted and mangled to produce a result that demands tolerance and respect only from some. These legal challenges could have been opportunities to reimagine a shared space for peoples of different groups, and to reconcile the competing claims and affronts but instead, they end up propping a spurious civilizational superiority of vegetarianism over non-vegetarianism by couching it in the language of compassion. So alongside a survey of notions and practices of religious tolerance propagated by Akbar and other Mughal rulers in Medieval Indian history, the court harks back to the 7-judge Constitution Bench, which while upholding the ban on slaughter of cow and her progeny had invoked 51 A in a novel way:

> The concept of compassion for living creatures enshrined in Article 51-A (g) is based on the background of the rich cultural heritage of India the land of Mahatma Gandhi, Vinobha, Mahaveer, Buddha, Nanak

> and others. No religion or holy book in any part of the world teaches or encourages cruelty. Indian society is a pluralistic society. It has unity in diversity. The religious, cultures and people may be diverse, yet all speak in one voice that cruelty to any living creature must be curbed and ceased.[43]

By assigning the value of compassion to vegetarianism alone, and coupling cruelty with non-vegetarianism, respect and tolerance, harmony and brotherhood are to be wrested out through executive and 'lawful' fiats that affect specific caste and community groups that do not place a premium on vegetarianism. It is they who must be burdened with the responsibility for the attainment of this ideal state of tolerance and harmony.

But where the executive and the judiciary elevate the state's positive recognition of some religious groups and their sentiments to almost a constitutional duty – vapid and cynical neutrality is evoked to evade ethical questions of responsibility for protecting the life and liberty of minority groups. The violence in the state of Gujarat in 2002 saw targeted attacks on mosques, hospices and graveyards by riotous mobs. Public interest litigation was filed by Islamic Relief Committee Gujarat in the Gujarat High Court, which in 2012 held the state liable to pay for the repair and restoration of "all religious places including those of worship" that had been damaged during the violence. It appointed district principal judges as special officers for determining the amount of compensation for the religious place under their jurisdiction.

The matter immediately travelled up to the Supreme Court where the state government contested the high court's directive on a number of counts, but mainly took the plea that the

> State cannot be commanded to repair or restore any place of worship as such an act on the part of the State will create a dent in the secular fabric and further the expenditure from the State exchequer is impermissible in view of the language employed the Article 27 of the Constitution.[44]

Article 27 forbids utilizing the tax-payer's money "for the promotion or maintenance of any particular religion or religions denomination." The state, which had in the first place expressly failed to protect the places of worship, surely a failure of a secular state if there was one, now took cover behind the establishment clause. Denying the 'special' nature of the destruction of these religious places, the government insisted that it fell under a generic "Right to property" and thereby relief could be sought in civil law alone where individual parties could seek compensation and not public or tort law under 226, as the petitioners had done. What the original petitioners had sought was the acknowledgment of the humiliation and the debasement of the community by the attacks on places held most sacred to them. By overruling the High Court order and settling for a scheme of compensation devised by the state government, the apex court in its final judgment participated in the evasion of the question that was moot for the petitioners: recognition by the state and law of the grievous harm done by a dominant group to a weak section of society. Article 51-A and pious homilies of brotherhood and amity surrendered meekly before the might of the separation of state and religion.

I want to take one last example before turning to the essays in this collection. This is the case of Hadiya/ Akhila, in the news recently. It coalesces disparate concerns that have been the staple of political rhetoric (conversion, marriage, purity of communities etc.) and judicial scrutiny (individual rights, freedom of choice in marriage, but also conversion). What it also helps us do is to question the standard legal historical narrative, which sees a breach between criminal and personal/ civil laws – only the latter being the playground of communities and religion. The ways in which criminal law can reify communities and assign properties to social groups have been largely overlooked, as has been the traffic between the civil/personal and the criminal. One arena of such objectification is the anti-terror legislation and its workings. The structure of these laws which recognize and privilege guilt by association, and the widespread prosecution – though not necessarily conviction – of those belonging to certain caste and community groups under these laws, end up creating suspect communities very much in the manner that colonial Criminal Tribes Act 1871 created "hereditary criminals". The figure of the Islamist terrorist, as an 'essential type', ought to be seen as much a product of law as of popular culture and politics.

Hadiya/ Akhila was a homeopathy student who embraced Islam, and thereafter entered into a marriage with a Muslim boy. Public attention was first drawn to it when the Kerala High Court annulled Hadiya's marriage and subsequently when the Supreme Court ordered the National Investigative Agency to enquire into the issues arising from the writ petition moved by her husband. Feminists have also noted the gross infantilization of Hadiya, the erosion of her agency and the silencing of her voice by the heavy hand of patriarchy.

Certainly, in voiding the marriage and granting Haidya's custody to her father, the High Court assumed the mantle of *parens patriae*. Her vociferous denial of the charges of force was dismissed with assertions about her mediocre intelligence, young age and incapacity to think properly and independently. Nonetheless, this infantilization is not merely symptomatic of the state's relationship with its female citizenry. It draws upon the long history of post-colonial state's attitude to religious conversion. Though Article 25 granted the freedom to practice and propagate one's religion, conversion was always looked upon with suspicion and as an attempt to sunder the Hindu community by preying on the weak. Whilst attempts to pass a central law to prohibit conversion failed thrice, Orissa and Madhya Pradesh successfully enacted anti-conversion laws very early.[45] These laws were cast in the language of vulnerability and weakness and criminalized conversion by force, fraud or allurement. O.P. Tyagi who moved a private member's bill in the Parliament in 1978 said that the "Constitution has given special protection to Harijans", and he wished to bestow upon "them dharmik protection as well".[46] Under the Orissa and MP act, the punishment would be doubled if those converted were minors, women, or belonged to scheduled castes and scheduled tribes.

The inherent paternalism of these acts has been upheld by the court rulings when these laws were challenged. The Supreme Court's ruling in *Stainislaus* interpreted freedom of conscience to be the right to be not influenced or even exposed to persuasion by the followers of another faith.[47] Pratap Bhanu Mehta's argument that to the state and Law, religious speech appears to be a site of "passion and unreason",[48] which stultifies the listeners and renders them susceptible, zombie-like, to allurements, inducement and force, applies well here.

The Kerala government pleader stated in the court that Hadiya was

> influenced by feeding her with graphic details of hell and the torments that sinners are subjected to in their life after death. She has also been made to believe that in order to escape from the torments of hell, acceptance of the Islamic faith was the only way.

A police report said, "Akhila believed that Islam would help her reach heaven after earth". Under the sundry freedom of religion laws, these would comprise as certain proof of conversion by fraud. Though there is no such law in force in Kerala, this judgment emerges in the legal universe where Law can construe anything more than "exposition of tenets" as a crime and the courts feel compelled to protect those so enfeebled and incapacitated by religious propaganda.

High Court's assessment of Hadiya compares with the Orissa High court's observation in *Yulitha Hyde*: "Threat of divine displeasure numbs the mental faculty; *more so of an undeveloped mind* and the actions of such a person thereafter, are not free and according to conscience."[49]

The state's anxiety about religious conversions of course has a more fundamental source than simply the fear of religious speech: the spectre of debilitating numbers of Hindus. Does not the Government of India 1950 order that excludes from the purview of reservation those who have converted to Islam and Christianity offer material incentives (as opposed to divine displeasure) for conversion back into the Hindu fold?[50]

The Supreme Court while hearing the case invoked the Blue whale challenge to imply that Hadiya's apparently 'free' will may not necessarily be her own. The comparison is apposite at another level too. The Deep Internet and this dystopian sport luring adolescents into committing suicide are very much how the petitioner, the government pleader and ultimately even the high court have portrayed Akhila's transformation into Hadiya through "indoctrination" and "fanatic interpretations of Quran", and the need to "rescue" her from "evil influences" and the "dangers she is exposed to".

The HC admits that there have been many cases of marriages across religious divides but the courts have had no trouble accepting them. What stumps the court is not that Hadiya converted to Islam for love – for that would be understandable as a purely utilitarian choice – but out of piety. This court seems to be at a cognitive loss to make sense of it and clings to the only frame available to comprehend Islamic piety: that of radicalization and extremism.

It's "inquisitive mind" worries if any radical organisations have been behind her interest in Islam; it also censures the police for not investigating two people Hadiya was in touch with despite "clear indications that the said persons are persons involved in the study of Muslim religion." The husband's Facebook posts "unmistakably show his radical inclination", according to the court. His past links with SDPI (which is not banned but regularly referred to as being connected to the banned SIMI), his employment in the Gulf, an old criminal case arising out of a dispute with a rival youth organization, and the arrest of a former SDPI member by the NIA though unconnected to him, summon all the tropes familiar to us in terror cases: the vagueness of charges, nebulous conspiracies, criminalization for political affiliations or just simply a public expression of faith, seen as too extreme – and the creation of a suspect community. Interesting that Hadiya's father first habeas corpus petition alleging that Hadiya was in the illegal custody of her friends and their father was dismissed. The second petition claiming that she would be transported to Syria to join ISIS by extremist organizations that had forcibly converted her was treated more favourably.

The Supreme Court has ordered the country's premier anti-terror agency, NIA, to unearth the 'truth'. The apex court may or not may overrule the High Court's invalidating the marriage but its choice of the agency tells us the extent to which a girl's turn to Islam can only be interpreted in the legal matrix of terrorism.

We are returned in the end to the sovereign's power to define religion – and even good piety and bad.

Organization of the special issue

The present collection is divided into three sections. In the first, John and Sethi address a question that has been central to the Law-Religion debate: If the very purpose of the law is to "transform life" and to "transmute reality into rules and regularities legible to law", should we even expect the law to "recognize and protect religious lives and complexities?"[51] Is Law (like Anthropology perhaps) fated to misrecognize religion? John's answer to this in the opening essay is a pessimistic yes.

To be sure, the relationship has been posed several times in the past.[52] While agreeing with Sen that the adjudication of religious freedom triggered a process of 'rationalisation' of Hinduism, where the practice was collapsed into doctrine – John sees this as far more pervasive, and applicable to all forms of Indian religiosity. In determining the "essential" core of religious practices being founded on doctrine alone, the courts have "passed over the experiences, intuitions and practices of religious practitioners and communities". Where many other legal scholars have assumed this to be a dilemma for constitutional liberalism torn between individual rights and group rights – in which the latter triumphs over the former, and thus necessitates even greater rationalisation[53] – John draws our attention to the very epistemic frames which structure the Constitution's normative claims over religion, and how they "misunderstand, distort and flatten out local conceptions of religion, spirituality and ethical striving."

The question of ethical striving assumes centrality in the Jain defence of the practice of ritual self-killing (sallekhana/ santhara), which was struck down by the Rajasthan High Court in 2015. Sethi explicates the ways in which the opposition to the practice (both by the petitioner and the High Court) was cast in the very language of reform and rationalization that John alludes to. It in fact draws upon a long history of reform, invoking the practice of Sati and judicial interventions to criminalise it. Sethi embarks on a historical exercise, looking at colonial attitudes to sallekhana and comparing them with hectic penal energies they devoted to the proscription of Sati, and asks why the British ignored sallekhana. Sethi also examines how the defence of sallekhana is mounted by the community. What happens when belief and practices enter the precincts of a courtroom, filtered through the prism of texts and authoritative sources, which must testify to its authenticity? Are they fundamentally altered?

The second section focuses on Muslim personal law (MPL) – a subject that always excites attention, but which at the present moment is especially significant in light of the recent Supreme Court judgment declaring instant triple talaq invalid and the wide-ranging discussions that have followed it. In spite of the history of personal laws as a product of colonial state administration – and the existence of a great deal of case law which has reinterpreted MPL in more gender-just ways – in the popular imagination, it is seen as frozen in time, beyond the purview of Constitutional tests, more like an isolated island, where hapless women have been marooned from where they send out signals of distress which the courts are fated to helplessly ignore.[54]

In part, the notion that personal laws cannot be fiddled around by the courts has been set up *Narasu* where Justice Gajendrakar ruled that personal laws being divinely ordained are not subject to the fundamental rights enumerated in Part III of the Constitution, saying famously that "The foundational sources of both the Hindu and the Mahomedan laws are their respective scriptural texts."[55]

The articles do not engage with the question of whether MPL is religiously ordained and thus beyond the remit of constitutional or state law. Majumdar's essay shows how the state continued to rework and reform Islamic personal law. He speaks of one such endeavour – albeit unsuccessful – where the state of Kerala attempted to codify and reform certain aspects of Islamic law resulting in a report entitled 'The Final Report of [*sic*] Law Reforms Commission Kerala' (hereinafter referred to as the 'Report'), and also a draft Bill called the Kerala Muslim Marriage and Dissolution by Talaq and Khula (Regulation) Bill 2009 (the 'Bill)'.

Incidentally, the architect of the initiative was Justice Krishna Iyer who in *Assan Rawther* had outlined his disagreement with Justice Gajendrakar's Narasu ratio by insisting that "Personal law so called is law by virtue of the sanction of the sovereign behind it and is, for the very reason, enforceable through Court. Not Manu or Muhammad but the Monarch for the time makes 'Personal law' enforceable."[56]

Though Majumdar's essay can be located in the wider field of the study of legal reform, his interests are quite different. By tracing the lineage of the Kerala reform initiative to the Muslim Family Law Ordinance (MFLO) enacted in Pakistan in 1961 – a lineage which is not acknowledged by the Kerala Law Reforms Commission – Majumdar also explores the downsides of legal reform through comparative law. He shows that while MFLO teetered between demands of 'pristine' law and 'modernity', the Kerala initiative's failure lies in its inability to recognise this tension, which in turn could be attributed to the inexplicit nature of its borrowing. As a result, the tension between 'pristine' law and 'modernity' inherent in MFLO is compounded by another tension, *i.e.*between tacit borrowing and deviating from MFLO's precepts.

Going beyond the usual explanations of shari'a and politics interplay, Neshat Quaiser's essay captures the dynamics of this interplay by examining shari'a as immanently contested terrain acquiring specific connotations due to its entanglement with extra-legal phenomena such as communalism in post-colonial India. But what it also does is to travel beyond the normative law machinery (whether as state-sanctioned or ulema) and quite a distance from 'official' courts to show us how ordinary folk – both men and women – negotiate and manipulate the normative codes while remaining within the four corners of Sharia. Ethnographic studies of dar ul qazas (or Sharia courts) are rare. Vatuk in her study of women initiated divorces in Sharia as well as family courts in south India has challenged both the exaggerated victimhood attributed to the Muslim woman as well as the notion that the right to initiate divorce (khula) granted women the power to assert themselves.[57] Vatuk, however, assumes both law and religion to be static categories, producing fairly predictable results. Quaiser urges us to see Sharia normativity as inherently contested.

While on the one hand, the ʿulamā assert the authority of fixed fiqh and accrue to themselves the power to interpret the sharia (heightened especially in the backdrop of the rise of majoritarianism), there is also, Quaiser shows, the realm of everyday laity ijtihād which constitutes the field of conviviality. He draws out the contours of this field populated by 'sensible' wives, 'undesirable' husbands and bazar qazis. The practices of conviviality crafted largely by women do not involve an alternative interpretation of the Sharia, nor the renunciation of one's Muslim/ Islamic identity. The prism of conviviality allows us to understand the workings of personal law adjudication beyond the dualities of conservative Ulama and reformists.

The third section dwells on the relationship between religion/ religious identities and the conjoined figure of 'law and order'. While the subject of both Rehman's and Fazal's papers is religious conflict in the colonial period, unlike most scholarly works on the theme which focus on Hindu-Muslim disputes, Rehman approaches this through the rather unusual lens of Parsi-Muslim conflict in Bombay and a Shia-Sunni dispute in Amroha (Uttar Pradesh). These are situated in a longer history of the colonial state being called upon by religious communities to referee their quarrels and to rationalize their acts and selves. In arbitering these disputes – in determining who was right and who the wrong, and in handing out resolutions – the state acted as a neutral referee but this neutrality could only be a chimera, guided as the state was by its own needs and imperatives. It thus played these disputes to its own advantages, resulting in the reification of communities as perpetually in conflict.

While Rehman looks at arbitration outside the courts, Fazal turns to a dispute between Muslims and Sikhs over the ownership of Shahidganj Gurudwara as contested in the colonial courts. Tracking its career from the Sikh Tribunal to the Privy Council – where the key question was whether the mosque was a sacred entity protected by religious laws or simply a piece of land to be governed by state laws, Fazal notes that each judicial conclusion dismissed Muslim claims over the mosque on grounds that it had been in possession of the Sikhs for years even while recognising that it had been originally a mosque. Why did the courts insist on the principle of adverse possession and favour status quo, asks Fazal. He replies that it was the desire for the maintenance of 'public order' that drove the colonial courts to weigh in on the side of the Sikhs in this case. If the colonial state lacked popular sovereignty and preferred non-interference and status quo in such conflicts to keep the peace, the post colonial states suffering from no such lack, succumbed to majoritarianism. It was the courts on whom the task of conflict resolution fell, and they embraced too, the logic of public order, and sided with the status quo, as reflected in the Babri Masjid judgment.

Maheshwari follows the trials of artists under attack by the Hindu Right – both through physical attacks and vandalism, and by the filing of cases for hurting religious sentiments, through the 1980s to the present. She shows how anxieties surrounding 'offence' and the rise in attacks on free speech came to be produced through multiple processes in the realm of politics, culture and economy, but most importantly, how this violence came to relocate itself in the courts. Rather than act as a bulwark against violence, Law itself contributed to the precariousness of free speech by turning into a medium of harassment particularly favoured by the right-wing. Though the essay is based on the post-colonial present, it is fused with the concerns especially outlined in Rehman's paper. The enactment of sections 153 A and 295 A of the Indian Penal Code by the British government as a way to deal with supposed unremitting hostility between communities, and the avowed, but patently false, neutrality of the government resonate throughout Maheshwari's essay.

What then of secularism? In his thoughtful Afterword, bearing principally on the 'analytics' of secularism, Hegde seeks to apprehend the contours of normative secularity – as an ideal – and to trace its legal/ moral commitments. Hegde ventures on this task through three interlocutors: the first of these is Taylor who insists on moving away from the fetishization of institutional arrangements in defining secularism, to goals or ideals (or goods) such as liberty and equality. The second is Agrama for whom modern secularism is riddled with a fundamental contradiction, namely one between suspicion of religious belief and the practice of religious freedom. Hegde holds his third conversation with Laborde who highlights the paradox of secular modernity: How (and why) do we protect freedom of religion in an age where religion is not special".

I hope that this collection of essays goes some way in adding to these debates and questions – questions that are more urgent today than they were ever.

Notes

1. McCutcheon, "The Category 'Religion' in Recent Publications: A Critical Survey."
2. Geertz, "Religion as a Cultural System."
3. Smith, *The Meaning and End of Religion*, 48, 141, 142. Others not so keen on abandoning the category wholly continued to provide defining features of religion. Brian K. Smith, for example, following Bruce Lincoln, distinguishes religious discourse from all others by the distinctive "types of claims to authority" it mobilizes and the bases on which these claims rest. To Lincoln's two primary bases on which religious authority is poised, namely, transcendence and timelessness, Brian Smith adds a third: universalism. Thus religious discourse establishes its claims to absolute, objective truth. see Smith, "Authority, Power, and the Definition of 'Religion'," 416.
4. Smith, "Religion, Religions, Religious," 269.
5. Asad, *Genealogies of Religion*, 45.
6. Lambek, "Interminable Disputes in Northwest Madagascar," 1.
7. Benda-Beckmann et al., "Introduction: On the Pervasiveness of Religious Normativity in Disputing Process," viii.
8. Sandberg, "A question of Belief," 55.
9. Comaroff, "Reflections on the Rise of Legal Theology," 197, 98.
10. Sullivan, "The World That *Smith* Made," 202.
11. Tayob, "Contested Religious Rituals and Practices in South Africa's Post-Apartheid Constitutional Order."
12. *Overview of the Court's Case Law on Freedom of Religion*, 8.
13. For how such a legal definition of religion has pernicious consequences for minorities in the ECHR see Peroni, "Religion and Culture in the Discourse of the European Court of Human Rights: The Risks of Stereotyping and Naturalizing."
14. Sullivan, 235.
15. Sullivan, 236.
16. Kirsch and Turner, *Permutations of Order: Religion and Law as Contested Sovereignties*.
17. Larson ed., *Religion and Personal Law in Secular India*.
18. *Dr. Noorjehan Safia Niaz And 1 Anr vs State Of Maharashtra*.
19. I.A. no. 10 of 2016 in the matter of *Indian Young Lawyers' Association and Anr vs The State of Kerala and Ors.* Writ petition (civil) 373 of 2006.
20. *Mohammed Zubair Corporal vs Union of India* (2017) 2 SCC 115.
21. *Wp(C). No. 6813 Of 2016 (B) vs Unknown* in the High Court of Kerala, AIR2016Ker115. On SC's position, see "Faith Is Something Different from Wearing Some Kind of Cloth: Supreme Court on Plea against CBSE Dress Code."

22. "Civic Body Bans Sale of Meat during Jain Fast." *Business Standard*, 7 September 2017.
23. *Shayara Bano vs Union of India, Writ Petition (C) No. 118 of 2016. Judgment delivered on.*
24. WP(Crl.).No. 297 of 2016 (S) in the High Court of Kerala, Ernakulum, 24 May 2017. 2017(2)KLJ974; Supreme Court's order in *Shafin Jahan vs. K.M. Asokan and Ors. Supreme Court order on* 16 August 2017.
25. *The Haryana Gauvansh Sanrakshan and Gausamvardhan Act 2015.*
26. *Jharkhand Freedom of Religion Bill 2017.*
27. Washbrook, "Law, State and Agrarian Society in Colonial India," 653–654.
28. Galanter, "The Displacement of Traditional Law in India."
29. On the point of how orientalism created Hinduism, see King, "Orientalism and the Modern Myth of 'Hinduism'."
30. Rocher, pace Derrett, has insisted that Dharmasastras be viewed above all as scholastic books, whose subject is not merely law; its authors and commentators were not lawyers owing allegiance to different schools of thought. The common (and to Rocher's mind, mistaken) British view of commentaries as legal texts led to the creation of schools of law by Colebrooke and other orientalists. See Davis Jr, "Introduction," 19–25.
31. Gallanter, 19.
32. Derrett, *Religion, Law and the State in India,* 438–440.
33. Chigateri, "Negotiating the 'Sacred' Cow: Cow Slaughter and the Regulation of Difference in India," 142–146.
34. Sullivan's point about multi religious coalitions coming together in defence of religion is not entirely absent in India. For example, the appeal against decriminalization of homosexuality saw the congealing of such a coalition. Several religious organisations belonging to different faiths filed interventions in the Supreme Court, though not under a single banner. These included Trust God Missionaries, The Tamil Nadu Muslim Munnetra Kazhagam, All Indian Muslim Personal Law Board, Utkal Christian Council Apostolic Churches Alliance, Sanatan Dharma Pratinidhi Sabha, Bharat Swabhiman Patanjali Yogpeeth. *Suresh Kumar Koushal vs Naz Foundation* (2014) 1 SCC 1.
35. Veena *Das,* "Cohabiting an Interreligious Milieu: Reflections on Religious Diversity," 84.
36. Comaroff, *op.cit.*, 198.
37. Mehta, 'Not allowed to sell her flat to a Muslim, Pune woman takes on entire 'society'. The seller was asked by a member of the Cooperative Society if slaughter of goats on the lawn would be ok with her. See Khaitan, 'Vegetarianism, tolerance and discrimination'. In another case in Mumbai, a housing cooperative society similarly passed a resolution disallowing the sale of flat to a Muslim family. An FIR was filed against the cooperative society. See 'Bakri-eid and a Militant Vegetarian Housing Society' and 'Meat Row: Its Veg vs Non-veg in Mumbai Housing Societies'.
38. Positive here does not imply of a higher value or order but merely proactive.
39. *Om Prakash & Others vs State of Up*. (2004) 3 SCC 402, para 35.
40. Article 51 A was introduced by the 42nd amendment in 1977.
41. Om Prakash, (2004) 3 SCC 402, para 38.
42. *Hinsa Virodhak Sangh v. Mirzapur Moti Kuresh Jamat* . A.I.R. 2008 S.C. 1892. All further citations from the judgment.
43. *State of Gujarat vs. Mirzapur Moti Kureshi Kassab Jamat & Ors* cited in *Hinsa Virodhak* . A.I.R. 2008 S.C. 1892.
44. *State of Gujarat & Anr. Vs. Islami Relief Committee, Gujarat (I.R.C.G.) & Anr,* Civil Appeal No. 3249 of 2016.
45. See Neufeldt, "To Convert or Not to Convert."
46. Louis and Menezes, "Religion Bill: Fears of Persecution."
47. *Rev. Stainislaus vs State of Madhya Pradesh & Ors* 1977 AIR 908.
48. Mehta, "Passion and Constraint."
49. *Mrs. Yulitha Hyde And Ors. vs State of Orissa And Ors* AIR 1973 Ori 116.
50. Fazal, "Scheduled Castes, Reservations and Religion."
51. Sullivan, Hurd, Mahmood and Danchin, *The Politics of Religious Freedom*, 8.
52. See especially, Baird, "Introduction," and Sen, "The Indian Supreme Court and the Quest for a 'Rational' Hinduism."
53. See for example, Dhagamwar, "Women, Children and the Constitution."
54. Vatuk notes how pervasive this tendency is, even in scholarly writings. *Marriage and its Discontents*, vii.
55. *The State of Bombay vs Narasu Appa Mali* AIR 1952 Bom 84.
56. *Assan Rawther v Ammu Umma* (1971) KLT 684.
57. Vatuk, *Marriage and its Discontents*, 116–153.

Bibliography

Asad, T. *Genealogies of Religion: Discipline and Reasons of Power.* Baltimore and London: The John Hopkins University Press, 1993.

Baird, R. D. (ed.). *Religion and Law in Independent India.* 2nd ed. Delhi: Manohar, 2005.

Benda-Beckmann et al. (ed.). *Religion in Disputes: Pervasiveness of Religious Normativity in Disputing Processes.* New York: Palgrave Macmillan, 2013.

Chigateri, S. "Negotiating the 'Sacred' Cow: Cow Slaughter and the Regulation of Difference in India." In *Democracy, Religious Pluralism and the Liberal Dilemma of Accommodation*, Studies in Global Justice, vol. 7, edited by Mookherjee M. Dordrecht. Springer, 2011. https://doi.org/10.1007/978-90-481-9017-1_8.

Comaroff, J. L. "Reflections on the Rise of Legal Theology: Law and Religion in the Twenty-First Century." *Social Analysis: The International Journal of Social and Cultural Practice* 53, no. 1 (Spring 2009): 193–216.

Das, V. "Cohabiting an Interreligious Milieu: Reflections on Religious Diversity." In *A Companion to the Anthropology of Religion*, edited by J. Boddy and M. Lambek. Sussex: Wiley Blackwell, 2013: 69–84.

Davis Jr, D. R. 'Introduction'. In *Studies on Hindu Law and Dharmasastra* by Ludo Rocher. UK and USA: Anthem Press, 2014, pp. 17–37.

Derrett, J. M. *Religion, Law and the State in India.* London: Oxford University Press, 1968.

Dhagamwar, V. "Women, Children and the Constitution: Hostages to Religion, Outcaste by Law." In *Religion and Law in Independent India*, edited by R. D. Baird, 2nd ed. Delhi: Manohar, 2005, pp. 283–324.

Fazal, T. "Scheduled Castes, Reservations and Religion: Revisiting a Juridical Debate." *Contributions to Indian Sociology* 51, no. 1 (February 19, 2017): 1–24.

Galanter, M. "The Displacement of Traditional Law in India." *Journal of Social Issues*, 24 (1968): 65–91.

Geertz, C. *The Interpretation of Cultures.* New York: Basic Books, 1973.

Khaitan, T. "Vegetarianism, Tolerance and Discrimination." *The Hindu*, May26, 2008.

King, R. "Orientalism and the Modern Myth of 'Hinduism'." *Numen* 46, no. 2 (1999): 146–185.

Kirsch, T. G. and B. Turner (eds.). *Permutations of Order: Religion and Law as Contested Sovereignties.* England and USA: Ashgate, 2009.

Lambek, M. "Interminable Disputes in Northwest Madagascar." In *Religion in Disputes: Pervasiveness of Religious Normativity in Disputing Processes*, edited by Benda-Beckmann et al., 1–18. New York: Palgrave Macmillan, 2013.

Larson, G. J. (ed.). *Religion and Personal Law in Secular India: A Call to Judgment.* Bloomington and Indianapolis: Indiana University Press, 2001.

McCutcheon, R. T. "The Category 'Religion' in Recent Publications: A Critical Survey." *Numen* 42, no. 3 (October, 1995): 284–309.

Mehta, P. B. "Passion and Constraint." *Seminar* 521 (January 2003). Available at: https://www.india-seminar.com/2003/521/521%20pratap%20bhanu%20mehta.htm

Neufeldt, R. W. "To Convert or Not to Convert: Legal and Political Dimensions of Conversion in Independent India." In *Religion and Law in Independent India*, edited by Robert D. Baird, 2nd ed. Delhi: Manohar, 2005.

Peroni, L. "Religion and Culture in the Discourse of the European Court of Human Rights: The Risks of Stereotyping and Naturalizing." *International Journal of Law in Context* 10, no. 2 (2014): 195–221.

Sandberg, R. "A Question of Belief." In *Religion and Law*, edited by N. Spencer London: Theos, 2012, pp. 51–63.

Sen, R. "The Indian Supreme Court and the Quest for a 'Rational' Hinduism." *South Asian History and Culture* 1, no. 1 (2009): 86–104.

Smith, B. K. "Authority, Power, and the Definition of 'Religion'." *Historical Reflections / Réflexions Historiques* 25, no. 3 (Fall 1999): 413–422.

Smith, J. Z. "Religion, Religions, Religious." In *Critical terms for Religious Studies*, edited by M. C. Taylor. Chicago and London: University of Chicago Press, 1998, pp. 269–284.

Smith, W. C. *The Meaning and End of Religion.* New York: Mentor Books, 1962.

Sullivan, W. F. "The World That *Smith* Made." In *The Politics of Religious Freedom*, edited by W. F. Sullivan, E. S. Hurd, S. Mahmood, and P. G. Danchin. Chicago and London: University of Chicago Press, 2015, pp: 231–239.

Sullivan, W. F., E. S. Hurd, S. Mahmood, and P. G. Danchin (eds.). *The Politics of Religious Freedom.* Chicago and London: University of Chicago Press, 2015.

Tayob, A. "Contested Religious Rituals and Practices in South Africa's Post-Apartheid Constitutional Order." Paper presented at International workshop on 'Religion and Law in India', Jamia Millia Islamia, March 2016.

Vatuk, S. *Marriage and Its Discontent: Women, Islam and Law in India.* New Delhi: Women Unlimited, 2017.

Washbrook, D. A. "Law, State and Agrarian Society in Colonial India." *Modern Asian Studies* 15, no. 3 (1981): 653–654.

Bills and reports

Jharkhand Freedom of Religion Bill 2017, accessed at: http://files.constantcontact.com/523942c3501/9c2fd470-ffb4-4c21-a485-9138a10a2896.pdf

Overview of the Court's Case Law on Freedom of Religion, Council of Europe/ ECHR, first published 19 January 2011, updated on 31 October 2013. p. 8. http://www.echr.coe.int/Documents/Research_report_religion_ENG.pdf

The Haryana Gauvansh Sanrakshan and Gausamvardhan Act 2015, Government of Haryana Gazetteer Extraordinary, 19 November 2015.

Newspaper reports

"Bakri-eid and a Militant Vegetarian Housing Society' and 'Meat Row: Its Veg vs Non-veg in Mumbai Housing Societies." http://www.rediff.com/news/column/bakri-eid-and-a-militant-vegetarian-housing-society/20150923.htm.

"Civic Body Bans Sale of Meat during Jain Fast." *Business Standard*, 7 September 2017.

"Religion Bill: Fears of Persecution." *India Today*, 30 April 1979.

"Meat Row: Its Veg vs Non-veg in Mumbai Housing Societies." *Midday*, 15 September 2015.

"Not Allowed to Sell Her Flat to a Muslim, Pune Woman Takes on Entire 'society'." *Indian Express*, 2 April, 2008.

"Faith Is Something Different from Wearing Some Kind of Cloth: Supreme Court on Plea against CBSE Dress Code." *Livelaw*, www.livelaw.in/faith-is-something-different-from-wearing-some-kind-of-cloth-supreme-court-on-plea-against-cbse-dress-code/.

Cases

Assan Rawther v Ammu Umma (1971) KLT 684.

Dr. Noorjehan Safia Niaz And 1 Anr vs State Of Maharashtra 2016(5)ABR660.

Hinsa Virodhak Sangh v. Mirzapur Moti Kuresh Jamat A.I.R. 2008 S.C. 1892.

IA No. 10 of 2016 in the matter of *Indian Young Lawyers' Association and Anr vs The State of Kerala and Ors*, Writ petition (civil) 373 of 2006.

Mohd. Zubair v. Union of India, (2017) 2 SCC 115.

Mrs. Yulitha Hyde And Ors. vs State Of Orissa And Ors. AIR 1973 Ori 116.

Om Prakash & Others vs State of Up & Others (2004) 3 SCC 402.

Rev. Stainislaus vs State of Madhya Pradesh & Ors 1977) 1 SCC 677.

Shafin Jahan vs. K.M. Asokan and Ors, order of the Supreme Court, 16 August 2017.

Shayara Bano vs Union of India, Writ Petition (C) No. 118 of 2016. Not reported yet. 22 August 2017.

State of Gujarat vs. Mirzapur Moti Kureshi Kassab Jamat & Ors 2005(8) SCC 534.

State of Gujarat & Anr. Vs. Islami Relief Committee, Gujarat (I.R.C.G.) & Anr, Civil Appeal No. 3249 of 2016. Not reported yet. 29 August 2017.

State of Bombay vs Narasu Appa Mali. AIR 1952 Bom 84.

Suresh Kumar Koushal v. Naz Foundation, (2014) 1 SCC 1.

WP(Crl.).No. 297 of 2016 (S) in the High Court of Kerala, Ernakulum, 2017(2)KLJ974.

Wp(C).No. 6813 of 2016 (B) vs Unknown AIR2016Ker115.

Part 1

Religion and Law

Competing Sovereignties?

Framing religion in constitutional politics: a view from Indian Constitutional Law

Mathew John

ABSTRACT
Modern constitutional power is organized to secure ever-expanding state control over vast swathes of social and cultural life. Though religion is classically thought to be a domain of human experience that is to be left independent of state power, it is in fact deeply structured by contemporary government. Against this background, this paper examines the manner in which the Indian constitutional state exercises its power over religion and religious practices. It does so by arguing that the epistemic forms through which control is exercised over Indian religious practices operate to misunderstand, distort and flatten out local conceptions of religion, spirituality and ethical striving. That is, by following classic decisions on the bounds of religious freedom as decided by the Indian Supreme Court, it is argued that religion understood primarily as traditions of continued inter-generational practice are transformed in judicial description as practices founded in an imagined doctrinal foundation. This judicial transformation of religion is presented as being counter-intuitive to the nature of religious experience of almost all religious traditions in the Indian sub-continent. And in turn, this is presented as a challenge to secure the allegiance and consent of the Indian people to the ever-widening reach of state power over religion in contemporary India.

Introduction

Constitutional texts and practices manifest the form in which a political formation pulls together in an act of self-expression. In its detail, this constitutional self-expression illustrates judgements about the order, unity, and the form in which a common will is to be mobilized. In other words, constitutional government is not only about technical legal responses to specific challenges but also about the deeper commitments on the very orientation and ends of the sovereign state power. Viewed in this manner constitutions are the ground on which the popular will that founds legal authority crafts specific engagement with the range of issues that define a constitutional community over time.[1] From this vantage point, all domains of social and cultural power are subject to the workings of state power, especially as witnessed by the elaboration, expansion and working of constitutional government over the course of the twentieth century. Set against this background of state power, the present essay examines the impact of constitutional power on religious practice in India.

Examining the government of religious practice as a mobilization of state power is particularly apt in the Indian context as its Constitution has been explicitly organized to enable the exercise of state power over what are widely viewed to be backward and ethically deformed nodes of religious, social and cultural power. However, this assertion of state power is often entangled in the normative or ideological language of secularism, equal rights and, social revolution – the forms through which state power over religion is organized.[2] It is undoubtedly true that the dispositions that animate these normative responses have been crucial to shape the ethical horizons of Indian constitutional practice and in ensuring the legally valid exercise of state power. However, normative analysis often masks the specific nature of the claims that sovereign power makes on religious practice and whether they are indeed legitimate, the presumable object of constitutional government.

Accordingly, outlining the practice of religious freedom in the Indian Constitution, this essay will argue that the power exerted by the epistemic frames structuring the Constitution's normative claims over religion, misunderstand distort and flatten out local conceptions of religion spirituality and ethical striving. In turn, this throws in doubt the legitimacy of claims that constitutional practice has made over religious traditions and their freedoms. To make this case, it is first useful to elaborate in greater detail the idea of constitutional power as a force that enables a political community to act in concert rather than a mere constraint on state action.

Constitutionalism, community and the enablement of religious freedom

The conception of constitutional power as a force that enables collective action, lurks in the background even of discussions of religious freedom understood as a space autonomous from state control. Michael Oakeshott traces this enabling conception of modern state power to strands of thinking about state formation in Europe that he terms the *universitas* and the *societas*. Drawing on forms of association in Roman law, the *universitas* is a state imagined on the lines of a corporation established to pursue a common end.[3] The *universitas* is accordingly 'telocaratic' in its orientation to facilitate the management of common concerns. A *universitas* is contrasted with the state understood as a *societas*, a condition where, as Oakeshott puts it:

> [T]he ruler of a state when it is understood as a societas is the custodian of the loyalties of the association and the guardian and administrator of the conditions which constitute the relationship of socii. He cannot, for example, be the owner or trustee of its property, because it has none; and he is not the manager or director of its activities, because there are no such activities to be managed. This ruler is a master of ceremonies, not an arbiter of fashion. His concern is with the 'manners' of convives, and his office is to keep the conversation going, not to determine what is said. Thus, a state understood in terms of societas is ... a civitas, and its government (whatever its constitution) is a nomocracy whose laws are to be understood as conditions of conduct, not devices instrumental to the satisfaction of preferred wants."[4]

Conventionally religious freedom as it is understood in the liberal democratic playbook is solely associated with the *societas*. However, Oakeshott argues that the *societas* and the *universitas* should not be understood as mutually exclusive models that coincide with particular regimes of state power. On the contrary, he argues that they are to be seen as reflecting contrary dispositions in human nature to be autonomous as well as to be part of a common venture respectively which contingently leave their imprint on political association.

Consequently, drawing on Oakeshott, Martin Loughlin explains that the *societas* and the *universitas* are part of a 'polarized consciousness' which contains the possibility of different contingently possible forms of association that pragmatic motivations of human agents might generate.[5] Therefore, as an expression of collective action, protecting religious freedom in different political contexts could foreground and display the imprint of this polarized consciousness.

For the purposes of this paper, it is not necessary to evaluate the psychology of human action on which this conception of state power is founded. Instead, it is sufficient to note that as expressions of popular will, both the *universitas* and the *societas* are entirely legitimate forms of mobilizing the consenting will of a sovereign political community. And, equally importantly both of these forms have as a matter of fact constituted the spirit and form in which state and governmental power has been organized across the course of the twentieth century.[6]

Conceiving state power primarily as a product of collective action raises the challenge of potentially unlimited and arbitrary sovereign power, especially when it takes the form of the *universitas*. This is of course a complex subject that cannot be resolved in a couple of sentences. Even so, Loughlin's answer to this problem draws on a long and venerable tradition of political thought that ties the legitimacy of sovereign state power to limitations that it is subjected to when expressed in the form of law and rules and, by extension to the allegiance of the people. Thus, Loughlin links the enormous augmentation of state power over the last century to the ability to work through the limitations of legal forms and thereby secure the consent of those over whom the ruler seeks to rule.[7]

Whatever be the success of law as a form of limiting arbitrary state power there can be little doubt that the legal form of modern constitutional states has played some part in the enormous augmentation of state power. And it is against this background that this paper examines the working of the constitutionally protected right to religious freedom. It does so by examining the epistemic forms through which the Indian Constitution frames religious freedom and argues that constitutional practice produces a crisis in legitimacy as it misunderstands and mischaracterizes significant aspects of social practice and ethical striving that mark the Indian religious traditions.

The structure of religious freedom in the Indian constitution

In what is now a well-worn description of the problem religion posed for constitutional politics in India, B. R. Ambedkar intervened in a debate on impending reform of religious personal laws in the Constituent Assembly in the following manner:

> *(t)he religious conceptions in this country are so vast that they cover every aspect of life, from birth to death.* There is nothing which is not religion and if personal law is to be saved, I am sure about it that in social matters we will come to a standstill... There is nothing extraordinary in saying that *we ought to strive hereafter to limit the definition of religion in such a manner that we shall not extend beyond beliefs and such rituals as may be connected with ceremonials which are essentially religious* .. I personally do not understand why religion should be given this vast, expansive jurisdiction so as to cover the whole of life and to prevent the legislature from encroaching upon that field.[8] (emphasis added)

In other words, Ambedkar expressed a reasonably widely held belief that far too much of social life was tainted by religion. Consequently, the search for beliefs and practices which Ambedkar calls 'essentially religious' was an attempt to reduce its expansive and pernicious reach over social life. This mission to reform and reduce religion to its essential core is significant as it has been at the heart of the Indian constitutional practice of religious freedom, and the procedures through which this essential core is determined require closer examination.

Social reform through social compact

Only a cursory glance at the discussions on religious freedom in the processes of the Indian Constituent Assembly reveal the importance that the state vision for reforming practices associated with religious beliefs played in the drafting of provisions on religious freedom. The right to religious freedom took early shape in the Assembly when the Fundamental Rights Sub-Committee[9] adopted a draft clause presented to it by K.M. Munshi granting all persons equal rights to freedom of conscience and the right to freely *practice* religion, subject to the maintenance of public order, morality or health. A clarifying clause stated that 'the right to profess and practice religion shall not include economic, financial, political or other secular activities associated with religious worship.'[10] However, this provision was almost instantly subjected to strong and sustained opposition by the reformers in the assembly.

Speaking for the reformist position, Rajkumari Amrit Kaur expressed apprehensions about Munshi's clause 'inasmuch as it might invalidate legislation against anti-social customs which might have the sanction of religion.'[11] To facilitate such legislation Rajkumari Amrit Kaur thought it appropriate to limit religious freedom by conceiving of it narrowly to include only the right to conscience and worship and not the right to religious practice.[12] Thus when another committee addressing the concerns of Minorities suggested that the right of religious freedom be tied to 'religious practice', it was again opposed by Amrit Kaur who feared that

> they would not only be a bar to future social legislation but would even invalidate past legislation such as the Widow Remarriage Act, the Sarda Act or even the law abolishing Sati. Everyone is aware how many evil practices, which one would like to abolish, are carried on in the name of religion, e.g., purdah, polygamy, caste disabilities, animal sacrifice, dedication of girls to temples, to mention a few.[13]

Amrit Kaur's concerns were not unusual and many other powerful voices in the assembly expressed similar positions[14] and, her arguments for constraining religious practice formed an important part of the constitutional vision seeking to narrow religion to its essential core.

The ambitions of the reformers as expressed by Amrit Kaur were driven by the entirely laudable and almost unquestionable objective of eradicating unethical practices that were understood to be associated with the Hindu religion. However, as Shyama Prasad Mookherjee and others pointed out, a reform agenda that sought to target and restrict religious practices would impose potentially unjustifiable burdens on the Indian religious traditions which as a matter of fact emphasized practice and practices over worship. Consequently, Mookherjee suggested that the assembly provides a significantly greater leeway for practice, permitting reform of religious practices only in exceptional circumstances. Recognizing these challenges, it was decided on the suggestion of C Rajagopalachari that a more comprehensive provision would be drafted in which practices would be included as part of the right to freedom but one that also empowered the legislature to reform religious practices as a separate proviso[15] A re-drafted clause was accordingly adopted as Article 25 of the contemporary Constitution.

Various aspects of the right to religious freedom are of course dealt with in the Constitution in three articles besides Article 25.[16] However, it is in Article 25 that the constitution lays out both the general contours of the right to religion and the power of the state to reform aspects of religious practice. In its detail, one part of Art 25 is structured like a standard liberal freedom where the right to practice profess and propagate religion is qualified by standard liberal restraints demanding that such practice does not affect the similar rights of others (Article 25(1)). However, in addition the Constitution also includes an altogether different kind of restraint on religious practice which permits the State to restrain religious freedom by subjecting it to the state's power to 'regulate or restrict economic, financial, political or other secular activity which may be associated with religious practice' (Art 25(a)) or, 'provide for social welfare and reform or the throwing open of Hindu religious institutions of a public character to all classes and sections of Hindus.' (Art.25(2)(b)). It is this explicit mandate for the exercise of state power to reform religion that has permitted and even required that constitutional practice structure religion into a core set of essential beliefs and practices protected by the right to religious freedoms and a not so essential periphery which has been subject to state-led reform. This distinction has been most clearly elaborated in judicial decisions on the essential core of a religious tradition which must now be examined to understand the impact of state power on religious practice.[17]

The search for the truth of religious practices

In one of the earliest and definitive decisions on the issue of essential religious practices,[18] the Supreme Court was called to decide on the constitutional validity of the Madras Hindu Religious and Charitable Endowments Act 1951. It was contended by the petitioner in the case that this statute, which granted the government power to take over mismanaged Hindu religious institutions as a trustee, violated the community's right to religious freedom and to manage religious institutions as permitted by Art 25(1) and Art 26[19] of the Constitution.

Countering the claims of the petitioner, the State contended that it had the broadest powers of regulating all 'secular' aspects related to a religious tradition under Art. 25(2)(a) – an argument made by many of the reformers in the constituent assembly to assert state power to reform socially unjust practices. Though the Constituent Assembly resolved this question to facilitate religious practice, a stretched reading of Art 25 and 26 might perhaps suggest that the State could regulate and reform religion as long as it did not completely extinguish the right to religious freedom. However, the court categorically refused to accept this contention that the right to religious freedom extended only to the essential bonds of belief and conscience between believers and their deities.

Instead, it held that

> what constitutes the essential part of a religion is primarily to be *ascertained with reference to the doctrines of that religion itself*... and the mere fact that they involve expenditure of money or employment of priests and servants or the use of marketable commodities would not make them secular activities..(emphasis added)[20]

In other words, the court stressed that the essential core of a religion was to be determined by taking into account those doctrines and practices that a community *subjectively* viewed to be essential to their religion. This exercise of judicial power clearly seeks to ground state intervention in religious practice, quite like Martin Loughlin argues, so as to enhance the reach and legitimacy of state power. However, in what manner would the court arrive at a subjectively satisfactory account of essential religious beliefs and practices that would command the allegiance of a practitioner or a community?

It is important to note here that it is the court itself that will have to ultimately make a 'subjective' and sympathetic determination about whether the claims of an individual or a community forms part of the core of its religious tradition. As a matter of fact, Indian courts have over the years acted almost as theologians sifting between different kinds of religious claims, establishing some while denying others. Thus, for example, the Supreme Court has held that the sacrifice of cows did not constitute an essential part of the Islamic faith[21]; overruled Muslim claims that prayer in a mosque was crucial to the Islamic faith[22]; refused to accept traditional rights of the Tilkayats of the Shrinathji temple at Nathdwara which was taken from them by the Nathdwara Temple Act, 1959[23]; stipulated that the tandava dance was not a significant part of the Anand Margi community[24]; declared that the followers of Aurobindo did not constitute a distinct religion[25] and so on. As in any hermeneutic exercise, there are many equally valid candidates that could claim to be the essential religious truth leaving the court open to the charge that its determinations of essential religious practice are entirely ad hoc.[26]

Nonetheless, this essay will suggest that it is possible to discern the working of a common conceptual grid in the judicial representation of essential religion that is common across interpretative differences in specific cases. To do so we must extrapolate two inchoately articulated conceptions of religious practice as it was fashioned by Justice Mukherjea in his decision in the *Shirur Mutt* case. The *first* of these draws on an intuitive sociology of Indian religions that emphasizes the importance of traditions of religious *practice*. In the words of the court,

> (t)here are well known religions in India like Buddhism and Jainism which do not believe in God or in any Intelligent First Cause ... A religion might not only prescribe rituals and observances, ceremonies and modes of worship which are regarded as integral parts of religion, and these forms and observances might extend even to matters of food and dress"[27]

However, tied into this intuitive sociological account of religion is a second conceptual scheme through which essential practice might be characterized. In the words of the court,

> *A religion undoubtedly has its basis in a system of beliefs or doctrines* which are regarded by those who profess that religion as conducive to their spiritual well-being,.[28] (emphasis added)

Thus, though the court places considerable emphasis on traditions of practice and ritual as the distinctive markers of religion, it collapses practice into doctrine when it asserts that practices are *founded* in doctrine. This then is a second frame that the court employs to characterize religion.

Most importantly as we will note presently, the court has also come to describe religion as practices founded in the truth of its doctrines.

However, the link between doctrine and practice or the lack of it requires more explanation. Pratap Bhanu Mehta illustrates this bond by drawing out different senses of being religious from two important figures in Roman antiquity. Extracting from Cicero's *De Natura Deorum* Mehta presents a practice-oriented religion by contrasting it with superstition

> *religion has been* dissociated from superstition not only by philosophers but by our own ancestors as well. I may mention as to these two terms that men who used to spend whole days in prayer and sacrifice in order that their children might survive them (*essent superstites*), were called *superstitiosus*, a title which afterwards extended more widely, while such as heedfully repeated and, as it were, "regathered" (*relegerent*) everything that formed a part of divine worship, were named *religiosus* from *relegere*,. . . . It was in this way that with the words *superstitiosus* and *religiosus*, the one became the designation of a fault, the other of an excellence.[29]

Cicero is contrasted with Lactantius, a Christian who took issue with this characterization of religion a few centuries later. According to Lactantius, religion is a bond of piety that ties man to God. Countering Cicero's account of religion he argued that

> (t)he word is not as Cicero interpreted it from "re-reading," or "choosing again" (*relegendo*)... it is important, really, why you worship, not how you worship, or what you pray for... We have said that *the name of religion is taken from the bond of piety, because God has bound and fastened man to Himself of piety, since it is necessary for us to serve Him as Lord and obey Him as father... They are superstitious who worship many and false gods; but we, who supplicate the one true God, are religious.*[30] (emphasis in original)

There are therefore three different sensibilities that could be drawn from Mehta's discussion of religiosity. First, religion as the devotion to regathering and repetition of much that is excellent or valued in a tradition; second, religion as a commitment to superstitious, excessive or absurd practice; and third, religion as commitment to true theology. For Cicero, religion is a way of life or a set of inherited and excellent practices. The only reason for its practice is pre-existing practice whose repetition regathers the sense of an ongoing tradition. That is, the significance of practice is nothing but repetition such that it can re-create a valuable social and cultural milieu, with superstition or excessiveness being the contrasting value against which it acquires salience. Significantly, the truth or falsity of belief or doctrine is unimportant to Cicero's conception of religion while it is the basis of Lactantius' conception of his religion.

Mehta glosses over the significance of the distinctions between these different conceptions of religion.[31] However, Ronojoy Sen in an excellent essay, reviewing the Indian Supreme Court's adjudication of state power to reforms religious practice, employs these distinctions to describe what he understands to be the legal and judicial rationalization of religion and especially of the Hindu religion. That is, he argues that the adjudication of religious freedom results in a collapse of practice into doctrine where courts reform, re-characterize or rationalize the everyday practices of 'Hinduism' (in particular) in the image of a doctrinal or Vedic Hindu religion. The present essay draws on this conception of rationalization but argues that it is far more widespread than claimed by Sen. That is, it makes the case that rationalization or doctrinalization through judicial intervention applies to all forms of Indian religiosity. More importantly, it is also argued that this rationalizing approach to the Indian religious traditions commits a category mistake that misidentifies and distorts the Indian religious traditions in the process of rationalization. That is, that law's rationalizing approach operates with an epistemic and conceptual outlook that is unable to recognize subcontinental religiosity as traditions of ethical practice, whether these be tied to canonical or ritual driven Hinduism or indeed any other religious tradition.[32]

Justice Mukherjea, who decided the Shirur Mutt case and shaped the judicial approach to essential religious practices could potentially have captured this practice-based approach to religiosity. However, his decision already had elements of a rationalized form of religion where practice was understood to be founded in the truth of doctrine. Consequently, as he had no clear conceptual manner of accounting for and defending practice based traditional religiosity, subsequent decisions were unable to defend a conception of religion founded on ethical and spiritual striving and practice against the rationalizing and reforming dispositions of the Indian state and judiciary. The specific form in which this rationalizing distorts Indian religious experience or is unable to engage with the contours of religious experience, however, requires closer scrutiny and is elaborated in the following sections.

The peculiar presence of religion in Indian Constitutional adjudication

Understanding 'religion' as traditions or cycles of practice and striving (even when ethically deformed) is deeply ingrained in the intuitions of almost all religious and cultural traditions in India and the approach of rationalization or doctrinalization impacts almost all of India's religious traditions. The present essay will, therefore, examine this problem through two classic decisions of the Supreme Court on the reform or rationalization of two very different religious traditions to illustrate the difficulties produced by the rationalization of these traditions in terms of essential religious doctrines. In both cases, the religious practices concerned are by most counts ethically unpalatable calling for some kind of state intervention. However, the question that follows is whether state intervention fashioned by the Supreme Court is organized in a manner that is likely to secure the allegiance of the adherents. This problem is examined in greater detail in what follows.

In *Sardar Syedna Taher Saifuddin Saheb v. The State of Bombay*[33] the Indian Supreme Court considered a constitutional challenge brought by the *Dai-ul-Mutlaq* or religious head of the Dawoodi Bohra community against the validity of the Bombay Prevention of Excommunication Act 1949. The statute was a social reform initiative of the then Bombay legislature and was passed on the back of a Privy Council judgment which had decided that the *Dai* was the head of the Dawoodi Bohra community and had the right to excommunicate any member of the community after calling for a fair hearing. Responding to this judgment the statute penalized acts of excommunication which abridged community members' access to religious property, places of worship, burial grounds and so on. Consequently, defending excommunication as an important aspects of the Bohra tradition, the Dai on behalf of the Dawoodi Bohra community approached the Court on grounds that that the statute violated various aspects of their right to religious freedom.

Delivering the decision of the majority, Justice Dasgupta recounts the claims of the petitioners regarding excommunication in the following manner:

> According to the petitioner it is "an integral part of the religion and religious faith and belief of the Dawoodi Bohra community" that excommunication should be pronounced by him in suitable cases. It was urged that *even if this right to excommunicate is considered to be a religious practice as distinct from religious faith such religious practice is also a part of the religion of the Dawoodi Bohra community.(emphasis added)*[34]

The Bohras, therefore, sought to make a defence of their religion based on their traditional practices and challenged the ban on excommunication on these grounds as violating religious freedom. As already mentioned these claims, of course, say very little about whether these claims are ethically fair or justified. Perhaps Bohra practice would even qualify as superstitious or excessive practice from a Ciceronian perspective as discussed earlier or perhaps just downright unjust.[35] Nonetheless, it is important to note that the Dawoodi claim is advanced solely in traditional terms as a practice held with high regard. But that is not how the court characterized the practice of excommunication even as it decided in favour of the Dai that the statute was a violation of essential religious freedoms.

Justice Dasgupta considered the question of excommunication to be indispensable to the sustenance of a religious community in general and noted that it was a practice common to Muslim communities from the earliest histories of the faith. As mentioned in his decision – "the Prophet and the Imam had this right; and it is not disputed that the Dais have also in the past exercised it on a number of occasions. There can be little doubt that heresy or apostasy was a crime for which excommunication was in force among the Dawoodi Bohras also."[36] Accordingly, he held that the

Bombay statute abridged rights of a community to manage its affairs as granted under Art. 26(b) and was therefore unconstitutional. It is important to notice that though Dasgupta J. defended the rights of the Bohras, he equivocates on his support for their claims about their traditional practices through a discussion of the status of excommunication within Islam. Thus, even though he affirms the centrality of excommunication to religion in general and to Islam, in particular, it is not entirely clear whether the practice is grounded in traditional practice or in Islamic doctrine. Nonetheless, it is precise as a traditional religious practice that the *Dai* argued his right to excommunicate errant members by drawing a distinction as they termed it between religious practice and faith. This distinction acquires far greater salience in the dissenting decision of Justice Sinha.

The rationalist in Justice Sinha comes to the fore when he casts the problem of excommunication in terms of individual belief. Thus, he asks whether an individual can 'be compelled to have a particular belief on pain of a penalty, like excommunication? One is entitled to believe or not to believe a particular tenet or to follow or not to follow a particular practice in matters of religion. No one can, therefore, be compelled, against his own judgment and belief, to hold any particular creed or follow a set of religious practises.' Casting the practice of excommunication in this manner allows him see it as not being *essentially or doctrinally* connected to the Bohra faith, a claim also made by a dissenting member of the community in submissions to the court. Consequently, drawing on the Supreme Court's decision in *Durgah Committee, Ajmer v. Syed Hussain*,[37] Justice Sinha asserts that constitutional protection extends only to essential and presumably doctrinally essential features of a religion and not to incidental and superstitious accretions to religion. Consequently, by casting excommunication as a superstitious accretion and also as one affecting civil rights of dissenting members of the Bohra community, Justice Sinha is able to disregard its status as a practice to hold that the excommunication law was legally valid.

The Sardar Syedna case is not an exception as judicial interpretation of essential practices has in numerous cases passed over the experiences, intuitions and practices of religious practitioners and communities by casting traditional practice as being founded in doctrine.[38] However, the problem is particularly stark in relation to the 'Hindu' traditions where it has always been considerably more difficult to speak of these traditions in doctrinal terms. And, this problem is sharply illustrated through the much-discussed Swaminarayan decision of the Supreme Court addressing temple entry reform.

Accordingly, in *Sastri Yagnapurshdasji v. Muldas Bhudardas* Vaishya,[39] the Satsangis or followers of Swaminarayan, a nineteenth-century social reformer, claimed immunity from the provisions of a temple entry statute, the Bombay Hindu Places of Public Worship (Entry-Authori zation) Act 1956. Like all other temple entry legislations in India, the statute barred Hindu temples of a public character from refusing entry to any class or section of Hindus on the ground that they belonged to an untouchable caste or community.

Arguing for their traditional and perhaps essential freedoms, the Satsangis claimed they were not bound by the temple entry statute because they were a religious sect entirely distinct from the Hindu religion. They argued that though they could be considered socially and culturally Hindu, they were not part of the Hindu 'religion' because

> Swaminarayan, the founder of the sect, considered himself as the Supreme God, and as such, the sect that believes in the divinity of Swaminarayan cannot be assimilated with the followers of Hindu religion. It was also urged that the temples in suit had been established for the worship of Swaminarayan himself and not for the worship of the traditional Hindu idols .. It was further contended that the sect propagated the ideal that worship of any God other than Swaminarayan would be a betrayal of his faith, and lastly, that the Acharyas who had been appointed by Swaminarayan adopted a procedure of "Initiation" (*diksha*) which showed that on initiation, the devotee became a Satsangi and assumed a distinct and separate character as a follower of the sect.[40]

That is, the Satsangis offered a subjective and traditional account of what made them into a distinct religious community with practices they viewed as distinct from the Hindu 'religion'.

However, it was not clear whether and how this description of their practices set them apart from the Hindu 'religion'. What was the Hindu religion from which the Satsangis claimed distinctness? This question was considered at length by Justice Gajendragadkar and formed the basis of his decision.

Delivering the unanimous opinion of the Supreme Court, Chief Justice Gajendragadkar disallowed the Satsangi claims, pronounced them 'Hindu' and subjected them to the demands of the temple entry statute. However, there was an irresolvable contradiction in Justice Gajendragadkar's account of the Hindu religion. On the one hand, he argued that the Hindu religion

> does not claim any one prophet; it does not worship any one God; it does not subscribe to any one dogma; it does not believe in any one philosophic concept; it does not follow any one set of religious rites or performances; in fact, it does not appear to satisfy the narrow traditional features of any religion or creed. It may broadly be described as a way of life and nothing more.[41]

This account of the Hindu religion might perhaps seem far too vague to refer to any well-defined or discrete entity. However, despite its fuzziness, this account of the Hindu religion is precisely what this essay has identified as traditional religiosity. Of course, in the specific facts of this case, it would be very difficult to associate the narrow and insular vision of the Swaminarayan's as having much to do with a quest for spiritual truth. Nonetheless, it is sufficient for the moment to note the resolutely non-doctrinal forms of sub-continental religiosity that Gajendragadkar intuitively drew upon to both locate the Swaminarayan tradition and to consider whether they were Hindu.

On the other hand, however, Justice Gajendragadkar's opinion also advanced a much more formalist, reductive definition of the Hindu religion. Drawing significantly from the writing of Dr S. Radhakrishnan and other modern commentators on the 'Hindu' traditions, Justice Gajendragadkar went on to note that the wide variety of practices and philosophical reflections found in the tradition were nevertheless held together by a common philosophy of monistic idealism. That is,

> (b)eneath the diversity of philosophic thoughts, concepts and ideas expressed by Hindu philosophers .. lie certain broad concepts which can be treated as basic. The first amongst these basic concepts is the acceptance of the Veda as the highest authority in religious and philosophic matters ..[42]

With this rationalizing turn, Justice Gajendragadkar defined the Hindu religion, not in traditional terms as has been described earlier, but in terms of ideas such as rebirth and predestination which he likened to doctrine. It is this doctrinal account of Hinduism that he ultimately used to refute the Swaminarayans' claim that they were sufficiently distinct from Hinduism as to constitute a separate religion, which he dismissed as simply a product of 'superstition, ignorance and complete misunderstanding of the *true teachings* of Hindu religion and of the real significance of the tenets and philosophy taught by Swaminarayan himself.'[43] (emphasis added)

Of course, Gajendragadkar used a doctrinal account of Hinduism to justify a conclusion that few can disagree with – that the state had to intervene in and redress some of the worst excesses of social exclusion in Indian society. Even so, both in this case and in the Syedna case the court collapsed a practice based traditional account of religion into an essential or doctrinal entity in the process of determining the legitimate domain of essential religious practices and by extension of religious freedom. However, if religious experiences in India stem largely from traditions of practice, and if the task of regulating religion requires some form of balancing between the right to traditional practice and that of the state to intervene in objectionable practices then it is unlikely that rationalizing forms of judicial intervention as we have described them in this essay are the most likely candidates to generate consent within the communities whose practices the state seeks to reform and govern. In fact, the epistemic framework in which the Supreme Court has cast religious freedom mischaracterizes religious practice and experience and perhaps even comes in the way of generating a genuine conversation about those practices and securing the consent of the adherents for state intervention. It is this aspect of state power that this essay has attempted to foreground and it is on this note that we must now draw towards a conclusion.

Conclusion

This essay has outlined the manner in which constitutional power has shaped the contours of religious freedom. While the imprint of the *universitas* in particular has shaped the contours of religious freedom in contemporary India, its embodiment in the essential practices test has been unable to draw on the traditions of practice and truth-seeking that have defined Indian traditions of religious and spiritual striving. Of course, this is not to suggest in any manner that there is anything that is inherently morally and ethically superior in traditional and practice-based religion.[44] In fact, the examples discussed by the essay only demonstrate that there is much that might be odious ethically degenerate in traditional practice. Nonetheless, to the extent that liberal democratic power is structured by the bond of consent that ties citizens to states, it would only seem proper that attempts are made to organize state power in ways that can best seek the allegiance of the people it seeks to govern.

Thus, state power can and must intervene in practices like excommunication, temple entry or indeed any other practice that the legal process deems worthy of regulation. However, the challenge posed by the existing model of regulation based on judicial determination of essential practices is that of one of fashioning an ethic of intervention that is able at the same time to grant some form of epistemic recognition to the Indian religious traditions. This task requires a reconsideration of the essential practices model and a consideration of alternative models of fashioning intervention that are consistent with traditional religiosity. Set against that task, this essay must be viewed as a preliminary effort in clearing the ground towards that end.

Notes

1. For an account of the strands of thinking reflecting the deeper constitutional commitments that inflect juridical rules, see Martin Loughlin, 'Droit Politique' (2017) 17 Jus Politicum: Revue de Droit Politique 295.
2. For a sample of the Indian debate see Derrett, *Religion, Law and the State in India*; Dhavan and Nariman, 'The Supreme Court and Group Life: Religious Freedom, Minority Groups and Disadvantaged Communities'; Galanter, 'Hinduism, Secularism, and the Indian Judiciary'; Surendranath, 'Essential Practices Doctrine: Towards Inevitable Constitutional Burial'; Bhatia, 'Freedom from Community'.
3. Oakeshott, *On Human Conduct*, 205–6.
4. Ibid., 202–3.
5. Loughlin, *Foundations of Public Law*, 163.
6. See Loughlin, *Foundations of Public Law* Especially Chapter 7 which discusses law as embodying the spirit of a people.
7. See also Arendt, *On Revolution*.
8. *Constituent Assembly Debates*, 7:781.
9. The Indian constituent assembly was advised by an Advisory committee set up under the Cabinet Mission Statement. In turn, the Advisory committee constituted sub-committees on various aspects of Constitutional governance. A considerable part of the structure and design of religious freedom took shape in the deliberations of this committee process especially in the sub-committees on fundamental rights and on minority rights.
10. Rao et al., *The Framing of India's Constitution*, 2:122, 140.
11. Ibid., 2:122.
12. Ibid., 2:146–47.
13. Ibid., 2:213.
14. For instance, draft clauses submitted by Ambedkar included provisions abolishing 'any privilege or disability arising out of rank, birth, person, family, religion or religious usage and custom', as well as preventing the State from making or enforcing 'any custom which shall abridge the privileges or immunities of any citizens'. Art. II, Section 1, (1)&(2); Additionally Govind Ballabh Pant expressed similar opinions in the advisory committee discussing the issue of religious freedom when he argued against inclusion of a right to religious practice in the right to religious freedom. According to him 'To say that it will be open to people to

claim a safeguard against a thing done by the legislature in the Supreme or other courts on the ground that the law infringes the practices that come under the name of religion is to make any Constitution utterly unworkable ... by introducing the word "religion" it will militate against any real right of religious worship.' Ibid., 2:79,86, 265.

15. Ibid., 2:265–67.
16. This essay only deals with Article 25 and to some extent Article 26 (which addresses the freedom of religious denominations to manage their affairs). However, the Constitution also makes provision for freedom from religious tax (Article 27) and freedom from religious instruction in schools (Article 28).
17. See Sen, 'The Indian Supreme Court and the Quest for a 'rational' Hinduism'.
18. *The Commissioner Hindu Religious Endowments, Madras v. Sri Laxmindra Thirtha Swamiar of Shirur Mutt* MANU/SC/0136/1954.
19. Article 26 reads "Subject to public order, morality and health, every religious denomination or any section thereof shall have the right – (a) to establish and maintain institutions for religious and charitable purposes; (b) to manage its own affairs in matters of religion; (c) to own and acquire movable and immovable property; and (d) to administer such property in accordance with law.
20. *Shirur Mutt* Case MANU/SC/0136/1954., para 20.
21. *M.H. Qureshi v. State of Bihar* AIR 1958 SC 731.
22. *Ismail Faruqui v. UOI* (1994) 6 SCC 360.
23. *Tilkayat Shri Govindlalji Maharaj v. State of Rajasthan* AIR 1963 SC 1638.
24. *Jagdishwaranand v. Police Commissioner, Calcutta* AIR 1984 SC 51.
25. *S.P. Mittal v. Union of India* AIR 1983 SC 1.
26. Dhavan, 'Religious Freedom in India,' 209.
27. Shirur Mutt Case., para 17.
28. Ibid.
29. Mehta, "On the Possibility of Religious Pluralism," 67.
30. Ibid., 67–68.
31. For a more elaborate discussion of the distinctions Mehta makes it is useful to note the more elaborately argued position by S. N. Balagangadhara on the role that the Christian idea of *religion* played in the transformation of the Roman *tradition*. See Balagangadhara, "The Heathen in His Blindness," chap. 2.
32. This is an observation made by Balagangadhara and De Roover though they describe its operation in relation to the secular state and its ability to treat religions equally. Balagangadhara and Roover, 'The Secular State and Religious Conflict'. Ashish Nandy also makes a similar point when we notes the distinction between religion as ideology and religion as faith. Nandy, 'The Politics of Secularism and the Recovery of Toleration', 322–23.
33. MANU/SC/0072/1962.
34. MANU/SC/0072/1962 para 43.
35. Mehta, "On the Possibility of Religious Pluralism."
36. See note 34 above. 42.
37. MANU/SC/0063/1961.
38. See Supra notes 9–14.
39. AIR 1966 SC 1119.
40. Ibid., 1123.
41. Ibid., 1128.
42. Ibid., 1130.
43. Id. at 1135.
44. See Discussion of Mehta in the section, 'The search for the truth of religious practices'.

Disclosure statement

No potential conflict of interest was reported by the author.

Bibliography

Arendt, H. *On Revolution*. New York: Penguin Books, 1965.

Balagangadhara, S. N. *The Heathen in His Blindness: Asia, the West, and the Dynamic of Religion*. 2nd ed. New Delhi: Manohar, 2005.

Balagangadhara, S. N., and J. De Roover. "The Secular State and Religious Conflict: Liberal Neutrality and the Indian Case of Pluralism." *Journal of Political Philosophy* 15, no. 1 (2007): 67–92. doi:10.1111/j.1467-9760.2007.00268.x.

Bhatia, G. "Freedom from Community: Individual Rights, Group Life, State Authority and Religious Freedom under the Indian Constitution." *Global Constitutionalism* 5, no. 3 (November, 2016): 351–382. doi:10.1017/S2045381716000228.

Constituent Assembly Debates: Official Report. Vol. 7. 12 vols. New Delhi: Lok Sabha Secretariat, 1999.

Derrett, J., and M. Duncan. *Religion, Law and the State in India*. Delhi: Oxford University Press, 1999.

Dhavan, R. "Religious Freedom in India." *The American journal of comparative law* 35 (1987): 209–254. doi:10.2307/840167.

Dhavan, R., and F. S. Nariman. "The Supreme Court and Group Life: Religious Freedom, Minority Groups and Disadvantaged Communities." In *Supreme but Not Infallible: Essays in Honour of the Supreme Court of India*, edited by B. N. Kirpal, A. H. Desai, G. Subramanium, R. Dhavan, and R. Ramachandran, 256–287. New Delhi: Oxford University Press, 2000.

Galanter, M. "Hinduism, Secularism, and the Indian Judiciary." In *Secularism and Its Critics*, edited by R. Bhargava, 268–295. Delhi: Oxford University Press, 1999.

Gandhi, M. *Hindu Dharma*. New Delhi: Orient Paperbacks, 1978.

Loughlin, M. *Foundations of Public Law*. Reprint ed. Oxford: OUP, 2010.

Mehta, P. B. "On the Possibility of Religious Pluralism." In *Religious Pluralism, Globalization, and World Politics*, edited by T. Banchoff, 65–88. Oxford: Oxford University Press, 2008.

Nandy, A. "The Politics of Secularism and the Recovery of Toleration." In *Secularism and Its Critics*, edited by R. Bhargava, 321–344. Delhi: Oxford University Press, 1999.

Oakeshott, M. *On Human Conduct*. Oxford: Clarendon Press, 1975.

Rao, B. S., V. K. N. Menon, S. C. Kashyap, and N. K. N. Iyengar. *The Framing of India's Constitution*. Vol. 2 vols. 6 vols. New Delhi: Indian Institute of Public Administration, 1966.

Sen, R. "The Indian Supreme Court and the Quest for a 'Rational' Hinduism." *South Asian History and Culture* 1, no. 1 December 22 (2009): 86–104. doi:10.1080/19472490903387258.

Surendranath, A. "Essential Practices Doctrine: Towards Inevitable Constitutional Burial." *Journal of the National Human Rights Commission, India* 15 (2016): 159–176.

Cases

Durgah Committee, Ajmer v. Syed Hussain MANU/SC/0063/1961

Ismail Faruqui v. UOI (1994) 6 SCC 360

Jagdishwaranand v. Police Commissioner, Calcutta AIR 1984 SC 51

M.H. Qureshi v. State of Bihar AIR 1958 SC 731

S.P. Mittal v. Union of India AIR 1983 SC 1

Sardar Syedna Taher Saifuddin Saheb v. The State of Bombay MANU/SC/0072/1962

Sastri Yagnapurshdasji v. Muldas Bhudardas Vaishya

The Commissioner Hindu Religious Endowments, Madras v. Sri Laxmindra Thirtha Swamiar of Shirur Mutt MANU/SC/0136/1954

Tilkayat Shri Govindlalji Maharaj v. State of Rajastan AIR 1963 SC 1638

Ritual death in a secular state: the Jain practice of Sallekhana

Manisha Sethi

ABSTRACT

The Rajasthan High Court criminalized the Jain practice of ritual voluntary death, variously termed sallekhana or santhara in 2015. The petition that sought its criminalization, and the court judgment were both framed in the language of religious reform and invoked judicial memory of sati. The Jain defenders of the practice, insisted on its difference from sati on the one hand, and suicide and euthanasia on the other, which too continued to remain beyond the pale of legality. However, in setting it up as an 'essential practice', which would afford it the protection of Article 25, they simultaneously drew upon Jainism's ethical teachings – mobilizing a range of ancient texts, providing a list of their religious figures and historical personalities who met 'death with equanimity' – and the moral and legal arguments utilized by euthanasia advocates, in particular the debates around the Right to Life. This paper thus examines the anxieties that have framed the debate on both sides, and asks what happens when piety and belief enter, or rather, are dragged into the courtroom: when one party seeks its denunciation and another its validation, or indifference even, from modern, rational law? The paper also examines if the High Court judgment is the result of the Christian/colonial legal legacy, which abhorred and outlawed suicide, as claimed by many commentators, by scrutinizing the colonial attitudes to sallekhana.

According to the Jains, their ancient texts enjoin them under certain circumstances to progressively renounce food and water, till life ebbs away. This vow is termed variously as sallekhana, santhara, samadhimaran or panditamarana.[1] In 2015, the Rajasthan High Court adjudicating on a Public Interest Litigation writ petition challenging this ritual fast unto death ruled that the state was obliged to abolish it, and register a criminal case under sections 309 and 306 IPC should anyone pursue or abet this outlawed practice.[2] The judgment was the climax of almost a decade-long case that played out in the High Court even as a small number of Jain men and women continued to terminate their lives in the manner prescribed in the Jain texts.

This essay does not set out to defend or critique sallekhana, nor to explicate its meaning for those who perform it.[3] Instead it asks what happens when this piety and belief enter, or rather, are dragged into the courtroom? When one party seeks its denunciation and another its validation, or indifference even, from modern, rational law? This paper examines the anxieties that have framed the debate on both sides: those that triggered the lawsuit and the response of the court on the one hand, and the vigorous defence of the practice and the fear of loss of faith on the other hand.

Dying as social evil

There are no reliable statistics about the total number of Jains who voluntarily meet death every year in this fashion. Community journals and newsletters regularly publish accounts of those who have undertaken the fast or those who have passed away following sallekhana or santhara with extravagant commentaries about the virtues of this path. Writing in 1992, Billimoria put the figure at '5 to 6, or up to 10' cases each year though he conceded the numbers could be slightly higher if one took account of those cases which were not publicized.[4] Babulal Jain Ujjwal who publishes an annual newsletter on Jain affairs from Mumbai has counted an average of 550 santharas in 2009 and 465 in 2008.[5] Baya has presented a sample of 350 cases in a decade, between January 1994 to December 2003, on the basis of which he extrapolates the figure of 20 voluntary deaths per month, and 240 per year for the same period – a figure he calls a 'conservative estimate'.[6]

The data even so available are not gender disaggregated, but a cursory look at the public announcements confirms that both men and women undertake the vow of sallekhana. In fact, Baya's sample shows to the contrary that among the Digambars, the number of men who undertake sallekhana outstrips that of women; while among Shvetambars, there is a marginal excess of women in this pool. More than the gender ratios, Baya's sample is interesting for sectarian differences among lay and ascetic proclivities for voluntary death. While 46% of monks and 39% of nuns among Digambars undertook sallekhana, as opposed to a mere 1 and 0.6% of lay men and women – among the Shvetambars, it was overwhelmingly the lay followers who led in the field.[7]

Nonetheless, gossip and insinuation are always rife that women outnumber men in this endeavour, and that sallekhana is in principle, patriarchy's way of getting rid of women who have outlived their usefulness, or a clever means to deprive women of their property rights. Indeed, the framing of sallekhana as a 'social evil' depends at least in part on the idea that it is a gendered practice.

And in framing it so, sallekhana comes to be identified with Sati. Judicial memory about sati is invoked prominently in the petition filed by Nikhil Soni, the Jaipur lawyer who approached the Rajasthan High Court seeking the practice's criminalization. The Sati Prevention Laws were promulgated in the aftermath of the infamous burning of a young widow Roop Kanwar on her husband's pyre in 1987 in Rajasthan. Soni locates his petition squarely in that historical stream of legal reforms. In its language and formulation, the petition constantly reminds the court of sati prevention laws, which deemed not only the performance of sati but also, and even primarily, its glorification as unlawful. Soni places special emphasis on the ceremonial nature of sallekhana and the participation of the 'entire community' in its designing 'under the shelter of custom and religion'. Soni's petition summons the imagery of sati temples as sites of pilgrimage and draws parallels with the 'gathering for darshan' and 'converting the place as pilgrimage and paying honour to the person who adopts "santhara"'. 'People use to visit the person for "darshan" and visit to witness the occasion. Large number of people gathers there and the house becomes a place of pilgrimage [sic].'[8] Further, that these visitors 'prayed for redemption and salvation of the holly soul, in a nutshell glorified the event and hence abated the santhara' [sic].[9] Indeed, Soni states boldly that the Jains' collective participation amounts to 'glorification' as defined in the sati prevention law and should thus attract the same penal consequences.[10] Interestingly, Soni is not a Jain himself and his knowledge of santharas is based entirely on the Internet.[11]

Taking this argument forward while appearing in person in the court, Soni denied the voluntariness of the practice. In describing Santhara as 'notorious, abhorrent and tribal practice in the religion', Soni conjures colonial accounts of the rite of sati, with the woman as a wretched and powerless victim of religious customs, which necessitates the civilizing intervention of the court. His portrayal of santhara closely approximates the descriptions of sati by its opponents:

> ...adoption of Santhara, an act with criminal content, has become a means of climbing social ladder. Any person adopting Santhara is not allowed to go back on his vow, and the entire family and community forces him/her to complete the process in which he has to go through inhuman and intolerant conditions. He/she is some times tied to the chair or bed and is not allowed to eat and drink, even if he/she wants to come out of the vow or suffers from pain on the ground of criticism. A person adopting Santhara is surrounded by the groups singing Bhajan and Kirtan and he/she is made to loose conscience and drawn by religious fanaticism, to accept the process of death. It is nothing but killing a person, who may or may not have in the religious belief vowed to adopt Santhara as a means to end his/her life [sic].[12]

Compare the above, for example, with the narration of a fact-finding team comprising women journalists, which recreated the hours before the burning of Roop Kanwar.

> Preparation for the sati began immediately after Maal Singh's body was brought to the village at about 1 am. Roop Kanwar, who got an inkling of this escaped from the house and hid in one of the dhanis (barns) in the surrounding field... Roop, finally found cowering in the barn, was forcibly dragged to the house and put on the pyre at around 1.30. She is said to have screamed and struggled to get out when the pyre was lit, but Rajput youths with swords surrounding her made escape impossible.[13]

Agent of one's own death?

Like sati, Soni claims, santhara is nothing less than murder imposed on an unwilling and defenceless victim, in whose killing the entire community is complicit. The argument here turns on the (im)possibility of a person freely choosing to give up life. As a commentator confessed, he could not 'resist the argument that old women in the Jain community are socially pressurized to believe that suicide is their real, perhaps only, salvation.'[14] In such a reading, not only is santhara not voluntary but also gendered, again bringing to mind debates on the question of agency in the aftermath of Roop Kanwar's burning.

Feminists found it difficult to imagine an act of self-immolation flowing from a woman's personal volition rather than an outcome of the internalization of patriarchal religious ideology. As a scholar remarked, speaking purportedly for her comrades, that feminists would be steadfast in their view of sati as murder 'even if Roop Kanwar's volition could be established without doubt, by some magical replay of linear time'.[15] There could be therefore no 'true' or authentic sati. Another feminist disquiet with argument that women had *a right to choose* to burn themselves arose from the highly 'public and participatory nature of the funeral',[16] which in the first place is what renders it an act of sati. That is, its 'publicness' – the music, the gathering of people to witness the event, the celebrations that accompany and then follow it – cannot simply be squared with private and personal motivations that are being attributed to the woman.

Santhara is also a public ritual par excellence. It is not usually conducted secreted away in one's home – the taking of the vow is announced in local newspapers or Jain magazines, sermons are organized and a stream of visitors ceaselessly flows in and out of the house of the one who has undertaken the fast. Where for Soni, the 'public' is a community of complicity in crime, for the anthropologist James Laidlaw, it is this very extended spectacle of fasting and collective participation that authenticates the volition of the person at the centre of the ceremony. Thus, despite the fact that Laidlaw too draws on similarities between sati and sallekhana – joined as the two are, according to him by the underlying principle 'of extraordinary virtue being able to will and regulate the manner of its own death, as well as the imagery of purifying death by sacrificial burning,' – in his view the 'sceptical or secular sensibility' is able to discern the will that lies at the heart of the action in sallekhana in the public event. Therefore, he concludes, 'as far as I know, the legal prohibition of suicide has never led to police or court intervention to prevent a Jain fast to death, although they are frequently very well publicized as they proceed.'[17] Laidlaw had spoken too soon it appears.

In a state which had seen Roop Kanwar's 'sati' polarizing public opinion, Soni seems to be reminding the courts of its own historic role in ushering in social change. The Jain community's 'economic dominance' – rather like the Rajputs' social and political dominance, the chief custodians of sati dharma – must not be allowed to deter the courts' from stripping santhara of the protection afforded to religious practices. 'When the State of Rajasthan can stop Sati', Soni argued, 'and those abetting Sati are treated as offenders, in which case, the investigations are carried out and punishment is awarded, the Santhara is no different and it is also a process to commit suicide in the name of religion as in the case of Sati. There is absolutely no need to protect the practice of Santhara by the State.'[18]

This recalls the complaint raised by the defenders of sati in Rajasthan, among them, for example, politician Kalyan Singh Kalvi, who charged: 'Jains are known to die by fasting. Buddhists are known to immolate themselves. So why apply this law only to us?'[19] Kalvi and others like him had accused the state of interfering with the religious practices of Hindus alone, leaving others free to follow their traditions.

What's so 'essential' in a practice?

The Jain respondents had assembled a range of evidence – its ancient scriptures *Acharanga Sutra, Ratnakaranda Sravakcara, Bhagwati Sutra*, opinions of religious leaders, modern jurists and scholars such as Justice Tukol and Colonel Baya – in support of their contention that santhara was an ancient religious practice undertaken by spiritual adepts in the pursuit of salvation, markedly distinct from what was legally defined as a suicide. They also provided a veritable list of their religious figures and historical personalities who met 'death with equanimity' in this way, citing epigraphical, textual and media records.[20] For them, this contended that sallekhana was an 'essential practice' protected under Article 25.[21]

The route the court adopted to ascertain santhara's essentialness was its universality. The fact that not every Jain meets her end in this way becomes crucial in informing the court's decision. For the petitioner, it is only an occasional practice undertaken by an individual at the 'instigation' of others. Rejecting the material placed before it, the court ruled that since it is not 'necessarily required for the pursuit of immortality or moksha', it is not an essential practice.[22] Thus, it is not enough for the belief to be held sincerely by the community and for some to pursue it. It must be fairly universally practised and deemed to be the only means of salvation as laid out in Jain books – the discontinuance of which would imperil the very foundations of Jain faith. The court struck down sallekhana as an essential and integral practice of the Jains worthy of receiving the protection of Articles 25, 26 or 29.

It is obvious that the judgment in the Sati case is never far from the court's mind. It wishes to emulate that 'piece of great legal work, which reaffirmed the rule of law in the State of Rajasthan, in which the sections of people glorified the practice of Sati as a religious practice protected by Article 25 of the Constitution of India'.[23] The court reminds all that in *Onkar Singh*, the challengers to the Rajasthan Sati (Prevention) Ordinance had presented before the division bench of the Rajasthan High Court scriptures which accepted sati and studies which showed its prevalence – and yet the challenge to the ordinance was dismissed. Having established a dubious parity between sati and santhara – on the basis of little else but petitioner's allegation that santhara is coercive – the court cannot imagine but follow in its predecessor's footsteps.

In addition to Constitutional provisions pertaining to religious rights, what became central here was the meaning inscribed in Article 21. Did the right to life to include the right to die? Interestingly, all sides in this matter invoke the judicial pronouncements on the question of suicide and euthanasia to either condemn and criminalize sallekhana, or to uphold it. While judicial conclusions on this question have been varied,[24] the current law flows from the Constitution Bench's judgment in *Gyan Kaur*, which upheld S. 309's constitutionality.[25] Even so, the highest court recognized the right of a person to die with dignity 'when life is ebbing out', especially in cases of terminal illness of persistent vegetative state. A month before the Rajasthan High Court pronounced its judgment in the Santhara case, in a hospital in Mumbai, a woman who had lain lifelessly in a state of PVS for the past 42 years passed away. She was Aruna Shanbaug, on whose behalf a writ filed by her 'next friend' led to the Supreme Court to deliver its judgment allowing for passive euthanasia under certain conditions and monitoring by the high courts.[26]

While the Jain respondents cited the inconclusive and equivocal pronouncements of the Supreme Court in both these judgments on the morality and expediency of taking one's life to defend sallekhana – the petitioner clutches at the legal effects of the judgments, namely the continued criminalization of suicide. The court agrees with the petitioner and concludes that the Constitution 'does not permit nor include under Article 21 the right to take one's own life, nor can include the right to take life as an essential religious practice under Article 25 of the Constitution.'

It appears that since it was not legal to kill oneself for non-religious reasons, killing oneself for religious motivations could not be permitted. Thus, in a sense, a religious practice's essentialness to the tradition's adherents could only be determined by what was external to it – namely, the Indian Penal Code – not by the values held by the adherents themselves.

Death and modern legal rationality: the problem of translatability

If the Rajasthan High Court had presumed that its judgment would be received as an heir apparent to the *Onkar Singh* case and extolled as a progressive step towards ending egregious and odious practices that continue in the name of religion and custom, it was not to be. Indeed, a range of writers and commentators picked on it as an illustration of law's blindness to religious belief, in particular Western Law's hubris and its inability to understand traditional notions of death and dying. Unlike in the case of sati, where even the most ardent critics of modern legal rationality recognized Roop Kanwar's sati to be murder, the scholarly response to the outlawing of sallekhana on the whole followed a very different path.

The judgment was roundly critiqued on several counts. The first argument was that the language of secular law itself is too arid to capture the multivalent meanings inhering in the concept of death. Whereas santhara is distinguished from suicide by the 'quality of intent', law and courts were simply ill-equipped to make sense of the different intents in the different forms of deaths.[27] This inability – or 'unmusicality' – to fathom these different intents results in the court treating sallekhana as suicide, or sati, or any other kind of self-destruction, and necessitates the invocation of S. 309 in all cases. At times this is seen as the inadequacy of the English language itself, and the insurmountable problem of translating such an idea as encapsulated in sallekhana, into English. The process of (un)translation is bound to result in loss of meaning.[28]

A corollary to this argument is that secular law, despite its pretensions to secularism, is inflected with Christian theology, crafted as the Indian Penal Code was by a 'devout Christian',[29] Lord Thomas Babington Macaulay. 'Certainly', charges Mehta, 'IPC has traces of Christian view of life and dying.' Its Christian theological core does not allow law to 'contemplate alternative modes in which that event in life has been imagined.'[30] The court's response is not to apprehend the internal logic of sallekhana but to mobilize Christian theology and Anglo-Saxon law against it.[31] For one commentator, the rationale of a practice like sallekhana collides with the religious values of Christianity which conceive of the body in fundamentally different ways: while in the former, the body is viewed as a prison house of the soul, whose maintenance and fulfilment lead only to relentless embodiment in the cycle of birth and death; in the Judeo-Christian worldview, the body is the temple of human soul, whose wilful destruction is regarded as sin.[32]

Macaulay's inclusion of suicide as a crime derives, it is argued, from his Christian convictions about good and evil. The clash then is not really between secular sensibilities and religious ones – or between 'faith-based societies' and law-based institutions of governance – but two competing religious world views, for secularism is barely concealed Christian theology.

Though this kind of critique was hardly uniform, we can still discern a central twain that runs through all these scholars. This can be posited in terms of two equal and opposing arms of an equation. On the one hand of this equation stands this formulation: colonizer – Judeo Christian theology – legal rationality – English language – nation-state – fetishization of body. This is in conflict with another set of interrelated values: colonized – Eastern worldview – pluralist ethics – multivalent Indian language – civilization – body as a prison.

Once the terms are set like this, the santhara judgment can only be seen as a 'clash of civilizations' by the commentators. These are, however, too easy conclusions drawn from the santhara judgment. It is true that the court here assumes the mantle of a modernizing reformer in striking down the practice of santhara as illicit. It is true also that nation-states wish to monopolize the meaning over death. Nonetheless, the tendency to fetishize a civilizational difference, an opposition even, is not necessarily warranted, or even justified, for it ends up simplifying what are messy negotiations over law and communities. But above all, it ignores the way in which postcolonial courts have dealt with the religion and understood their own authority in doing so.

First, the state of Rajasthan's response to the writ in the court was identical to that of the community's. It asked for the writ to be dismissed on grounds that it lacked substantive research and failed to provide evidence of any specific incident of coerced sallekhana. Denying any illegality to the practice, the state echoed the Jain respondents' plea that sallekhana was an ancient and venerable religious practice protected by Article 25 of the Indian Constitution. Rejecting the meagre newspapers reports marshalled by Soni in his petition, the state instead turns to the text favoured by the Jains themselves, i.e., Justice Tukol's treatise *Sallekhana is not Suicide*, to bolster the claim for a valid and perfectly licit religiosity of sallekhana.[33] The court terms this response as 'curious', 'protectionist', 'confused' as well one mixed with 'respect and reverence of the religion'.

The contention that Rajasthan High Court decision is rooted in Christian theological ideas about death, which is unable to then recognize alternative attitudes to dying, also deserves a closer examination. It is true that in the last few centuries, especially when Macaulay was codifying the penalties for crimes against the body, Christian ideas, both Catholic and Calvinist, about suicide were heavily influenced by St. Augustine's injunction against self killing as a terrible sin and a violation of the Biblical commandment 'Thou shalt not kill'. Eight hundred years after Augustine, the Catholic theologian Thomas Aquinas was to draw on him to denounce suicide as an act against self, community and God, concluding, 'To God alone belongs the power over death and life.'[34] This has proved to the basis of the Christian prohibition on self-killing, which then entered Anglo-Saxon law. Even so, suicide does not exhaust the category of voluntary death in Christianity as a spate of recent scholarly studies has shown. Martyrdom represented a noble form of self-killing in early Christianity which guaranteed a 'crown of immortality'.[35] This ideal drew upon, and reworked classical Pagan ideas about honour, persecution, suffering and heroic death. In fact, martyrdom became the ultimate evidence of one's faith and piety as the martyr's death mimicked Christ's suffering and victory on the cross.[36] The numbers of martyrs ran into thousands,[37] and even the great opponent of suicide, St Augustine, praised Christian martyrs whose piety and numbers, according to him, far surpassed those of Roman martyrs. The point here is not to engage in an exercise in comparative religion, but merely to emphasize that the Christian tradition itself had variegated attitudes towards voluntary death, with one martyr even declaring, 'we conquer death and are not conquered by it', and another asking, 'what is more glorious..than by dying to have overcome death itself, which is feared by all?'[38]

Santhara in the colonial view

As a 'devout Christian', Macaulay is said to have brought his religious beliefs into the draft of the penal code he designed for India. In outlining the 'offences effecting the human body' (sections 294–362) covering a range of crimes from murder through manslaughter to 'unnatural offences',

Macaulay listed voluntary culpable homicide *by consent* (emphasis added) as section 298, when a 'person whose death is caused, being above twelve years of age, suffers death, or takes the risk of death, by his own choice'.[39] Such a killing was not to be punished as severely as murder by the sentence of death, nor even as suicide, whose abetment under S. 306 also attracted the possible penalties of death or transportation for life.

Clearly for Macaulay, this was a special and mitigated form of homicide. The motives, from which this form of homicide springs, says Macaulay, are far more respectable than those that cause the commission of ordinary murder. Such a killing, which is qualified twice over – both as 'voluntary' and 'by 'consent', could be the effect of 'a strong sense of religious duty'.[40] Moreover, Macaulay warns that such motives would not be thought culpable, 'except in Christian societies and even in Christian societies, would not be regarded by the public, and ought not to be treated by law as assassins'. Such suicides or homicides are utterly devoid of evil in the eyes of the Macaulay, as they do not cause alarm or terror among others, as do assassins otherwise.[41]

The principal illustration of this form of killing for Macaulay is the one who lights the pyre of a Hindu widow 'who consents to be burned with the corpse of her husband'.[42] He provides different examples in his explanatory note. However, there is no reference to sallekhana under those cases of suicide motivated by religious or normative reasons. Indeed, sallekhana does not seem to have attracted the attention of the colonial administrators at all.

One must remember that Jainism was a rather late arrival to the study of Indian religions, confused as it was for a long time, either as a sect of Hinduism, or a version of Buddhism. Its texts waited long to be translated into English and other European languages, missionaries and orientalists ignored it for the most part, it's practices remained in the shadows despite the hectic production of 'customs and manners' variety of scholarship in this period. Till the mid 19th century, Jainism had still to emerge as a bounded and reified entity.[43] The Calcutta school of orientalism, epitomized in the writings of Jones, Colebrooke, Wilson, and Prinsep, and whose interests lay elsewhere, comprehensively dominated the European study of Indian religions.[44] Moreover, Jains' low numbers in the Bengal Presidency – coincidentally also the site of a large number of satis in this period – did not spur any Orientalist interest in the independent study of Jains,[45] or indeed of any campaign to abolish sallekhana.

Some key Jain texts that had been translated and included in the *Sacred Books of the East* series by the mid 19th century, did refer to the Jain practice of starvation to death, but only fleetingly. Georg Buhler in his lecture in 1887 invokes these texts while noting that 'Voluntary death by the withdrawal of nourishment is, according to the strict doctrine of the Digambara, necessary for all ascetics.... The milder Svetambara do not demand this absolutely, but regard it, as a sure entrance to Nirvana.'[46] Buhler is certain of the continuation of the practice in contemporary times.[47]

Buhler was associated with the Bombay Asiatic Society and as such it was largely the Bombay and Madras school of orientalists,[48] who provided a picture of the community and its practices in a more full-blooded way. A.K. Forbes, for example, a British judicial officer and a connoisseur of Gujarati language compiled a history of Gujarat, *Ras Mala* (first published in 1856) based partly on Jain sources. Here he described the taking of the vow of santharo (Gujarati colloquial) by Jain ascetics, during the period of *paryusan* that 'pledges them to produce their death by abstaining from food'.[49] His description, even if brief, of the announcement of the santharo, the gathering of other Jain adherents to worship the 'juttee' (the vow taker), the care with which his feverish body is dabbed with moist clothes, the preparations for the funeral, and the scrambling for the fragments of the deceased ascetic's clothes as blessings by childless women is based on accounts of his Jain interlocutors and not simply on a text.

The Archaeological Survey of Mysore's extensive work in Sravan Belgola in the late 19th century under the leadership of B. Lewis Rice, not only unveiled the history of Jainism in the South, it also pointed to the centrality of sallekhana in Jain history as the site itself was linked to the death of Bhadrabahu, the last of the Jain elders who knew the srutis. In his voluminous analysis of the inscriptions of the site – the last of which was from as late as 1809 – Rice informs us of the many cryptic recordings he finds of the deaths of 'both clerics and laics, male and female, who had given themselves up to fasting with the express object of quitting the body'.[50] Identifying the vow of 'religious suicide' as sallekhana, Rice then proceeds to quote and translate portions of the *Ratna Karandaka*, the principle text which deals with the householders' duties, including the vow of fasting to death.[51]

Rice cannot constrain remarking on the practice itself, whose fastidious recording he had stumbled upon:

> The bitterest satirist of human delusions could hardly depict a scene of sterner irony than the naked summit of this bare rock dotted with emaciated devotees, both men and women, in silent torture awaiting the hour of self-imposed death. The irony is complete when we remember that avoidance of the destruction of life in whatever form is a fundamental doctrine of the sect.[52]

The most cogent Christian view on santhara comes from one of the early western chroniclers of the Jains, Mrs Stevenson of the Irish Mission in Surat, who acknowledges the help rendered to her by her Gujarati Jain interlocutors while expressing her indebtedness to Reverend G.P. Taylor of the Divinity College Ahmedabad. She discusses the 'terrible vow' of santharo in some detail in *The Heart of Jainism*.[53] To her the theory of karma and rebirth 'naturally encouraged belief in suicide as a form of prudential insurance!'[54] Though it is in a matter-of-fact tone that she narrates the undertaking of the vow as death approaches,[55] she is unable to come to terms with the religious sanction of voluntary death. 'It is strange', she writes 'that a religious system which begins with the most minute regulations against the taking of the lowest insect life should end by encouraging human suicide.'[56] Her bafflement was amplified by the knowledge that Jainism otherwise disapproved of 'simple suicide'.[57] Her pronouncement on the ethicality of the practice is stinging:

> The sadhu climbs some sacred hill such as Parasnatha, Girnar, or Satrunjaya; and there, in order to do nothing that may lead to karma, he does absolutely nothing at all, but awaits death without moving hand or foot, head or body. The influence of a negative religion is then worked out to its irresistible conclusion, and with all the sorrows and ills of the world waiting to be relieved, the soldier deserts his post in order to free his own soul from suffering.[58]

Towards the end of her book, Mrs Stevenson embarks on what had become standard missionary practice: to denounce the religion described as absurd and false, and to uphold the superiority and truth of the Christian faith. She does this through a comparison between the three jewels of Jainism, i.e., Right Knowledge, Right Faith and Right Conduct and what she sees as the '*tri-ratna*' of Christianity, faith, hope and love. While the former creates an impersonal system that bestows no redemption save self-mortification and death, in the latter the Good Lord offers eternal hope. In the absence of a personal redeemer, she declares the heart of Jainism to be empty.[59]

The above survey of the colonial discourse on santhara tells us this: Western authors were aware of the existence of this practice and this was based not only a study of the texts, but also through their interaction with the Jains themselves; that the attitude of these authors towards the practice was typical of that period, whether it was the archaeologist Rice or the missionary, Mrs Stevenson – santhara represented despair and hopelessness and presented an enigma to the Orientalist mind, since 'religious suicide' seemed incompatible with the value of ahmisa. This attitude nonetheless did not lead to any denunciation of santhara as a heinous practice, nor to the launching of any campaign to suppress it – as against sati, or infanticide or human sacrifice. It remained a philosophical puzzle, or at the most, as yet more evidence of the falsity of the non-Christian faith.

Why did the British feel no impulse to criminalize santhara? Was it the relative ignorance about Jainism itself – the fact that most of the Orientalist scholars who recorded the practice were not based in the heart of the Empire where the policies were being drafted but in its outposts in Gujarat or Mysore?[60] Or perhaps, religious suicide of this kind did not evoke the same repugnance that infanticide or sati did amongst European orientalists, trained as they were in the Classics and familiar with ancient Roman suicides.

Rice, for instance, quotes the formidable historian of European morals, William E.H. Lecky, to show that sallekhana-like practice was scarcely unique to the Jains or to Indians. He cites Lecky's examples from the Pagan Empire of Rome, where '[T]he conception of suicide as an euthanasia, an abridgement of the pangs of disease, and a guarantee against the dotage of age was not confined to philosophical treatises. We have considerable evidence of its being frequently put in practice.' Lecky also mentions according to Lewis, the practice of 'Endura' by means of which the Albigenses, a gnostic sect in the South of France, accelerated death, 'by fasting and sometimes by bleeding'.[61]

It is interesting to note that none of these writings – paltry in comparison to the writings on sati – had any impact on the law commissions that were working to create a codified law for India around the same time. One could speculate that the considerable weakening of the theological arguments against suicide in England by the 19th century and its reduction to a medical or legal problem rather than a religious one[62] could have played a role in the absolute penal neglect by the colonial rulers towards sallekhana. By the 1820s, just a decade before Macaulay was to lecture the House of Commons on the benefits of a codified law for India, suicide no longer even appeared in the category of homicide – with suicides increasingly being allowed burial on consecrated grounds, and sentences for attempted suicides now reduced to a mere two years.[63]

One case, which was brought before the Supreme Court in Calcutta and then subsequently appealed in the Privy Council, is significant to understanding the British attitudes towards suicide among their subjects. The life of this case, *Advocate General of Bengal (on behalf of her majesty) Vs. Ranee Surnomoye Dossee*, straddles two periods of what Galanter calls the 'expropriation of Indian law', the first inaugurated by Warren Hastings in 1772 with the expansion of government's judicial functions in Bengal through various charters, mayor's court and subsequently the Supreme Court; and the second, the period of extensive codification of law beginning from 1860 onwards, also marking the shift of power from the Company to the Crown.[64] In 1832, Raja Hurrynauth Roy of Calcutta, a Hindu of considerable property, made a will and soon passed away leaving behind his mother, his wife, a son and a daughter. In 1839, the mother and wife of the deceased man moved the Supreme Court against the son for the proper implementation of the will. In 1843, the Supreme Court asked a fund to be created for the maintenance of the two women. The following year, the young heir, Kistonauth Roy, committed suicide. He was survived by his childless widow who received her dead husband's estate. On the passing of the mother, Kistonauth's widow moved the court seeking transfer of the fund that had been setup by the Supreme Court to maintain her husband's female kin. At this stage, the Indian government staked claim to this fund on grounds that the coroner's finding of death by suicide should lead to the forfeiture of property to the Crown. The case turned on whether English law applied to Hindu subjects in Calcutta when the Raja 'destroyed himself' in 1844. The government's plea was that it did, via the Charter of George the 1st in 1726, and then through the 33rd Geo III C. 52, s. 157 (when the Governor General was authorized to appoint as many coroners as he deemed fit). The Supreme Court, however, rejected this contention, leading the Advocate General to appeal the decision in the Privy Council, which upheld the Supreme Court's decision.

Among the many issues that were raised in the course of the trial and the appeal, were the Supreme Court's and the Privy Council's differential legal understanding of suicide in England, or Christian territories and India and among non-Christian peoples. In the Privy Council, the appellants' attorneys invoked in addition to the charters and statutes, the Indian Penal Code which had clearly criminalized suicide. Nonetheless, the members of the Privy Council were not impressed. Recognizing that '[T]he laws and usages of Eastern countries where Christianity does not prevail are so at variance with all the principles, feelings, and habits of European Christians', the Privy Council held that:

> Self-destruction, though treated by the law of England as Murder, and spoken ... as the worst of all Murders, is really, as it affects society, and in a moral and religious point of view, of a character very different not only from all other Murders, but from all other Felonies. These distinctions are pointed out with great force and clearness in the notes attached to the Indian Code, as originally prepared by Lord Macaulay and the other Commissioners. The truth is, that the act is one which in countries not influenced by the doctrines of Christianity has been regarded as deriving its moral character altogether from the circumstances in which it is committed:–sometimes as blameable, sometimes as justifiable, sometimes as meritorious, or even an act of positive duty.
>
> In this light suicide seems to have been viewed by the founders of the Hindoo Code, who condemn it in ordinary cases as forbidden by their religion; but in others, as in the well-known instances of Suttee and self-immolation under the car of *Juggernauth*, treat it as an act of great religious merit.[65]

If sati was an articulation of tradition, and its abolition a reformulation of tradition and embrace of enlightened rationality[66] – suppression of infanticide allowed colonial rule to expand in territories hitherto inaccessible[67]; similarly, allegations – rumours it turned out – of self-immolations under the wheels of the mighty Jagganath car were linked to imperial health and sanitation policies.[68] Besides, these interventions provided justification for the continuance of the paternalistic hand of the ruler. The effects however of this moral-legal civilizing mission were not uniform. And certainly, much more was at stake here than simply a Christian view of Eastern religions, and to understand colonial governmentality as merely a reflection of Christian beliefs would be erroneous. There was panoply of religious, ideological, political and material interests that shaped and shifted colonial policies on law and religion. Possibly, sallkehna was not marked out on this grid of interests and thus escaped the attention of colonial lawmakers.

The Jain response

If sallekhana escaped colonial law and legal action even later, as Laidlaw says, and as Jain spokespersons are often wont to remind that the practice was never prohibited or regarded as a 'contravention of law' by any regime in Indian history,[69] it has remained nonetheless in the pale of controversy. Thus, Baya's survey of sallekhana conducted in early 2000s – before the PIL was filed – includes several questions that are clearly aimed to allaying its controversial aspects, namely if the santhara was accepted voluntarily (question number 7).[70] The questionnaire also asks if there were any legal fallouts of the undertaking of the vow. Further, in a case study from Rajsamand (in Rajasthan) in 1996, Baya tells us that a 'miscreant lodged a police complaint' and that a section of the press too attempted to equate santhara with sati. He reports that the matter was resolved after the '*ksapaka*' explained to the police and the press about the 'spiritual purport of the practice' and persuaded them that he was not committing suicide.[71]

From much before Baya's wide-ranging survey of the practice, Jain scholars have felt the need to respond to critics and sceptics. Champat Rai Jain (1867–1942) was a barrister and a scholar of comparative religion who founded a Jain mission in London – in particular he took upon himself the task of responding to Christian criticisms of Jain doctrines, publishing a series of books and tracts in English targetting both a European audience as well as the western educated Jains nearer home.[72] Jain translated into English *Ratnakarana Sravakcara*, one of the key texts which lays out the philosophical foundations of the practice. His translation appeared in 1917, barely a few years after Mrs Stevenson's monograph. Jain's erudite introduction though does not refer to her or any other colonial writings on sallekhana. His concerns are instead to engage with emerging ideas from the field of modern psychology, cognitive sciences and physics in order to explicate Jain perspective on matter, consciousness and soul. In 1933, however, an article published in the *Simla Times* by one 'ASP', alleging among other things that Jainism encouraged suicide roiled Jain to respond. In his letter to the editor (which was never published to his chagrin but appeared later in his collected works), Jain cites 'Jain Shastras', draws parallels between sallekhana and the views of the ancient Europeans (especially Seneca) on voluntary death, and refers to modern advocates of euthanasia in the West, in order to first, dispel the notion that sallekhana is suicide, and second, to prove that it was hardly 'the only culprit in this regard'.[73] In a later piece, he returns to this theme at greater length. Though it lacks the polemical bite of the rejoinder to the *Simla Times* piece, one can discern that the topic has been taken up in the knowledge that certain 'misconceptions' about this practice need to be dispelled. Jain starts by listing out the fears associated with death and delineates how Jainism conquers this fear of death and disease through the vow of Samadhi-marana. 'This is a kind of invitation to death itself', though he warns it is 'not in the nature of suicide'. Making a distinction between the two on the basis of several factors, such as 'mental clarity, peace and tranquillity, the absence of wish to end life on the instant, that is to say the determination to continue to face one's troubles as long as there is a chance of life left, and the hire, which characterize the former but are wanting in the latter.' He concludes, 'The man who dies a suicide is a coward; he who resorts to samadhi-marana is a hero!'[74]

It is Justice Tukol, a retired judge of the High Court of Karnataka, who can be credited with preparing an exhaustive response to the critics of sallekhana. A respected figure of the South Indian Jain community, both as a judge and as a scholar, he published widely on Jainology. His lectures at the L.D. Institute of Indology in 1975 were published the following year as a brief treatise, *Sallekhana is not Suicide*. It remains till date the template on which Jain advocates of sallekhana have mounted their defence of the practice. The model it constructed proceeded thus: philosophical background of sallekhana and what it means; inscriptional evidence from various Jain archaeological sites, a survey of voluntary deaths in different traditions, comparison with suicide and euthanasia, and law on suicide. In his preface, Tukol writes that his studies of jurisprudence, IPC and the cases decided by him affirm his belief that sallekhana and suicide are two different orders of death. While he counters Rice (unsubstantiated imaginary and sentimental outpourings based on hearsay) and Mrs. Stevenson (uncharitable and superficial), Tukol's primary move is to introduce legal interpretation and constitutional rights, into the discussion, thus taking the defence of the practice beyond the metaphysical into the legal domain.

Without naming anyone, Tukol trains his guns at those commentators who, in his view have misread Section 309 to include within it fasting or refusal to take bodily sustenance. Tukol, insisting on the primacy of the principle of interpretation of a criminal statute, namely, that it should be construed directly and concludes that '[T]here is no law which casts an obligation on every individual not to fast.'[75] Raising sallekhana to one of the cardinal principle of Jainism, he clarifies that only the select few adepts who have advanced spiritually undertake it. Tukol's argument is based largely on the constitutional protection offered by Article 25, which overrides any penal code, and would render it impossible to punish any act sanctioned by religion and performed in accordance with prescribed rites. Any provision that attempts to do this, he says, would not have the authority of law. He also dismisses the suggestion that sallekhana could possibly interfere with public order, health and morality.

When Tukol was writing in the mid 1970s, the 42nd Law Commission report (1971) on the Indian Penal Code had already recommended the repeal of section 309 terming it 'harsh' and 'unjustifiable'.[76] If Macaulay's impulse in promulgating the crime of suicide was Christian, then the Law Commission cited the Laws of Manu to demonstrate that 'suicide was regarded as permissible in some circumstances in ancient India', and quoted Max Muller's note that 'Jaina ascetics, too, consider it particularly meritorious' in its support.[77] Tukol's lectures ignore the Commission's recommendation. Why is this so? It is hardly possible that Justice Tukol was not aware of it.

I argue that a perceptible shift occurs between Tukol's book and the time that the practice comes to be challenged legally. First, the debates around the right to life (and die) under Article 21 emerge prominently through a series of judgments.[78] A general environment sympathetic to the decriminalization of suicide and euthanasia, advances in law and philosophical debates across the world make available a new framework of 'right to die with dignity' from within which to argue for the legality of sallekhana. To be sure, the Jain spokespersons do not give up on the claim of sallekhana's distinctiveness from suicide and euthanasia and yet draw upon the same set of moral and legal arguments as utilized by euthanasia advocates. This is, of course, evident in the Rajasthan HC where the Jain respondents invoked *Gyan Kaur* and *Aruna Shanbaug* judgments. This point was reiterated even in the more academic discussions that were held in the aftermath of the High Court judgment.[79]

Besides, the entrenchment of the essential practices doctrine, from *Shirur Mutt* to *Anand Margi* case, renders the courts into pseudo theologians pronouncing whether this or that practice was essential or not to the followers of a faith. By raising sallekhana to a cardinal principle, the cornerstone and the most essential of all Jain practices – as its defenders *must do* in order to secure its legal protection – an ascetic model of Jainism comes to overwhelm and completely elide the model of worldly well-being.[80] It perforce ends up exaggerating the dualism of the soul and body, where the body is shown to be a prison cage of the soul, whose destruction is an essential step towards liberation. While certainly, the *Ratnakaranda Sravakacara* calls it the 'fleshy prison',[81] it also lays out that sallekhana must be undertaken only 'when the body is no longer capable of serving its owner as an instrument of dharma'.[82] Thus Jainism also envisions the body as an ally, as both the tool and the site where Jain ideals are rendered legible, for example, through fasting, which may allow the pursuit of both renunciatory and worldly ends concurrently.[83] However, the judicial process forces a monochromatic rendering of Jainism – a vision that even cultural critics unwittingly replicate in their critique of the judgment.

When the courts craft a definition of religion and its practices it also effectively shifts the language of the debate from metaphysical and religious to rights and liberty.[84] Communities then have little choice but to mutate philosophical and ethical arguments into legal-historical ones, as happens with the invocation of a hoary historical tradition of sallekhana supported by sacred texts. In fact, in a move that mimics the juridical, it has been proposed by some members of the community that guidelines or SOPs be framed to govern the vow in order that custom and law may be united and doubts about coercion allayed.[85]

Conclusion

How does one understand the judgment of the Rajasthan High Court? I think it is not helpful to reduce it to a clash of civilization argument as many commentators did indeed, since the colonial view of sallekhana itself was fractured at best. Even on the question of suicide, the response was more complex than a simple Christian-secular-colonial versus pluralist-indigenous binary allows for, as the Privy Council judgment illustrates. Moreover, the colonial attitude towards sallekhana was one of penal neglect (in much the same way that they ignored Jain bal diksha but pursued the reform of child marriages).[86] Instead, it might be more fruitful to locate the petition, the judgment as well as the Jain responses in a complex of legal and judicial developments. One is the reification of religious practices through the essential practices doctrine, which is meant to create a judicially acceptable definition of religious traditions. The second is the emergence and evolution of the Public Interest Litigation, allowing a person with no locus standi or little connection with a social question to approach the higher courts for intervention. This has transmuted the court into a super-legislature. The petitioner and the court can assume the mantle of vanguards of social change, working to produce a new nation-state.[87] Santhara is deemed to be deeply antithetical the petitioner's vision of a modernizing nation and ideal citizenship, which demands that the one must participate in the progress of the country rather than kill oneself.[88] The court too lauds the petitioner for his advocacy of 'modern thought and thinking' and reliance on 'governing law of the land'.[89] Bound together in the pact of social revolution, the petitioner and the court echo each other, and end up criminalizing sallekhana.

Notes

1. Caillat, "Fasting unto death according to the Jaina tradition."
2. *Nikhil Soni v. Union of India and others.* A rash of special leave petitions by Jain individuals and organisations were filed in the Supreme Court seeking a stay on the Rajasthan High Court judgment. The SC stayed the judgment vide its order on 31 August 2015. *Dhawal Jiwan Mehta versus Nikhil Soni and Others*, Supreme Court of India. S. 309 pertains to attempt to commit suicide and S. 306 to abetment to suicide.
3. On this, see the excellent studies by Bilimoria, "The Jaina Ethic of Voluntary Death"; Chapple, "Nonresistant Death"; and Laidlaw, "A life worth leaving."
4. Bilimoria, "The Jaina Ethic of Voluntary Death," 338.
5. *Times of India*, 18 March 2010.
6. Baya, *Death with Equanimity*, 260, 262.
7. Baya, *Death with Equanimity*, 262–4.
8. D.B. Civil Writ Petition no. 7414/2006 (henceforth Writ), Para 3.
9. Writ, Para 5.
10. Ibid., 9.
11. Ibid., 4.
12. *Nikhil Soni v Union of India* (henceforth judgment), para 19.
13. *Trial by Fire.*
14. Dhavan, "Did Supreme Court Just Allow Suicide."
15. Talwar Oldenberg, "The Roop Kanwar Case," 104.
16. Sangari and Vaid, "Institutions, Beliefs, Ideologies," WS-10.
17. Laidlaw, "A Life Worth Leaving," 193.
18. Judgment, para 19.
19. Hawley, *Sati, The Blessing and the Curse*, 10.
20. Judgment, see paras 11 and 12.
21. The Indian Constitution through its article 25 guarantees freedom of conscience and free profession, practice and propagation of religion with the caveat that this right will be subject to public order, morality and health. However, according to the petitioner, neither this, nor Article 26 that grants complete autonomy to a religious denomination or organization to manage its own affairs, nor for that matter Article 29, which guarantees the protection of interests of minorities by devolving on them the right to conserve their culture sanctions sathara.
22. Judgment, para 39.
23. Judgment, para 33.
24. The Bombay High Court in Maruti struck down S. 309, declaring it to be ultra vires articles 14 and 21 of the Constitution, and quashed all pending prosecutions under the section in the state of Maharashtra. *Maruti Shripati Dubal vs. the State Of Maharashtra.* In *State vs. Sanjay Kumar Bhatia*, 1985 Crl.L.J.931, the division bench of the Delhi High Court called S. 309 an 'anachronism unworthy of human society like ours'. In *Chenna Jagadeeswar and another Vs. State of Andhra Pradesh*, 1988 Crl.L.J.549, the Division Bench of the Andhra Pradesh High Court rejected the challenge to the constitutional validity of Section 309 IPC, and the argument that Article 21 included the right to die. The Supreme Court in *P. Rathinam vs. Union Of India* declared S. 309 to be void concluding that 'an act of suicide cannot be said to be against religion, morality or public policy, and an act of attempted suicide has no baneful effect on society. Further, suicide or attempt to commit it causes no harm to others, because of which State's interference with the personal liberty of the persons concerned is not called for.' The Mental Health Care Act 2017, which came into effect in 2018, has effectively decriminalized suicide by presuming that suicides are driven by extreme stress, and holding that those who attempted suicide would not be 'tried and punished under the said Code.' *The Mental Heath CareAct*, 46.
25. *Smt. Gyan Kaur vs. The State Of Punjab.*
26. *Aruna Ramachandra Shanbaug v. Union of India.*
27. Mehta, "Death and the Sovereign."
28. "Language and justice die or are diminished when language is deprived of its right to polysemy and to a multiplicity of meaning. When language is rendered captive, justice loses out in the long run." Viswanathan, "A Reductive Reading of Santhara."
29. Almost all commentators critical of the judgment reference Macaulay's Christian devoutness.
30. See note 27 above.
31. Viswanathan, "A Reductive Reading of Santhara."
32. Hattangadi, "Santhara in the eyes of the Law."
33. Judgment, paras 9 and 10.
34. *Summa Theologiae*, q. 64, article 5.

35. Droge and Tabor, *A Noble Death*, 129.
36. Straw, "A Very Special Death," 39.
37. Colt, *The Enigma of Suicide*,156. Augustine's stricture against suicide is said to have sprung from his desire to discredit the North African sect of Donatists amongst whom the numbers of martyrs was particularly high.
38. Flavian and Cuprian cited in Straw, 39.
39. A Penal Code prepared by the Indian Law Commissioners, 78.
40. Ibid., 61.
41. Ibid., 61.
42. Ibid., 78.
43. see Flugel, "Invention of Jainism."
44. See Orr, "Orientalists, Missionaries, and Jains."
45. Numark, "The Scottish 'Discovery' of Jainism."
46. Buhler, *On the Indian Sect of the Jainas*, 14. Durkheim drew upon upon Buhler's lecture while formulating his concept of altruistic suicide, where "the individual kills himself purely for the joy of sacrifice, because, even with no particular reason, renunciation in itself is considered praiseworthy." Durkheim, 181–82.
47. Buhler, *On the Indian Sect of the Jainas*, 15.
48. See Numark and Orr.
49. Forbes, Ras Mala, 328.
50. Rice, *Inscriptions at Sravan Belgola*, 15.
51. C.R. Jaini's translation of the text was still some years away.
52. Ibid., 17.
53. Stevenson, *The Heart of Jainism*, 221.
54. Ibid., 30.
55. Ibid., see especially 221–2.
56. Ibid.,168.
57. Ibid., 296.
58. Ibid., 168.
59. Ibid., 248.
60. Even so, santhara or sallekhana did not always receive attention. For example, John Wilson, a Scottish missionary based in Bombay who was engaging polemically with Jain scholars as early as 1835 makes no mention of santhara. In none of his interactions with the Jains does he debate or dispute the practice of starving to death. His theological and philosophical refutation of Jainism focuses on the absence of a creator God. See "Letter to the Jaina Priests of Palitana" in *Life of John Wilson*, 195–6. Wilson's penal and reformist energies were focused on infanticide in Kathiwar, whose suppression by the colonial government he detailed in a full volume. Wilson, *History of the Suppression of Infanticide in Western India*.
61. See note 50 above.
62. Barry, *Breaking the Thread of Life*, 48.
63. Ibid., 77.
64. Galanter, "The Displacement of Traditional Law in Modern India," 17–18.
65. 9 M.I.A. 387, decided on 30.06.1863.
66. Lata Mani, "Contentious Traditions."
67. Prakasi cited in Cassells, *Social Legislation of the East India Company*, 114.
68. Ahuja, "The Bridge Builders," 103.
69. Tukol, *Sallekhana is not Suicide*, 95.
70. Baya, *Death with Equanimity*, xxxvii.
71. Baya, 269–270.
72. Jaini, "The Jainas and the Western Scholar," 33.
73. Jain, "Some Misconceptions regarding Jainism," 177–82.
74. Jain, "Festival of Death," 110–15.
75. Tukol, *Sallekhana is not Suicide*, 83.
76. 42nd Law Commission Report, 244.
77. Ibid., 243.
78. See footnote above. Also see The 210th Law Commission Report on *Humanization and Decriminalization of Suicide*, 2008.
79. Justice Panachand, D.R. Mehta, Shugan Jain, etc., at 'The Legality and Jurisprudence of Sallekhana/Santhara/Samadhimrana/Pryopavesa in the Indian Traditions" at National Law University Dwarka, Delhi on 26–27 February 2016.
80. This tendency has blighted the scholarship on Jains and Jainism. See Cort, "Singing the Glory of Asceticism."
81. Jain, *Ratnakaranda Sravakcara*, 9.

82. Ibid., 58.
83. See Laidlaw, *Riches and Renunciation*, 152; On materialization of wifely bodies, see Kelting, "Candanbālā's hair." It is also important to note that among the temple going Jain sects, the idols of the Tirthankars represent their spiritually perfect bodies. On debates on iconography, see Cort, *Framing the Jina.*
84. Luithe-Hardenberg notes a similar trend in the context of child diksha as the current discussion centres almost exclusively on rights of children as opposed to 19th-century debates where those campaigning against the practice were mostly exercised by whether children could possibly uphold the rigours of an ascetic life, and the fear that this failure would bring ignominy.
85. Mridul Goswami, Shugan Jain, Justice Panachand and others at the NLUD conference.
86. On this see Luithe-Hardenberg.
87. For a discussion on this, see Bhuwania, *Courting the People.*
88. Since every citizen is a "valuable asset" and "integral part of nation," according to Soni, he must contribute "his best toward to his motherland" (sic). "Customs and rituals" such as voluntary death a good citizen cannot renounce his "rights and liabilities towards his family and nation."
89. Judgment, Para 8.

Disclosure statement

No potential conflict of interest was reported by the author.

Bibliography

Ahuja, R. "The Bridge Builders': Some Notes on Railways, Pilgrimage and the British Civilizing Mission in Colonial India." In *Colonialism as Civilizing Mission: Cultural Ideology in British India*, edited by H. Fischer-Tine and M. Mann, 95–116 London: Anthem Press, 2004.

Barry, R. L. *Breaking the Thread of Life: On Rational Suicide.* USA: Transaction Publishers, 2012.

Baya, D. S. *Death with Equanimity: The Pursuit of Immortality.* Jaipur: Prakriti Bharati Academy, 2007.

Bhuwania, A. *Courting the People: Public Interest Litigation in Post-Emergency India.* Delhi: Cambridge University Press, 2017.

Bilimoria, P. "The Jain Ethic of Voluntary Death: A Report from India." *Bioethics* 6, no. 4 (1992): 331–355.

Buhler, J. G. *On the Indian Sect of the Jainas.* Translated from the German by Jas Burgess. London: Luzac, 1903.

Caillat, C. "Fasting Unto Death according to the Jaina Tradition." *Acta Orientalia* 38 (1977): 43–66.

Cassels, N. G. *Social Legislation of the East India Company: Public Justice versus Public Instruction.* New Delhi: Sage, 2010.

Chapple, C. "Nonresistant Death." *Jinamanjari: Contemporary Jaina Reflections* 2, no. 2 (April, 1991): 51–62.

Colt, G. H. *The Enigma of Suicide.* USA: Touchstone (Simon and Schuster, 1991.

Cort, J. E. "Singing the Glory of Asceticism: Devotion of Asceticism in Jainism." *Journal of the American Academy of Religion* 70, no. 4 (December, 2002): 719–742.

Cort, J. E. *Framing the Jina: Narratives of Icons and Idols in Jain History.* Delhi: OUP, 2010.

Dhavan, R. "Did Supreme Court Just Allow Suicide." *Dailyo.* Accessed January 15, 2017. http://www.dailyo.in/politics/jainism-santhara-rajasthan-judgement-sati-roop-kanwar-irom-sharmila-badana-devi/story/1/6099.html

Droge and Tabor. *A Noble Death: Suicide and Martyrdom among Christians and Jews in Antiquity.* San Francisco: Harper, 1992.

Durkheim, E. *Suicide: A Study in Sociology.* Translated by John A. Spaulding and George Simpson. London: Routledge, 1952 (1897).

Flugel, P. "The Invention of Jainism: A Short History of Jaina Studies." *International Journal of Jain Studies* 1, no. 1 (2005): 1–14.

Forbes, A. K. *Ras Mala: The Hindoo Annals of the Province of Goozerat in Western India.* Oxford: OUP, 1924 edition (1856).

Galanter, M. "The Displacement of Traditional Law in Modern India." In *Law and Society in Modern India* edited by M. Galanter, 15–36. Delhi: OUP, 1994.

Hattangadi, S. "Santhara in the Eyes of the Law." *The Hindu*, August 15, 2015

Hawley, J. S., ed. *Sati, the Blessing and the Curse: The Burning of Wives in India.* New York: OUP, 1994.

Jain, C. R. *Ratnakaranda Sravakcara: The Householder's Dharma.* Arrah: The Central Jaina Publishing, 1917.

Jain, C. R. "Some Misconceptions regarding Jainism." In *Jainism and World Problems: Essays and Addresses Part II* edited by C.R. Jain, 177–182. Bijnore: Jaina Parishad, 1933.

Jain, C. R. "Festival of Death." In *The Change of Heart: Essays and Addresses Part III* edited by C.R. Jain, 110–115. Delhi, 1939.

Jaini, P. S. "The Jainas and the Western Scholar." In *Collected Papers on Jaina Studies* edited by P.S. Jaini, 23–36. Delhi: Motilal Banarsidas, 2000.
Kelting, M. W. "Candanbālā's Hair: Fasting, Beauty, and the Materialization of Jain Wives." *Religion* 39, no. 1 (2009): 1–10.
Laidlaw, J. *Riches and Renunciation: Religion, Economy and Society among the Jains*. Oxford: Clarendon Press, 1995.
Laidlaw, J. "A Life Worth Leaving: Fasting to Death as Telos of A Jain Religious Life." *Economy and society* 34, no. 2 (2005): 178–199.
Luithle-Hardenberg, A. "When Children Become Ascetics: Preliminary Considerations about Disputes on Jain Bal Munis in Western India." *The Oriental Anthropologist* 14, no. 2 (2014): 217–240.
Mani, L. "Contentious Traditions: The Debate on Sati in Colonial India." *Cultural Critique*, no. 7 (Autumn 1987): 119–156
Mehta, P. B. "Death and the Sovereign." *Indian Express*, August 19, 2015.
Numark, M. "The Scottish 'Discovery' of Jainism in Nineteenth-Century Bombay." *Journal of Scottish Historical Studies* 33, no. 1 (2013): 20–51.
Orr, L. "Orientalists, Missionaries and Jains: The South Indian Story." In *The Madras School of Orientalism: Producing Knowledge in Colonial South India*, edited by T. R. Trautmann, 263–287. Delhi: Oxford University Press, 2009.
Rice, B. L. *Inscriptions at Sravan Belgola: A Chief Seat of the Jains*. Bangalore: Mysore Government Central Press, 1880.
Sangari, K., and S. Vaid. "Institutions, Beliefs, Ideologies: Widow Immolation in Contemporary Rajasthan." *Economic and political weekly* 26, no. 17 (27 April 1991): WS. 2–18.
Smith, G. *The Life of John Wilson: For Fifty Years Philanthropist and Scholar in the East*. London: John Murray, 1878.
Straw, C. "A Very Special Death: Christian Martyrdom in Its Classical Context." In *Sacrificing the Self: Perspectives on Martyrdom and Religion*, edited by M. Cormack, 39–57. New York: OUP, 2001.
Talwar Oldenberg, V. "The Roop Kanwar Case: Feminist Responses." In *Sati, the Blessing and the Curse: The Burning of Wives in India*, edited by J. S. Hawley, 101–130. New York: OUP, 1994.
Tukol, T. K. *Sallekhana Is Not Suicide*. Ahmedabad: L.D. Institute of Indology, 1976. (LD Series 55).
Visavanathan, S. "A Reductive Reading of Santhara." *The Hindu*, August 24, 2015.
Wilson, J. *History of the Suppression of Infanticide in Western India under the Government of Bombay Including Notices of the Provinces and Tribes in Which the Practice Has Prevalence*. Bombay: Smith, Taylor and Co., 1835.

Reports

Trial by Fire: A Report on Roop Kanwar's Death. Bombay: Women and Media Committee of Bombay Union of Journalists, 1987.
42nd Law Commission Report on *Indian Penal Code*. Delhi: Ministry of Law, Government of India, 1971.
210th Law Commission Report on *Humanization and Decriminalization of Suicide*. Delhi: Ministry of Law, Government of India, 2008.
The Mental Health Care Act 2017, Ministry of Law and Justice, The Gazette of India, Extraordinary Notification, 7 April 2017.

Cases

Maruti Shripati Dubal vs State Of Maharashtra, (1986) 88 BOMLR 589.
State Vs. Sanjay Kumar Bhatia, 1985 Crl.L.J.931.
Chenna Jagadeeswar and another Vs. State of Andhra Pradesh, 1988 Crl.L.J.549.
P.Rathinam vs Union Of India, 1994 SCC (3) 394.
Smt. Gyan Kaur vs The State Of Punjab, 1996 SCC (2) 648
Aruna Ramachandra Shanbaug v. Union of India, (2011) 4 SCC 454.
Nikhil Soni v Union of India and others, 2015.
Advocate General of Bengal (on behalf of her majesty) Vs. Ranee Surnomoye Dossee 9 M.I.A. 387, decided on 30.06.1863.

Part 2

The Contested Field of Muslim Personal Law

Codification of Islamic law in South Asia, or how not to do comparative law

Abhik Majumdar

ABSTRACT

Comparative law is a fecund field of study capable of yielding insights not obtainable otherwise. It comprises a vital tool not only for academics but also for law and policymakers. It also happens to be a delicate undertaking, and prone to several pitfalls if not approached carefully. Given the shared legal and political antecedents of South Asian nations, a South Asia-specific comparative law discourse of at least some measure of robustness ought to have emerged by now. This expectation lies largely frustrated. Scholarly engagement with comparative law is both sporadic and unsatisfactory, the latter attributable to recurring shortcomings such as a tendency to cherry-pick. Such desultoriness is consequential, given comparative law's capacity to provide inputs to states' lawmaking and policymaking projects. In this paper, I explore a little-known instance, one that involves an initiative of the Indian state of Kerala to reform and codify certain aspects of Islamic personal law. It borrowed considerably from the reform initiatives of Pakistan and Bangladesh but, unusually, chose not to acknowledge this fact. It also deviated from the latter in several crucial respects. And in deviating, it also succeeded in undermining its own stated objectives. In this paper, I examine the two initiatives; their similarities and differences; and the implications that these similarities and differences carry, particularly in the light of avoiding pitfalls while doing comparative law.

Introduction

Law cannot evolve sequestered from other disciplines such as the social sciences and history. It must also continuously learn from itself. This involves absorbing from not only past experiences but also *shared* experiences, the experiences of other legal systems that are in some manner similarly situated, and have encountered similar issues. In the discourse of legal academics, the discipline of comparative law engages with issues of this sort.

It is surprising that the discipline counts for little in South Asia: judicial and academic discourses, as well as law school curricula, treat it in cursory fashion. The neglect is consequential for two reasons. The first concerns the singular inputs the discipline can provide to the praxis of law, which includes the adjudication of disputes, and the formulation of law and policy. This carries especial relevance in the South Asian context. Legal systems within the region share an enduring tradition of influencing one another's development. Take, for example, nations like India, Pakistan, and Bangladesh, whose common colonial antecedents reflect in many similarities across their respective laws. Even in today's post-colonial era, it is not uncommon for judges and lawmakers to draw from the evolution of these common features in other legal systems. An insufficient awareness of the modalities involved – such as how these evolutions have occurred; their causes; and their impact on systems other than their own – must surely impede them in their endeavours. Secondly, comparative law comprises a delicate undertaking. It remains meaningful only so long as it adheres to certain parameters; Frankenberg's seminal 1985 article, which we shall discuss a little later, characterizes them in terms of a balance between relativism and universalism.[1] And hence on occasions requiring a comparative approach, an unfamiliarity its modalities leaves us profoundly ill-equipped to address its challenges.

In this paper, I explore a little-known attempt at comparative law. Its roots lie in the reforms Pakistan initiated in the 1950s, culminating in the enactment of the Muslim Family Law Ordinance (MFLO) in 1961. The law remains in force in Pakistan and also Bangladesh, which separated from Pakistan in 1971 but chose to retain many of the laws it inherited. The legislation featured several types of innovation. Codifying and reforming the law's substantive aspects, particularly contentious practices such as polygamy and unilateral divorce, comprise one category. Another pertains to the larger issue of locating pristine Islamic law within the parameters of legislation, and particularly the procedural requirements of contemporary legal practices.[2]

Some years ago, the Indian state of Kerala attempted to codify and reform certain aspects of Islamic law. The initiative yielded a report entitled 'The Final Report of [*sic*] Law Reforms Commission Kerala' (hereinafter referred to as the 'Report'), and then a draft Bill called the Kerala Muslim Marriage and Dissolution by Talaq and Khula (Regulation) Bill 2009 (the 'Bill)'. Both drew considerably from parallel developments in Pakistan and Bangladesh. But this borrowing was not straightforward. For one, it was not acknowledged explicitly. And secondly, it was filtered through several considerations, including the Commission's perceptions of Islamic jurisprudence, existing court decisions on Islamic law, and even norms of morality as identified by the Commission. The initiative lies largely forgotten today, presumably as a consequence of the public outcry it evoked from conservatives in the Muslim community. Nevertheless, it is significant for us as subjecting it to scrutiny offers valuable insights into comparative law and its pitfalls. Earlier I had referred to comparative law as a delicate undertaking, which remains meaningful only if certain parameters are adhered to. The Kerala initiative represents a textbook example of what happens when these parameters are ignored. Thus, subjecting it to scrutiny enables us to understand the consequences of this disregard, specifically its impact on the objectives of the exercise.

I begin with an overview of the modalities of doing comparative law, particularly the kind of pitfalls it entails and how one may avoid them; followed by a brief overview of how comparative law has been done in the region so far. While I do reference examples from the Indian legal discourse, I do so for their illustrative value alone, i.e. because they constitute appropriate instantiations of what we discuss here. I then proceed to the main theme of this paper, which may be divided into two parts. One concerns developments in personal law change that occurred in Pakistan (and then also in what is now Bangladesh), in particularly developments relating to MFLO 1961. Here I present an account of the innovations the ordinance implemented in respect of both substantive law and legal procedure. The other part relates to the Kerala initiative. Here I look at how both the Commission Report and the Draft Bill took shape and what guided their development; the influence, tacit or otherwise, of MFLO 1961; in which respect and in what manner the Bill diverges from the former; and the consequences of these divergences.

Before I proceed, I must also identify the issues and perspectives I do not intend to pursue here. First, I forbear from engaging with the larger issue of legal reform, and particularly from endorsing any specific mode or paradigm of reform, even though the paper locates within this larger theme. My objective does not concern law reform *per se*: what I address here is a specific question about the role of comparative law in legal reform. To this end, the issue of Islamic personal law reform comprises a useful example, and it is only in this context that I engage with it. I also refrain from addressing specific questions relating to the discourse of personal law reform, such as its impact on gender issues, religious minorities, freedom of religion, and so forth. Neither do I examine the reform of other bodies of law, such as Hindu or Christian personal law; this is because my engagement with Islamic law reform is prompted by, and restricted to, the convenient instantiation it comprises of comparative law and its impact on the development of law.

Background

'Doing' comparative law

Doing comparative law is a delicate undertaking, and its successful execution entails avoiding several types of pitfalls. Frankenberg's seminal 1985 article constitutes a useful frame of reference in respect of both, i.e. the undertaking as well as its pitfalls. It locates them within the dialectic of the self and the other.[3] This may be optimally understood through what he identifies as the two extremes representing the non-dialectical, *viz.* relativism and universalism, which he also refers to as 'going native' and 'going rational', respectively.[4] To sustain this dialectic, he recommends two parameters. '*Distancing*' entails dissociating from 'settled knowledge' and particularly prejudice and ignorance entailing from the first, and thereby securing a measure of objectivity: 'From a distance old knowledge can be reviewed and new knowledge can be distinguished as it is in its own right.' '*Differencing*' is characterized as 'break(ing) the unconscious spell that holds us to see others by the measure of ourselves', that is, a 'conscious effort to establish subjectivity': 'Differencing calls into question the neutrality and universality of all criteria: it rejects the notion ... that the categories and concepts with which new experiences are grasped, classified, and compared have nothing whatsoever to do with the socio-cultural context of those who see in terms of them.'[5]

This carries particular resonance in the context of doing comparative law, particularly comparative personal law, within the framework of South Asia. It involves legal systems that on the one hand bear strong similarities, including a shared colonial past, and on the other hand, have developed further in their own distinctive ways. Negotiating these similarities and differences requires great skill, since the temptation to emphasize one at the cost of the other is considerable.

Comparative personal law in South Asia

It is not surprising that comparative personal law commands much interest from among scholars, judges, and lawmakers.[6] This has much to do with the character of the subject. Traditionally, religious doctrines have played a vital role in shaping personal law. These doctrines tend to apply across state boundaries, at times with little to no modification. This implies that personal laws belonging to different nations but sharing theological roots will bear significant similarities to one another. An offshoot of this is that the contentious aspects of religious doctrine have engendered similar controversies in the different legal systems in which they apply. Take the reform, and particularly the codification, of Islamic personal law. Legal systems the world over, including several that share much with India, have encountered problems of similar character. However, they have opted to address these in dissimilar manners. Legislation such as Malaysia's Islamic Family Laws (Federal Territories) Act (IFLA) 1984 and Singapore's Administration of Muslim Law Act (AMLA) 1968 are notable examples. In the South Asian context, MFLO 1961 of Pakistan and Bangladesh mentioned earlier represents surely the most radical development in this regard.

In contrast, South Asian law's engagement with the modalities of comparative law remains unsatisfactory on several counts. A brief overview of secondary literature underscores how negligently law scholars from within the region tend to treat the subject: it appears that almost all major contributions to the literature may be attributed to commentators from either outside South Asia,[7] or outside the discipline of law![8] It is certainly not my intention to denigrate these contributions for their provenance. Yet the fact remains that a robust engagement with comparative law from *within* South Asian legal scholarship is necessary, given its capacity to provide inputs to the praxis of law. And this engagement has remained thin at best, notwithstanding exceptions such as Mahmood's comparison of Indian and (pre-communist) Afghan law.[9]

A glance at this praxis suggests such inputs would be most valuable. In many instances, comparative law implications are simply overlooked. A series of Kerala High Court judgments[10] seeking to establish that polygamy *ipso facto* constitutes inequitable treatment and hence amounts to cruelty,[11] makes barely any mention of the legal position in other nations. At times this becomes a grave shortcoming. In 2009 the Law Commission of India published its 227th report on the theme of non-Muslims adopting Islam in order to marry polygamously. Now, this is by no means an issue peculiar to India alone: the law of Pakistan features cases such as *Mrs CM Samual v CM Samual*[12]; as do several Sri Lankan and Malaysian judgments, some of which[13] even discuss Indian decisions in considerable detail. But surprisingly, the 227th report does not carry any mention of them. Nor does it discuss how Malaysia[14] and Singapore[15] legislation have prohibited this practice. This applies also to other Law Commission reports dealing with issues relating to personal law, such as the secular law of divorce, the law of civil marriages, and evidence requirements of change in religion.[16] None of these reports even mention parallel developments in other jurisdictions.

At first sight, the 205th Report on Child Marriages comes across as a welcome exception.[17] It addresses at some length (p. 26–28) the legal position on child marriages in other legal systems. A closer look, however, reveals several shortcomings in this exegesis. For one, it spans a bewildering variety of jurisdictions, spanning (in that order) Australia, New Zealand, the United Kingdom, Egypt, the United States, Pakistan and Indonesia.[18] Given that they share little in common, the basis for selecting only them and not others remains obscure, leading to concerns about cherry-picking. The way the report seeks to address seven altogether distinct legal systems within about 420 words *sans* footnotes, only intensifies these concerns. Not surprisingly, the treatment accorded to these systems and their handling of child marriage is sketchy in the extreme. For the most part, it is confined to a bare recounting of one or two stray provisions selected from each legal system. Even the selection of the provisions appears haphazard: some deal with statutory rape; some void marriages of underage persons; other penalize child marriage, and so forth.

Similar instances may be identified in court judgments. *Shahulameedu v Subaida Beevi*[19] references within a single cursory observation the laws of Syria, Tunisia, Morocco, Pakistan, Iran, and the Islamic Republics of the erstwhile Soviet Union: it then infers that many Islamic nations had either prohibited or 'severely restricted' polygamy. This single reference comprises the judgment's entire discussion of other legal systems. It does not look at how these legal systems intersect; or whether at all they have intersected in terms of one influencing the legal development of the other. Nor does it venture to address the specifics of these laws, or even state which legislation these mandates derived from. It also eschews any discussion on the basis of these laws, beyond making two assertions: one, that these laws conform to the 'true spirit' of the Quran, which endorses monogamy and treats polygamy as an exception; and two, that polygamy was originally envisaged as a measure for rehabilitating war widows, which purpose no longer remained valid. No sources are offered in respect of either assertion. Subsequent judgments like *Habeebulla v Shakeela*[20] and *Saidali v Saleena*[21] allude to this with much approval. *Saidali* even makes a brief mention of MFLO 1961, but only to the extent of summarizing Sections 6 and 7 of the Ordinance.[22]

Such lack of rigour carries another fallout in addition to inducing distortions. It also decontextualizes enquiry. For instance, none of the foregoing examples countenance the possibility that two legal systems may arrive at similar conclusions from different starting points and through dissimilar lines of reasoning. Neither do they even mention, let alone subject to scrutiny, the reasoning that led each legal system to arrive at the conclusion that it did. Through its very act of making that assertion about Islamic countries prohibiting or severely restricting polygamy, *Shahulameedu* elides questions such as how prohibition and severe restriction differ in conception; why some have chosen the first and others the second; what exactly is meant by severe restriction; the consequences and implications of either approach when being implemented; and which is the more appropriate for India to adopt.

This leads to the central claim of the paper, *viz.* that the consequent unfamiliarity with the modalities adversely impacts on personal law development within the region's legal systems. My focus rests mainly on the inherent dynamics of the impact, that is, questions such as *how* or in what *manner* unsatisfactory engagement impacts on legal development. (While the impact also raises associated empirical questions such as how frequently attempts at comparative law are unsuccessful, or the extent to which they impact on legal development, I prefer not to address them as they constitute independent lines of enquiry in their own right.) And it is to explore these dynamics that I engage with the Kerala initiative, and how it borrows from Pakistan and Bangladesh law.

Personal law reform in Pakistan and Bangladesh

The narrative of MFLO must begin from the 1956 Commission on Marriage and Family Laws set up under the chairmanship of Justice Abdul Rashid, and its 1958 report which led to the enactment of the ordinance.[23] This legislation strove to achieve a balance between the needs of a perceived modernity and values traditionally associated with the Muslim community. Which is possibly why its drafters (and presumably also the authors of the 1956 report) drew much inspiration from conventional interpretations of Islamic personal law.[24] Notwithstanding these efforts, *Ulema* (members of the Islamic clergy) were quick to dub it a Western implant; some even claim that its 'main significance' today is as 'a focal point of conflict between the Muslim modernists, on the one hand, and the orthodox *ulama* and the fundamentalists, on the other.'[25] Be that as it may, it remains in force both in Pakistan and, with minor amendments, in Bangladesh too, which seceded from Pakistan in 1971 but still retains many of the latter's pre-1971 laws.

The Ordinance spans both substantive and procedural matters. The first pertains to questions such as when polygamy is permissible, appropriate maintenance amount, and so forth. Procedural aspects include setting up informal dispute settlement mechanisms called Arbitration Councils, how they are to be constituted, their jurisdiction, and other similar issues. The Ordinance is interesting, in that it attempts to tread a fine line between the mandates of pristine Islamic law, and the demands of contemporary conceptions of justice and equity. It clearly does not attempt to override pristine Islamic law. The Federal Shariat Court in *Allah Rakha v. Federation of Pakistan*[26] explored in some detail the issue of MFLO's consistency with Shar'ia. It concluded (para 105) that barring Sections 7 (3) and 7(5) that determine when divorce in the *talaq* form becomes effective, nothing in the Ordinance could be construed as inconsistent with the precepts of Islam.

And yet while remaining within the bounds of this pristine law, it seeks to subject the latter to substantive and procedural parameters associated more closely with contemporary legal discourse. A concrete illustration is useful here. The Malaysian IFLA 1984 mentioned earlier, specifies at s 23 (4)(d) that a polygamous marriage may be sanctioned only if it does not 'cause *darar syarie* to the existing wife or wives.' '*Darar syarie*' is defined in s 2(1) as 'harm, according to what is normally recognized by Islamic Law, affecting a wife in respect of religion, life, body, mind, moral or property'. In contrast, s 6(3) of MFLO requires only that such marriages be 'necessary and just'. The distinction is clear now. Both provisions reference values associated with justice and equity. The Malaysian law explicitly construes them in terms of how they have been understood in Islamic law: its Pakistani counterpart eschews keying the norms to the Shar'ia even though it does restrict itself to within the framework of pristine Islamic law.

Does this suggest a binary between pristine Islamic law and a constructed 'modernity'? The term 'pristine' might appear misleading. Shar'ia law is surely not static in character: it has evolved over centuries and continues to evolve. Moreover, its discourse features its own sites of debate and contestation just as any other body of laws does. What is significant here, however, is how little of this discourse MFLO takes into account, particularly when construing norms such as justice or necessity. We may contend this does imply a binary here, but not in the conventional sense: that is, a binary between that 'modernity' and not so much pristine law as its *inclusion* within the framework of the Ordinance even as a referent for construing norms.

Procedural innovations

While MFLO's substantive provisions on polygamy and similar issues have attracted the much greater share of attention,[27] its handling of procedure is no less interesting. The substantive and the procedural impact on one another at many levels. For instance, determining the validity and extent of litigants' claims is a matter of judicial discretion. And discretion, in turn, owes much to judges' perception, at times their individual predilections too. When it comes to socially and politically sensitive issues, the choice of judge matters even more. Polygamy, unilateral divorce, and other such issues relating to personal law clearly impact on gender, patriarchal hegemony, and also larger questions relating to the social organization in Pakistan.

Here the Ordinance takes the radical step of dissociating the clergy from all aspects of adjudication that it covers. It moots settling personal law disputes through *ad hoc* informal bodies known as Arbitration Councils. One may contend with some justification that the concept represents merely the modern iteration of a long-standing practice in Islamic jurisprudence: even the Quran says, 'If you fear a breach between two [spouses], appoint referees – one from his family and one from her family. God will bring them back together if they want to be reconciled.'[28] However, the Ordinance does not expressly acknowledge this. And hence the question whether or not the arbitration provisions draw inspiration from Shar'ia law becomes speculative.

These Councils are associated with three kinds of matters: polygamous marriages (Section 6); divorce (Sections 7–8); and maintenance (Section 9). Section 2(a) defines 'Arbitration Council' as a body that comprises of a chairman, and representatives of parties to matters addressed by the Ordinance. The chairman is drawn from established local government bodies. Pakistan's system of local government entails a three-tier hierarchy, comprising Zila, Tehsil, and Union Councils. The last mentioned are elected village-level bodies, and the lowest rung in this hierarchy.[29] The chairman of the Union Council also doubles up as the chairman of the Arbitration Council,[30] thereby lending a shade of permanency to the institution. The Bangladeshi version is slightly more elaborate, since local government is organized differently there. Consequently, it identifies a range of officials as qualified to act as chairmen of Arbitration Councils: this includes chairmen of Union Parishads and *Paurashavās* (urban municipal bodies), mayors and administrators of municipal corporations. These offices are essentially secular in character. And this secular orientation extends to the composition of Arbitration Councils also. Section 2(b) of both Pakistani and Bangladeshi versions provides that if the chairman of a particular Council or Parishad or other body is not a Muslim, then that body may for the purposes of the Ordinance elect one of its Muslim members or commissioners, as the case may be, to act as chairman. Beyond this, no further ecclesiastical qualifications are prescribed.

The other members of Councils are, as mentioned, representatives of the parties. And hence each Council thus constituted is specific to an individual dispute. Section 6(3) makes elaborate provisions for the constitution of a Council if a man desires to marry polygamously; entailing the chairman being required to ask the applicant, and also each of his existing wife or wives, to nominate their respective representatives. These then constitute the Council. In respect of matters concerning unilateral divorce (i.e. in the '*Talaq*' form) or maintenance (Sections 7(4) and 9(1) respectively), the chairman is required to constitute a Council as well. However, the manner of constitution is specified not in the Act itself (as Section 6(3) does) but in the Rules framed under the Ordinance. In Pakistan they are referred to as the 'West Pakistan Rules under the Muslim

Family Laws Ordinance, 1961'; and in Bangladesh as simply Muslim Family Law Rules, 1961'. We shall refer to them collectively as the 'MFLO Rules'.

Rule 6(1) requires the chairman to write to the parties and ask them to nominate one representative each within seven days. It also prescribes the same procedure for applications received under Section 6(4) of the Ordinance. This reference is puzzling, mainly because Section 6(4) does not actually deal with constituting Arbitration Councils. Even if we assume that the reference contains a typographical error and is actually intended at Section 6(3) (which does deal with the constitution of Councils), questions still remain. As we saw, Section 6(3) already provides for the constitution of Councils. Which makes the application of Rule 6(1) largely redundant, since the latter does not add much to it save peripheral details such as the time period for nomination. Beyond instantiating slapdash legislative drafting practices, this lapse does not carry much significance for us. What is more important is that neither the Ordinance nor the Rules specify any ecclesiastical qualification, or even religious affiliation, for nominated Council members.

Substantive aspects

The Ordinance's handling of substantive issues is instructive. As mentioned earlier, it does not seek to override pristine Islamic law. Neither does it attempt an exhaustive treatment of personal law. It restricts itself to just three issues, namely polygamy, divorce, and maintenance.[31] Even in respect of this limited range of issues, it operates within bounds set by pristine law. This, however, is subject to a qualification: the Ordinance does not make any explicit references to the Quran, or other religious treatises, in connection with any of the issues it addresses.

Each of the issues mentioned above envisages for Councils a specific role, and hence a form of engagement dissimilar from the others. Section 7 deals with unilateral divorce (i.e. in the *talaq* form), and specifies that Councils are required only to 'take all steps necessary' for reconciliation. In other words, in such cases Councils are not called upon to adjudicate on the matter, that is, decide or pass judgment of any sort. All they do is mediate between the parties to see if a compromise can be reached through goodwill alone. Through Section 8, this mediatory role of Councils is extended to other forms of divorce also. In respect of maintenance under Section 10, their role is more decisive: it is required to determine and then certify what maintenance amount is appropriate.

The Ordinance and Councils play a greater role in cases involving polygamous marriages. A cursory glance at the provision indicates that the Ordinance remains neutral to the theological, moral, and other debates on whether legally recognizing polygamy is desirable or not. It also seeks to function within Quranic mandates on polygamy, without in any way extending itself beyond the latter. The Quran specifies: 'If you fear to be unfair to female orphans, then marry those who appeal to you, two, three, or four, but if you fear to be unfair to them, then [marry] only one or a slave - that will be nearer to righteousness.'[32] The Federal Shariat Court, in *Allah Rakha v. Federation of Pakistan*[33] referred to earlier, has interpreted this to mean '[I]t should not be understood that the Qur'an is exhorting the believers to practise polygamy or that polygamy is considered as an ideal. In other words the Qur'an has tolerated or allowed polygamy and no more.' In legal theory terms, this amounts to a liberty accorded to the individual (i.e. the liberty to contract polygamous marriages), which is then both constricted and balanced by the obligation to be 'fair' to one's wives. And the Ordinance's provisions on polygamy reflect this liberty as well as obligations it is constricted by. Clause (1) of Section 6 states: 'No man, during the subsistence of an existing marriage, shall except with the *previous permission* in writing of the Arbitration Council, contract another marriage, nor shall any such marriage contracted without such permission be registered under this Ordinance' (emphasis added).

That the Ordinance construes prior permission of the Council as a *sine qua non* was recognized in a recent decision of the Pakistan Supreme Court, *Ishtiaq Ahmad v. The State*.[34] The facts involved here are interesting. The petitioner married polygamously without seeking permission from the Arbitration Council. He then claimed that since the term of the Union Council had expired, and local government elections had still not been held (which left vacant the chair of the Council chairman), there was nobody he could seek permission from. The Court rejected this contention, pointing out that the petitioner could have approached whichever official was designated to function as the Union Council chairman (as happens in such circumstances). Hence, the petitioner could not evade punishment on this ground.

Further, this emphasis on prior permission also establishes that polygamy is permissible *only* under specific circumstances, and *only* if the presence of these circumstances is validated by the Council. Can we contend here that that Ordinance treats monogamy as a default position of sorts, and countenances polygamy as valid only in special situations? Court decisions suggest this constituted the recognized position even before MFLO came into being. *Iftikhar Nazir Ahmad Khan v. Ghulam Kibria*[35] was decided in 1967, but on facts that predated MFLO. It involved a Lyallpur lawyer called Raja Ghulam Rasul, who already had four wives but then married for a fifth time, had a son by this fifth wife, divorced her, then married again and had another son by this new wife (it seems he had yet another woman living with him as his wife, but in court she failed to prove that she and Rasul were in fact married). In holding these marriages invalid but not altogether void, the court held (para 64) that 'Islam enjoins monogamy as the normal rule of marriage, the choice to marry more than one wife up to the limit of four (accepting the most liberal interpretation of the relevant Qur'anic text) . . . .' In the post-MFLO era, this was reaffirmed by the Supreme Courts of both Pakistan and Bangladesh in, respectively, *Syed Ali Nawas Gardezi v. Lt Col Muhammad Yusuf*[36] and *Abul Bashar v. Nurun Nabi.*[37] Both endorse the view that Section 6 is intended to 'restrict' polygamy. Admittedly the Pakistan decision does not amount to binding law since the facts of the case did not concern polygamy directly (it involved a woman living with another man without divorcing her husband, which amounted to adultery and not polygamy). But still, it carries significance as an indicator of judicial perception. The Bangladeshi decision suffers no such shortcoming.

Clause (3) requires the Council to merely satisfy itself that the proposed marriage is 'necessary and just'. It does not, however, specify what kind of grounds or parameters are to form the basis of this decision. For this, we need to turn once again to the Rules. Rule 14 states:

> In considering whether another proposed marriage is just and necessary during the continuance of an existing marriage the Arbitration Council may, *without prejudice to its general powers* to consider what is just and necessary, have regard to such circumstances, as the following *amongst others*:
>
> Sterility, physical infirmity, physical unfitness for the [*sic*] conjugal relation [*sic*], wilful avoidance of a decree for restitution of conjugal rights, or insanity on the part of an existing wife. (emphasis added)

Though it specifies five grounds validating polygamy, the language it uses is surprising. Through the use of phrases like 'without prejudice to its general powers to consider what is just and necessary' and 'the following amongst others' it confirms twice over that the Councils' discretion is not limited to these grounds alone, and that they are free to identify any other grounds not mentioned also as a valid reason for sanctioning polygamy. This appears to confer on Councils vast discretion in identifying grounds as valid reason for permitting polygamy: so vast, in fact, that it does not appear to be restricted in any manner, either by the grounds specified in Rule 14 or by any other law. This is formally known as 'uncanalised' or 'unfettered' discretion. Moreover, this Rule is not even a statutory provision, but only what is known as 'delegated' or 'subordinate' legislation framed under the Ordinance by the executive, not the legislature. Such subordinate legislation is subject to tight restrictions. Usually, if they confer discretion of such wide amplitude, they are liable to be promptly struck down by the judiciary as bad in law. So far, this has not happened here. Perhaps the wide amplitude was conferred so as not to antagonize the clergy? That said, the parameters that the Rule does specify are interesting. Sterility, physical infirmity, insanity and other such considerations are not dependent on theological sanction, and may well exist and operate without it. Nor does the Ordinance, or the Rules framed under it, specify considerations of pristine law as grounds for taking decisions.

Another weakness of the Ordinance concerns the consequences of violating Section 6. Clause (5) (b) does stipulate a year's simple imprisonment and/or fines of up to Rs 5,000 (Taka 10,000 in the Bangladeshi version) for polygamous marriages contracted without the prior permission of the Council. But as law courts have also recognized,[38] it stops short of declaring such marriages void, that is, a nullity in the eyes of the law. This serves to weaken the mandate of Section 6; a man may disregard it and marry polygamously secure in the knowledge that even if he is subjected to punishment, the marriage itself remains valid. The second point relates to the Penal Codes of all three nations, India as well as Pakistan and Bangladesh, which in this respect are virtually identical. The punishment for polygamy under Section 494 (of all the three Codes) is much more stringent, ranging up to even seven years' imprisonment, but the Section applies only in cases where the marriage is rendered void due to its polygamous character. This means that the punishment for flouting Section 6 of MFLO is restricted to one years' simple imprisonment only, and the much greater punishment under Section 494 rendered inapplicable to it. Moreover, the Ordinance does not prescribe any punishment for disregarding the maintenance amount certified under Section 9(1), which suggests violating it shall attract civil remedies only.

While on the issue of weaknesses, it must also be pointed out that many of its innovations have not succeeded in making a difference. As far back as 1969, commentators like Daniel Pearl claimed MFLO 'has not had too much success', attributing this to a flawed approach emphasizing legal restrictions on men's freedom while overlooking the need for greater literacy and education. Which is why Councils are apt to routinely pass applications without applying their minds.[39] Hossain observes in regard to the functioning of Councils in Bangladesh: 'Although women are seemingly taken into consideration in the decision-making process about multiple wives, the Arbitration Council lacks discretionary power. In practice, the Arbitration Council is composed of males who give permission to remarry even on the slightest pretexts.'[40]

Hence, in its vision of reconciling 'tradition' and 'modernity', the Ordinance perhaps overlooks the fact that the personal law conflicts may not always be among equals, that one side may be so much the stronger than the other. Moreover, the informality the process entails *ipso facto* subverts this end precisely because it makes it easy for one side to suborn the process to its own ends. Hence, while it is certainly a laudable initiative, the Ordinance as it stands is vulnerable to having its ends defeated.

The Kerala initiative

The provenance of the Kerala Law Reforms Commission can be traced back to an address made by RL Bhatia, the Governor of Kerala, to the state's Legislative Assembly, where he announced that the government proposed to treat law reform as a 'high priority item'.[41] Further impetus came from a statement by AR Lakshmanan, the chairman of the Law Commission of India, where he underlined the need for such a Commission given that many of the state's laws were obsolete, and that other states including Maharashtra, Gujarat, and Tamil Nadu had already established Law Commissions on their own.[42] On 17 November 2007, a notification was issued formally setting up the Commission under the chairpersonship of Justice VR Krishna Iyer, a former judge of the Supreme Court.[43] The notification conferred on it a wide remit, extending to rectifying defects in existing laws; repealing obsolete or unnecessary enactments; consolidating, modifying, reforming, simplifying, and modernizing existing laws; adopting better methods of administering the law, and so forth.

In 2009, the Commission submitted what it termed its 'Final Report'[44] (why it chose a title that appears to preclude further output is not clear). It addresses a wide range of issues: In respect of laws needing rectification of defects alone, the Commission drafted some thirty-nine Bills. (p 47)[45] Intriguingly, much of what the Report has to say premises on explicitly normative considerations:

'City robbery, cunning pick-pocketing flamboyant, flashy temptations and [*sic*] are the moral culpables behind lumpen bullies and sexy [*sic*] girls marring humility and innocence. The drug of showy godism, aggravated by the opium of religion in revelry, mafia malpractices, near-naked, promiscuous pleasure rackets and corruption ubiquitous, make social and economic sanity and equity a rarity' (p 17). It even proposes a Women's Code for Defense of Divinity [*sic*] and Dignity of Womanhood. The Report's discussion of it is preceded by a note on the theme 'Indian Womanhood – Its Dignity, Divinity and Defence by Law of its Defilement': 'Erotic misconduct takes various forms and mercenary institutions, including hotels and hostels, are covertly made use of for promiscuous operations which ruin the finer character of the youth. Publicity through advertisements in the print and electronic media and in public streets virtually abets the urge to commit sex offences' (p 97).

About religion or, to be precise, what it perceives as the perversion of religion, it asserts: 'Castes and communities, dubiously wearing "minority" apparel and masquerading as sacred religion, foment felonious tendencies. Much more mischief, with Godism as the tool, incendiary in its methodology, is achieved by politicizing religion, since faith is a flame which burns like wild fire' (p 28). And then, in the same page: 'We must save God, the Infinite, from goofy [*sic*], greedy, gold-hungry gods in parochial apparel and political haberdashery [*sic*]. Politicized godism slays sober secularism as a moral martyr. Kerala must overcome this sinister ploy of celestial belligerency and restore the splendour of the Universal Supremo by holistic law reform and humanistic pristine secularism. Yes, we can.'

This ponderous normativity also extends to the Commission's approach to Islamic law reform: 'If polygamy is taboo for the Hindu on the score of secular principles, public well-being and gender justice there is no reason why the Muslim brothers and sisters governed by the same Constitution and ethos should not surrender the *profligacy of polygamy* in favour of the *civilized culture of monogamy*' (p 33) (emphasis added). It then proposes the conjecture that 'the Koran enjoined monogamy upon Muslims and departure therefrom as an exception' (p 34). Surprisingly, it substantiates this assertion largely through Justice Iyer's own judgments in *Shahulameedu*[46] and *Yusuf Rowthan*.[47] Even the discussion on Quranic provisions found in p 40 are actually lengthy quotations from *Rowthan*.

The Kerala Muslim Marriage and Dissolution by Talaq and Khula (Regulation) Bill[48] was not intended as a comprehensive legislation. It restricts itself to a few specific areas, in this case, polygamous marriages (Clause 5) and divorce by *Talaq* and *Khula*. (Clause 11). While it does address some other minor issues such as divorce on grounds of irretrievable breakdown of marriage (Clause 9) and compulsory registration of all marriages (Clause 10), clearly the first two issues are dealt with more comprehensively.

Though neither the Bill nor the Commission's Report makes any explicit mention of MFLO, the latter's influence is palpable; it is hard to miss resemblances between the latter's Arbitration Councils and the 'Conciliation Councils' mooted in Clause 4 of the Bill (arbitration and conciliation are the two most prominent modes of 'alternate dispute resolution', or settling disputes outside law courts). These Councils do differ from their MFLO counterparts in some respects, though. Chairpersons are to be recruited from among retired subordinate judicial officers who are Muslims. More significantly, parties' nominees can only be 'scholars of Islam'. This qualification is surprising: why make such prescription parties' nominees, but not Chairpersons? Whatever be its purpose, this explicit concession to religion contrasts sharply with MFLO's policy of maintaining a distance of sorts from the clergy.

The Report's treatment of polygamy is marked by a moral slant MFLO avoids. The Commission's inference that the Quran actually endorses monogamy finds explicit mention in Clause 5, which addresses the issue of polygamous marriages. Even the title of the Clause boldly asserts: 'Monogamy shall be the Rule'. The provision then states, 'Monogamy shall be the rule binding on every Muslim, man or woman, but polygamy is permissible to Muslim male only to the extent provided for by this Act.' The bulk of the provision, particularly the parts that permit polygamy under controlled circumstances, are relegated to a proviso, where the 'rare' grounds justifying polygamy are specified. These include adultery; 'frigidity' [*sic*]; the wife's inability to bear children; and the first wife giving written consent. This departs from MFLO in two ways. First, here the grounds are enumerated in the main enactment itself and not in associated subordinate legislation. And secondly, in contrast to the wide discretion MFLO confers on Councils, the language used in the Bill precludes the recognition of any further grounds justifying polygamy: in technical terms this is known as an exhaustive enumeration. Further, unlike MFLO, Clause 7 voids polygamous marriages contravening Clause 5.

The Bill's deviation from MFLO in regard to the procedure outlined in Clause 5 must be termed inexplicable. After stipulating that a man 'may' remarry if the aforementioned 'rare grounds' exist, it goes on to state that if a dispute occurs about whether or not such grounds actually exist, the wife may raise the matter before the Council. It is not clear what the purpose behind this is; a misconceived practicality appears to be the best guess. However, its chief outcome is to undermine one of MFLO's key features, namely the requirement of prior permission. The merit of this arrangement is that it makes it feasible to intervene in doubtful cases at a time when the marriage has not yet taken place. The Bill, on the other hand, envisages intervention only after the first wife gets to know, which may well be after the marriage has already taken place. In which case all the Council can do is nullify a marriage that has already taken place, a more daunting task to contemplate than preventing a marriage before it occurs. Moreover, the initiative to secure this daunting outcome has to come not from the state but from the wife: surely not easy, and all the more so in deeply patriarchal circumstances. The matter does not end there either. The Bill appears to shift the burden of proof from the husband to the wife. Under MFLO, it is the husband who is required to establish before the Council the validity of his prospective marriage. But here, since it is the wife who is required to initiate proceedings, clearly it is she who must prove before the Council that the marriage is invalid. Does it mean she must now set about establishing that she is not 'frigid' (whatever that may mean), or that she has not actually committed adultery?

At a conceptual level also, this arrangement appears doubtful: it serves to contradict the Bill's own stated normative position. Clause 5 states unequivocally that 'Monogamy shall be the rule binding on every Muslim', thereby establishing monogamy as the rule and polygamy as an exception. However, the Bill then goes about enabling the husband to unilaterally take a call on the marriage's validity, and contemplates intervention only at a later stage. In such circumstances, does it not appear that the Bill treats polygamy as the default position, and subsequent nullification of unjustified marriages as the exception?

On the other hand, Clause 11 dealing with divorce suggests prior approval even if it does not expressly state so. The provision's heading explicitly references *Talaq* and *Khula*, two forms of divorce recognized under pristine Islamic law (the first is when a husband unilaterally divorces his wife by thrice uttering the word '*Talaq*'; and the second involves the wife initiating proceedings, and the husband consenting to it). The Clause then provides for either party initiating 'proceeding for that purpose (i.e. divorce) before the Council on the basis of grounds such as adultery (actually 'Leading an adulterous life); incompatibility of temperament; fraud; apostasy, and so forth as specified in the Clause itself. Clearly, this provision does not feature either the unilateral character of *Talaq*, or the mutuality of consent so characteristic of *Khula*. Hence, though it certainly represents an enlightened approach to divorce, it bears little resemblance to either pristine form. Which is why the references to *Talaq* and *Khula* appear surprising.

Concluding remarks

The Kerala Initiative does not figure prominently in the discourse of Indian personal law. And perhaps understandably so. It did not achieve much beyond evoking some measure of public outcry as newspaper reports indicate (e.g. *Daily News & Analysis*, 12 November 2008; *Indian Express*, 8 January 2009); following the outcry, it seems the Bill was quietly shelved, where it remains ever since. The question is, had it been enacted into law, how successful would it have been in resolving the issues it had set out to address? And to what extent can its potential success or failure be attributed to its relation with MFLO?

The two legislative initiatives share a similar mandate, one that seeks a balance between pristine law and prevalent conceptions of 'modernity'. MFLO sustains this balance through an overt distance from Shar'ia precepts while locating itself within the bounds of the latter. This enables it to avoid *invalidation* on grounds of inconsistency with Islam, while yet forbearing from overtly harnessing theological considerations for validation or justification. Whether this strategy has been successful, that is, whether it has enabled MFLO to secure its objectives, is a matter of debate. However, we may claim uncontroversially that the strategy does impart a conceptual coherence to the scheme of the Ordinance.

The Report and the Bill both explicitly reference moral standards. Does this indicate that they look to such standards for validation or justification, something MFLO consciously eschews? On the other hand, neither acknowledge MFLO as a source, though their debt to the latter is manifest. This recalls to mind Frankenberg's admonition about dissociating from 'settled knowledge' (the quotes are deliberate). The 205th Law Commission Report and judgments such as *Shahulameedu* appear to instantiate precisely this sort of 'settled knowledge': cherry-picking implies decontextualizing, which in these instances was coupled with a reluctance to subject borrowings to any detailed scrutiny. Their reluctance to go deeper suggests an unquestioning acceptance of what is being borrowed.

In the case of the Kerala initiative, though, at least the borrowing that we examined derives not from pristine law but from MFLO. And it is in this light, and not in terms of borrowing from Shar'ia law, that the reference to Frankenberg must be construed. MFLO certainly does not amount to 'old' knowledge, but its statutory character does bespeak a modicum of 'settled'. The Kerala initiative is unsatisfactory not because of its treatment of Shar'ia law but in its inadequately distancing itself from MFLO. But this also precludes any possibility of unquestioning acceptance, specifically due to the fact that neither the Bill nor the Report admits to having borrowed from MFLO! On the other hand, they do acknowledge the influence of moral, and particularly theological, precepts. This prompts the question, how does this affect the balance between pristine law and 'modernity' and, by extension, also the coherence that MFLO has achieved?

We may identify two forms in which Bill deviates from MFLO. The first involves a slant towards morality. Clause 5 declares monogamy to be 'the rule binding on every Muslim'; Clause 4 (c) requires parties' representatives in Councils to be 'scholars of Islam'. These conform to moral considerations that MFLO either avoids or at best recognizes tacitly. Their consequence is to expose the dispute resolution process to the influence of moral and theological considerations, and specifically the involvement of the clergy. The second concerns the procedure in Clause 5, which envisages intervention at a later stage, and that too at the initiative of the first wife. It is not clear what purpose this deviation serves. Possibly it is a concession to what the Commission thought was practicality. Its effect, however, is to only make things difficult for the aggrieved first wife. Moreover, this actually subverts the Bill's own stated normative position, since in cases of polygamous marriages, polygamy now becomes the default option and legal relief against unjustified marriages get relegated to the ranks of rare exceptions.

The character of the two deviations may differ considerably from one another, with one tilting towards morality, the other possibly a misconceived practicality. In terms of Frankenberg's dialectic, the first can be perceived instantiating 'going native', the second perhaps a flawed attempt at 'going rational'. But their consequences are similar. Sustaining a balance between the two forms comprises a key feature of MFLO, and plays an equally key role in securing its cohesion. But when the Bill borrows from MFLO without paying attention to what its key features are, it is this cohesion that stands compromized. For these reasons, the Bill must be treated as intrinsically flawed. And these flaws may be traced back to the manner in which it seeks to borrow from other legal systems.

Notes

1. Frankenberg, "Critical Comparisons: Re-thinking Comparative Law," 415.
2. I use the term 'pristine' in a technical sense here: it references the law that derives from scriptural and customary sources and has not been subjected to reform or codification.
3. Ibid.
4. Ibid.
5. Ibid., 414.
6. In the Asian context, the seminal contributions of MB Hooker on the law of Malaysia, Singapore, and other jurisdictions such as Hong Kong come readily to mind See e.g. Hooker, "The Relationship between Chinese Law and Common Law in Malaysia, Singapore, and Hong Kong"; Hooker, "Chinese Customary Law in Contemporary Malaysia and Singapore". Another instance is Hussain, "More Than One Law for All: Legal Pluralism in Southeast Asia" (Indonesia, Malaysia, Thailand). Examples pertaining to other jurisdictions include Ghandour, "Religious Law in a Secular State" (Israel and Palestine); and Tamanna, "Personal Status Laws in Morocco and Tunisia" (which also addresses Bangladesh).
7. See e.g. Galanter and Krishnan, "Personal Law and Human Rights in India and Israel"; and Subramanian, *Nation and Family*.
8. E.g. 'The present article ... is not a legalistic study. It views the problem from a political perspective.' Ghosh, "The Issue of Personal and Customary Law in South Asia," 180.
9. Mahmood, "Law and Social Development in India and Afghanistan: A Comparative Perspective".
10. See *K Muhamma Latheef v. Nishath*, All India Reporter (AIR) 2004 Kerala 22; *Abdurahiman v. Khairunneesa*, 2010 (1) Kerala Law Times (KLT) 891; and *Parakkattil Abu v. Pachiyath Beekkutty*. AIR 2011 Kerala 38.
11. Section 2(viii)(f) of the Dissolution of Muslim Marriages Act 1939 (DMMA 1939) recognizes as cruelty (and hence a ground for divorce) the failure to treat any wife within a polygamous marriage equitably in accordance with Quranic injunctions.
12. Pakistan Law Digest (PLD) 1967 Supreme Court (SC) 334.
13. See e.g. *Abeysundere v. Abeysundere*, (1998) 1 Sri Lanka Law Reports 185 (Sri Lanka); *Re Devendra*, (1920) 1 Malayan Cases 51.
14. Law Reform (Marriage and Divorce) Act 1976.
15. Singapore Women's Charter 1961.
16. See Law Commission of India, "The Indian Divorce Act (Report 164)"; Law Commission of India, "Laws of Civil Marriages in India (Report 212)"; Law Commission of India, "Conversion/Reconversion to Another Religion - Mode of Proof (Report 235)".
17. Law Commission of India, "Proposal to Amend the Prohibition of Child Marriage Act, 2006 and Other Allied Laws (Report 205)".
18. These include Australia, New Zealand, UK, Egypt, US, Pakistan and Indonesia, in that order. Why only these and not other countries find mention is not clear. See Law Commission of India, ibid., 26–28.
19. 1970 Kerala Law Times (KLT) 4, para 21.
20. 1984 Criminal Law Journal (Cri L J) 1062 (Kerala High Court), paras 3, 7.
21. 2008 (4) KLT 885.
22. Ibid., para 13–14.
23. Law and Justice Commission of Pakistan, "Reports of Ad hoc Law Reform Commissions".
24. Ahmad, "The Muslim Family Laws Ordinance of Pakistan," 39.
25. Ibid., 39–40.
26. Pakistan Legal Decisions (PLD) 2000 Federal Shariat Court (FSC) 1.
27. Cf. 'The most important aspect of the Muslim Family Laws Ordinance was its section on polygyny.' Ibid., 40.
28. The Quran, 4:35. See also Starkovsky, *The Koran Handbook*, 432.
29. See Mahmood, *Good Governance Reform Agenda in Pakistan*.
30. MFLO 1961, Section 2(b).
31. For some reason, Issues as vital as the validity of marriages; intestate succession; wills; gifts; *wakfs* (or trusts); and guardianship have been altogether left out.
32. The Quran, 4:3. See also Starkovsky, *The Koran Handbook*, 428.
33. Pakistan Legal Decisions (PLD) 2000 Federal Shariat Court (FSC) 1, para 82.
34. Criminal Petition No. 1252 of 2016, decided on 21 February 2017.
35. PLD 1968 Lahore 587.
36. PLD 1963 Supreme Court (SC) 51, para 35.
37. (1987) 39 Dhaka Law Reports 333, para 3.
38. See e.g. *Muhammad Aslam v. Ghulam Muhammad Tasleem* PLD 1971 Lahore 139, Para 10.
39. Pearl, "Family Law in Pakistan," 188–89 (further references omitted).
40. Hossain, "In Search of Equality," 100.

41. Mention of it can be found as of 14 May 2017 on the Kerala Law Reforms Commission website, http://www.keralalawcommission.nic.in/.
42. 'Law Commission Mooted for State'. 2007. *The Hindu*, 18 October.
43. Government of Kerala, "Government Order (Ms) No 253.2007/Law", Personnel and Administrative Reforms Department (PARD). 17 November 2007. http://pard.kerala.gov.in/pard_webservice/go/G.O. (Ms) No.253_2007_Law_16_17_11_2007.pdf.
44. Kerala Law Reforms Commission, "The Final Report".
45. Curiously, the contents page does not enumerate these specific issues. Indeed, a cursory look at the contents page does not make it entirely clear just how the document is organized.
46. *Shahulameedu v. Subaida Beevi*, 1970 KLT 4, para 21.
47. *Yusuf Rowthan v. Sowramma*, 1970 KLT 477.
48. Kerala Law Reforms Commission, "Kerala Muslim Marriage Bill".

Acknowledgments

Thanks are due to the following for their help and assistance: Ananya Bharadwaj, Bishwa Kallyan Dash, Md Saiful Karim, Satish Padhi, Shamita Sarkar, Sucharita Sengupta, and Tulip Suman.

Disclosure statement

No potential conflict of interest was reported by the author.

Bibliography

Ahmed, M. "The Muslim Family Laws Ordinance of Pakistan." *International journal on world peace* 10, no. 3 (1993): 37–46.

Frankenberg, G. "Critical Comparisons: Re-Thinking Comparative Law." *Harvard international law journal* 26, no. 2 (1985): 411–455.

Galanter, M., and J. Krishnan. "Personal Law and Human Rights in India and Israel." *Israel law review* 34, no. 01 (2000): 101–133. doi:10.1017/S0021223700011894.

Ghosh, P. S. "The Issue of Personal and Customary Law in South Asia: A Political Analysis." *Ethnic Studies Report* 19, no. 2 (2001): 179–194.

Hooker, M. B. "The Relationship between Chinese Law and Common Law in Malaysia, Singapore, and Hong Kong." *The journal of Asian studies* 28, no. 4 (1969): 723–742. doi:10.2307/2942408.

Hooker, M. B. "Chinese Customary Law in Contemporary Malaysia and Singapore." *Australian journal of Asian law* 1, no. 1 (1999): 34–54.

Hossain, K. "In Search of Equality: Marriage Related Laws for Muslim Women in Bangladesh." *Journal of International women's studies* 5, no. 1 (2003): 96–113.

Hussain, J. "More than One Law for All: Legal Pluralism in Southeast Asia." *Democracy and security* 7, no. 4, September 1 (2011): 374–389. doi:10.1080/17419166.2011.617621.

Kerala Law Reforms Commission. "The Final Report of [*Sic*] Law Reforms Commission Kerala." January 26, 2009. http://keralalawcommission.nic.in/WriteReadData/Report/LRC_Report_Vol._I.pdf

Kerala Law Reforms Commission. "Kerala Muslim Marriage and Dissolution by Talaq and Khula (Regulation) Bill 2009." Accessed May 14, 2017. http://www.keralalawcommission.nic.in/writereaddata/The%20Kerala%20Muslim%20Marriage%0and%20Dissolution%20by%20Talaq.pdf

Law and Justice Commission of Pakistan. "Reports of Ad Hoc Law Reform Commissions." Law and Justice Commission of Pakistan. Accessed April 23, 2017. http://www.ljcp.gov.pk/Menu%20Items/Publications/Summary%20of%20reports%20of%20Ad%20hoc%20Commissions/3-summary%20of%20reports%20adhoc%20commissions.htm

Law Commission of India. "The Indian Divorce Act (Report 164)." Law Commission of India. 1998. http://lawcommissionofindia.nic.in/101-169/Report164.pdf

Law Commission of India. "Proposal to Amend the Prohibition of Child Marriage Act, 2006 and Other Allied Laws (Report 205)." Law Commission of India. 2008. http://lawcommissionofindia.nic.in/reports/report205.pdf

Law Commission of India. "Laws of Civil Marriages in India (Report 212)." Law Commission of India. 2008. http://lawcommissionofindia.nic.in/reports/report212.pdf

Law Commission of India. "Conversion/Reconversion to Another Religion - Mode of Proof (Report 235)." Law Commission of India. 2010. http://lawcommissionofindia.nic.in/reports/report235.pdf

Mahmood, S. *Good Governance Reform Agenda in Pakistan: Current Challenges*. New York: Nova Publishers, 2007.

Mahmood, T. "Law and Social Development in India and Afghanistan: A Comparative Perspective." *Journal of the Indian law institute* 16, no. 2 (1974): 229–242.

Pearl, D. S. "Family Law in Pakistan." *Journal of family law* 9 (1985): 165–189.

Starkovsky, N. *The Koran Handbook: An Annotated Translation*. New York: Algora Publishing, 2005.

Subramanian, N. *Nation and Family: Personal Law, Cultural Pluralism, and Gendered Citizenship in India*. Stanford: Stanford University Press, 2014.

Tamanna, N. "Personal Status Laws in Morocco and Tunisia: A Comparative Exploration of the Possibilities for Equality-Enhancing Reform in Bangladesh." *Feminist legal studies* 16, no. 3, December 1 (2008): 323–343. doi:10.1007/s10691-008-9099-9.

Shari'a politics, ʿulamā and Laity Ijtihād: fields of normativity and conviviality

Neshat Quaiser

ABSTRACT

Contentiously debated shari'a (Islamic law) across the world has acquired specific political connotations. In India, this is so not only because the overbearing presence of fixity of maslaki-taqlīdi shari'a produce inverted truth that petrifies the true meaning, but also due to the deep entanglement of the legal with extra-legal phenomenon such as communalism, producing palpable theoretical–practical tensions. Employing the concepts of normativity and conviviality, the essay examines the normativity of dominant maslaki-taqlīdi shari'a-based Muslim Personal Law. Such a law aims at producing a conforming Muslim legal subject. On the other hand, this shari'a is rendered a contested terrain critically contesting the authority of the legal monotheism of codified taqlīdi shari'a by everyday laity ijtihād that constitutes the field of conviviality. Such conviviality is characterized by the laity's everyday idea of justice and democracy marked by a deep sense of defiance propelled by adverse and undesirable conditions of existence in everyday locations, viz., the Social. Thus, the field of conviviality is marked by a movement from normative subject to ontological self, enabling women/subjects to exercise their subjectivity to decode the occultated and petrified meanings of taqlīdi shari'a convivially. This signifies a movement towards making the canonized shari'a/law as an everyday social practice.

Answer of a question shall be according as to the custom of a people of their country.

Abu'l-Hasan `Ubaydullah bin Husain al-Karkhi

(873–952 AD) *Al-'Usul,*

My advocate told me that I would have won it ... in another court.

'That is very funny' I told him, 'so each court has its own laws'.

'Yes', he said.

(Voltaire in *Laws, in Philosophical Dictionary*).

Introduction

The essay is divided into three parts with sub-sections and a conclusion. Part I outlines the contexts and theoretical framework; part II, with reference to the field of normativity, addresses the questions of shari'a, fiqh, ijtihād and taqlīd debate; Muslim personal law and shari'a administration in India and the post-colonial turn; dār-ul-qaza and the Muslim legal subject; contemporary shari'a-reform practices; and the secular-shari'a-Hindutva divide. Part III, with reference to the field of conviviality, deals with the questions of everyday laity ijtihad; khul'a and dār-ul-qaza; convivially accessible shari'a; and the cases of bazaar qāzi and bazaar shari'a and of four women respondents. These cases are symptomatic of convivial negotiations with the field of shari'a normativity. Cases are drawn from the interviews with the women respondents and others conducted in a rather difficult situation due to their social locations, and also from the primary printed sources.

Preliminary statement

With the central focus on law as a social practice, the essay reflects on the politics, conceptions and everyday practices related to shari'a (Islamic law) in post-colonial India within the fields[1] of normativity and conviviality. The field of normativity is employed to mean the epistemological fixity of both the western/modern statist legal edifice and of literalist maslaki[2] shari'a law, which not so curiously remains entangled with extra-legal phenomena such as communalism in post-colonial India. The field of conviviality in this essay, on the other hand, is characterized by everyday laity ijtihād[3] through which the field of shari'a normativity, based on taqlīd,[4] is inventively manoeuvred by laity in their favour. This field is animated by the ideas of justice and democracy, and marked by a deep sense of defiance – unlike the field of normativity, which essentially constitutes a conforming subject. This essay examines the politics of shari'a-based Muslim Personal Law against the contentiously debated questions of shari'a, fiqh (Islamic jurisprudence), ijtihād and taqlīd, and reflects on the ways in which they contribute to the sustenance of the shari'a normativity; and further, the ways in which that normativity is contested from the field of conviviality.

Shari'a has acquired a more direct and wider political connotation today, as the politics around it is no more confined to the manipulations by state, ʿulamā (scholars of Islamic theology) and other dominants classes alone – it engulfs the entire gamut of Muslim social life.

Shari'a politics in the contemporary world has four distinct but often intersecting principal sources/locations: (1) Crisis faced by the Muslim countries/Islamic states where the pressing demands of modernity contend with that of an 'ideal' Islamic state; (2) Muslims living in European or other non-Muslim majority societies as religious minority; (3)'Reform the Shari'a', Islamic feminist and the 'Return to Shari'a' ideologies; and (4) Muslims, who once ruled a non-Muslim majority country, but are now recognized constitutionally to be a religious minority – India being the principal example.

This essay deals with the fourth location. The essay examines shari'a as immanently contested terrain and the ways in which shari'a is entangled with communalism. As a result of its unique trajectory, post-colonial Indian shari'a politics is marked critically by extra-legal factors of communalism and Hindutva[5] forces supported tacitly by the Indian state. The attempt, from time to time, by the state to change Shari'a or the threat by the communalists to impose a Uniform Civil Code (hereafter UCC)[6] is considered the main threat by the ʿulamā, not the reformists/modernists/secularists combine from within and outside the community. This situation has helped ʿulamā strengthen their position in sustaining the field of taqlīd-based shari'a normativity. In order to further consolidate their authority and strengthen their bargaining power, the ʿulamā adopted a two-pronged strategy: firstly, they have focussed on the constitutional guarantee to Muslims (as minority) to practise shari'a-based personal law in a Hindu majority country; and secondly, they have attempted to forge a unity among the vertically divided Muslims on caste and other lines, to construct a Muslim Ummah[7] in the name of protecting Shari'a in the face of anti-Muslim Hindutva onslaught. And yet the laity ijtihad transgress the codified boundary of shari'a normativity by drawing upon the personal or collective convivial resources.

The statist law and the taqlīdi shari'a, in effect, both produce inverted truth that petrifies the true meaning through a strategy of choreographic occultation of victim's true self by presenting other self as her own self, so that victim is implicated in her own punishment.[8] A comprehension of the occultating field of legal normativity demands what Paul Ricoeur called the 'hermeneutics of suspicion'. Ricoeur distinguished between two forms of hermeneutics: a hermeneutics of faith which aims to restore meaning to a text and a hermeneutics of suspicion which attempts to decode meanings that are disguised.[9]

Religions and religious laws across time and space have been considered as ubiquitously given phenomenon but in their social manifestations, even in terms of systems, they have always been organically evolving human experience as non-faith factors constantly come into play. Thus, religion/shari'a is not the sole and constant constitutive of social even a 'religious' subject. The field of religion then is quite flexible in everyday life – contrary to the ways in which it is presented in high literalist religious discourse, or in situations of intense binary religious conflict. Therefore, despite occultating hermeneutics of faith, shari'a normativity could become a field of struggle as it is penetrated through a human agency with counter-intuitive imagination paving the way for convivial practices.

Shari'a, Muslim personal law and dār-ul-qaza: the field of normativity

Shari'a-fiqh-ijtihād-taqlīd: debate and implications

The questions of ijtihād and taqlīd are the organizing principles through which the debate on shari'a reforms and Muslim personal law takes place.

The Revealed law of God, which cannot be altered, and its interpretation by legal scholars, which constitutes fiqh, are the two principal elements of the field of shari'a. Shari'a law therefore means Islamic law as presented in different schools of fiqh. The field of shari'a is marked not only by the differences among legal scholars, and deeply divided and antagonistic maslaki interpretations – but also by the conflict and tensions in both Islamic and non-Islamic states in different forms.[10]

Fiqh developed out of sunnah (what Muhammad did and approved of as a model) and was transmitted by the Prophet's companions and followers to the succeeding generations in the form of hadith (accounts and narratives describing the words, actions or habits of Muhammad) and their interpretations in the light of revealed law of God. This ultimately manifested in different schools of fiqh.[11] Islamic legal scholars developed different methods for interpreting shari'a rules, which are derived from the following main sources: The Qurán; hadith; ijma' (juristic consensus, when legal experts all agree on a point of law); and qiyas (legal reasoning by analogy).

Ijtihād in Islamic jurisprudence refers to independent reasoning and exertion of a jurist's mental faculty in finding a solution to a legal question, not specifically provided in Qur'an and Sunnah/hadith, with creative reinterpretation and application of Islamic injunctions to changed circumstances.

Traditionally, all the major schools of Islamic jurisprudence practised ijtihād but since the tenth century the 'gate of ijtihād' has been declared closed by the four Sunni schools of jurisprudence that demanded taqlīd (conformity to legal precedents without any critical thinking), which meant that '(A)ll the essential questions had been … finally settled … and that all future activity would have to be confined to the explanation, application and, at the most, interpretation … of the doctrines of established schools and authorities'[12] and any further use of ijtihād was declared bid'ah – sinful innovation.[13]

Therefore, the scope of ijtihād was gradually restricted, and taqlīd became the organizing principle for adjudicating disputes. In the absence of ijtihād, Shari'a adjudicated through dār-ul-qaza (Islamic Court) has almost been rendered into a fixed body of knowledge, and dār-ul-qaza an ineffective institution as it has refused to go beyond quoting the jurisprudents of bygone era.[14]

However, whether the gate of ijtihād really ever fully closed has been questioned,[15] with some scholars seeing ijtihād being favoured by Muslim reformers from since the eighteenth century as a means of returning to Islamic origins[16] as we shall see below in case of Ahl-e-Hadīs and Shah Waliullah in India.

Today, both modernists/reformists and Islamists favour ijtihād but from opposite vantage points. For the Islamists who raise the cry of 'Return to Shari'a', ijtihād is necessary to render modern Islam more authentic and to strengthen the faith of believers, which in turn would help re-establish the Golden Age of early Islam.[17] To Modernists/reformists, ijtihad implies the accommodation and reconciliation of Islam with modern society.[18] While in western world shari'a is viewed as being in direct conflict with the modern constitutional law, though it prescribes both religious and secular duties, western states are deeply worried about shari'a practice in their lands.[19]

In order to counter the Islamists' slogan of 'Return to Shari'a', attempts have been made to draw a neat distinction between shari'a and fiqh arguing that 'Shari'a is sacred, eternal and universal, whereas fiqh is human, mundane, temporal and local'[20] – ignoring the theological foundations of fiqh itself and how maslaki legal plurality operates within the framework of the shari'a. However, a historically informed ijtihād promotes plurality creating spaces within the given structured spaces, which could not only be located within the tradition of critical thoughts in Islam but would also check the closure of alternative possibilities and pave way for fresh critical reflections.

The debate on shari'a and fiqh is an indicator of the endemic tensions within Islamic jurisprudence that relates in part to the absence of its historical and social contextualization.[21] But, the question of contextualization and the modernists wanting to change shari'a have been rather strongly questioned. Representing the traditionalist view scholar, Seyyed Hossein Nasr has questioned the modernist project of ijtihād to make Shari'a 'conform to the times' advocating instead that 'it is the Shari'ah according to which society should be modelled not vice versa.'[22]

Closer home, Ahl al-Hadīth (Ahl-e-Hadīs) since the nineteenth century in Indian subcontinent has favoured ijtihād. They opposed taqlīd of any particular school of jurisprudence, but to them ijtihād meant strict itteb'a-e sunnah (supporting and following what Muhammad did and approved of as a model) privileging Quran and authentic hadīs as the only authority in matters of law and faith and opposed everything introduced after the earliest times of Islam, which in effect is no different from taqlīd.[23] And this is what the extremely influential eighteenth-century Indian subcontinental Islamic scholar and theologian Shah Waliullah too meant by ijtihād. However, his ijtihād also meant restoration of Islamic religious purity and a religiously just political system in the context of Indian subcontinent, where Islam and Muslims were faced with serious crisis and challenges since the early eighteenth century.[24] Sir Sayyed Ahmad Khan, considered to be a modernist in South Asia, had spoken in favour of ijtihād, but his influence in this regard was limited as he was opposed by ʿulamā for his pro-British views and his views on Islam and ijtihād were severely criticized,[25] and deemed to be colonially propelled. The influential Urdu poet Muhammad Iqbal strongly observed: 'The closing of the door of ijtihād is pure fiction suggested partly by the crystallization of legal thought in Islam, and partly by that intellectual laziness which … turns great thinkers into idols.'[26] But Iqbal was not part of the ʿulamā and hardly in a position to influence the course of legal thought in the Indian subcontinent. But more importantly, he could not have carried much weight as he was very much part of taqlīdi tradition and had extremely conservative views on several vital issues such as on women.

Despite the claim that ijtihād and taqlīd go together, in the Indian subcontinent it is taqlīd that is practised[27] in matters of personal law in the name of preventing the corrupt and un-Islamic practices and to counter what is seen as an anti-Islamic onslaught. A prominent Indian Islamic scholar represented the dominant view on the issue, when he stated:

> This demand to prepare a "modern edition" of fiqh is like throwing away your own precious gems and adopting pebbles from others. Any change in purely religious part of fiqh is not needed, and if this happened then the idea of change will permeate the mind of common people, and the dignity and importance of qanun (here Islamic rules, law) will go away from their heart, which will result in loosening of their grip over religion. As a result, like worldly law, religious law will also be rendered lifeless.[28]

In addition, contradictory hadiths on the same issues and their contradictory maslaki interpretations have further given rise to the strident rivalry among multiple maslak, producing blind adherence to one's own maslak, which has further strengthened the practice of taqlīd,[29] preventing ijtihād.

This situation has produced two principal critical manifestations in India: Firstly, in the absence of a non-taqlīdi dār-ul-qaza, adversely affected Muslims are denied a locally accessible family dispute resolution mechanism, forcing them to approach the expensive and time-consuming constitutional courts. While the financial hardship and mental agony which can ruin family and social life as a result of protracted litigation has been regularly employed by the ʿulamā in favour of the existing taqlīdi dār-ul-qaza. So while an ijtihad-driven moral economy of the dār-ul-qaza would have been worth pursuing, they have today emerged as an expression of ʿulamā saviourism. This has led to Muslim laity circumventing the authority of the taqlīdi ʿulamā through convivial practices.

Secondly, extra-legal intense communal politics has become the structuring principle for the representation of the self and the 'other' with reference to shari'a, with the result that a shari'a-based distinct Muslim legal subject is sought to be constructed. This in turn has additionally strengthened the practice of taqlīd.

It is obvious that the ʿulamā are busy in producing a meaning and context for a suitable shari'a and by doing so they are asserting the authority of a fixed fiqh, which has become a justificatory logic in the backdrop of a communal majoritarian agenda.

Muslim personal law administration in India

Muslim personal law during the medieval Muslim rule in India was just a part of a larger inclusive body of law that regulated the social and legal relations of all Indians. It would be significant to situate it within this larger body of law, which consisted of: (1) Civil Law (a) the pure Islamic personal law applied to Muslims only; and (b) the secular portion of the civil law relating to trade, barter, exchange, sale, etc. was applied to both Muslims and non-Muslims; (2) The religious and personal laws of the Hindus, Buddhists and other non-Muslims were based on their own religious and personal laws, and disputes were decided with the aid of the Pandits and Brahmans; in case of the other communities with aid of their learned men; (3) The laws of the land relating to the system of taxation relating to land revenue, manufacture, agriculture, excise, octroi, merchandise, etc. were adopted from India, and were applied to all including Muslims; (4) Criminal Law: (a) the Islamic shari'a relating to religious infringements such as drinking, apostacy, etc. was applied to Muslims only and (b) the Islamic law which punishes the acts such as adultery, murder, robbery, assault, etc. and which constituted crimes in the estimation of all nations was applied to Muslims and non-Muslims alike; (5) The Qānun-i-Shahī or the Edicts and Ordinances were common law of the country as opposed to canon law, and binding upon the judicial and executive officers of the State.[30] Outside the purview of Emperor's legal administration, there were numerous customary laws in operation. The multiplicity, inclusiveness and a relaxed shari'a cannot be missed.

The colonial rule with modernity's messianic message intended to impose the colonial-western knowledge in all spheres of social life including the legal sphere, but it did not disturb the personal laws of Hindus and Muslims as a requirement of stable colonial rule. Thus, the Judicial Plan of Warren Hastings of 1772 provided for establishment of civil and criminal courts and protected the right of Hindus and Muslims to apply their own personal laws in inheritance, marriage, etc. In the year 1791 under directions of Hastings, Charles Hamilton translated from a Persian version the Hedaya[31] into English. These endeavours systematized and gave shape to what is called Anglo-Muhammadan Law over many decades.

Anglo-Muhammadan Law, generally referred to as Muhammadan Law, was based on an interpretation of Islamic texts and practices. It was applied in British colonial courts in Indian subcontinent and included criminal and civil law. A comprehensive penal code (1860) ended its criminal application, but it continued to be applied in personal status law until the Muslim Personal Law Application Act (1937). David Gilmartin has drawn attention to Gregory Kozlowski's argument that the development of the law rested on the assumption that Muslims in India constituted a single community, which was defined by acceptance of a single, systematic set of personal laws, fixed and unchanging. In practice, Anglo-Muhammadan law did not apply equally to all Indian Muslims, and sometime the British courts favoured sect and customary laws.[32] In due course, the passage in 1937 of Muslim Personal Law (Shari'a) Application Act universalized the application of the Anglo-Muhammadan law for Indian Muslims.[33]

This owed not just to the 'colonial need for precise and reliable information about indigenous laws' but also to the endeavours to effect politico-ideological hegemony. In the process, they endorsed 'highly orthodox forms of Islamic law which were applied more widely and rigorously than in the pre-colonial period'.[34] Modern European legal standards, procedures and methods of interpretations were brazenly employed to judge the efficacy of Muhammadan Law.[35] Thus, the modern European legal epistemologies were the certified standard on the basis of which Muhammadan Law was tailor-made to suit the body of colonial requirements. The colonial politics of prefixing it with *Anglo* thus was to legitimize the Muhammadan Law.

Shari'a law: the post-colonial turn

During the anti-colonial struggle, an understanding was reached between the Indian National Congress and the Jami'atul-'ulamā-i-Hind[36] that the Muslim personal law would not be abolished after independence.[37] Muslims in India would continue to be guided by the Muslim Personal Law of 1937. However, when The Adoption of Children Bill, 1972 was tabled in the Parliament, the then Union Law Minister termed it as the first step towards UCC. The statement was dubbed by Muslim 'ulamā as a conspiracy to subvert shari'a law applicable to Indian Muslims through parallel legislation. It was against this alarmist background that the All India Muslim Personal Law Board (hereafter the Board) was formed in April 1973 to adopt suitable strategies for the protection and continued applicability of Muslim Personal Law, i.e. Shari'at Application Act 1937, in India.[38]

The Board was projected as a common platform of the Indian Muslims belonging to various schools of jurisprudence and thought to defend Muslim Personal Law. It has consistently insisted that shari'a is beyond the reach and scope of India's courts of law. The Supreme Court's judgement on Shah Bano led to nationwide protests that resulted in Indian Parliament passing the Muslim Women's Bill in 1986.[39] Ever since, shari'a politics in India has primarily revolved around Muslim personal law and the spectre of UCC.[40]

The question of UCC actually involves serious questions of citizenship, national identity vs. religious/community identity, difference and plurality. But increasingly, the debate on UCC and the demand for its implementation has primarily been driven by the Hindutva ideology to homogenize society on 'Hindu' line to establish a 'Hindu hegemony'.

Dār-ul-qaza, ideology and the Muslim legal subject

Dār-ul-qaza or shari'a court traditionally adjudicated problems of Muslims according to various schools of Islamic jurisprudence. Shari'a politics during medieval India took place through the system of qāzi court, which was central for the sustenance and continuation of the imperial rule, authority and legitimacy, thus it was never completely free from the political interventions exercised by Emperor, nobles and other dominant social classes and groups.

With the advent of European interventions, the traditional Islamic courts in Muslim lands began to change. For example, in addition to testimony of eyewitnesses, circumstantial evidence was given equal importance. Gradually, shari'a court was left to deal with marriage, divorce, custody, inheritance, adoption and waqf (religious endowments)-related matters. This trend continued in the twentieth century.[41] However, presently qāzi tries to play more of a mediatory role with an emphasis on resolving the problem.

Prior to the Board, it was the Imārat Shari'a Bihar, Orissa (and later Jharkhand) established in 1921, that had undertaken the promotion of the organized network of dār-ul-qaza in India in the light of continuing turbulence and crisis that the 1857 mutiny had produced for the high-born elite Muslims including ʿulamā. Imārat Shari'a (hereafter Imārat) projected itself as a socio-religious organization, which, in addition to preaching and propagation of Islam and protection of shari'a, takes pride in performing social service for the well-being of the suffering humanity.[42] The Board soon emerged as the shari'a-related umbrella organization, and the Board too, in addition to Imārat, began establishing and maintaining dār-ul-qazas. Shari'a courts set up by the Board are already functioning in Gujarat, Bihar, Uttar Pradesh, Assam, Rajasthan, Madhya Pradesh, Maharashtra, West Bengal and Orissa. Dār-ul-qaza, being the most important adjudicating body, the Board endeavours to establish its authority over it wherever they are.

Ummah and the legal subject

Imārat's self-image is premised on the concept of a Muslim ummah. Dār-ul-qazas are central to the formation of this ummah through the way in which it constructs a Muslim legal subject. According to the Imārat, the law of shari'a covers all of human activities in the religious, social cultural and political domains. This is based on Islamic 'principles of collectivism', as 'there is no place of individual life in Islam'. However, one must not lose sight of the consequences of loss of power of the Muslim high-born elite in the wake of colonial rule that the idea of ummah draws upon. For example, introducing the raison d'etre of the Imārat, it is observed:

> After the revolution of 1857 and the downfall of Mughal Empire in India, the ʿulamā of the day, in view of circumstances prevalent, were compelled to find out a suitable platform for the Muslim in India through which their social, cultural, religious lives and activities could be managed, controlled and guided in the light of Shariʿat laws. Collectivism is possible under a central power in an Islamic state, where the central force has been the Khalīfa (Caliph). But in non-Islamic countries, an organisation based on Shariʿat laws under one Ameer (Chief) who by virtue of his respectable status commands following among the Muslim is essentially required elected by the Muslims, to educate, inspire and guide the Muslim Ummah to enable them to lead a collective life under Islamic order.[43]

Imārat's emphasis on Islamic 'principles of collectivism' is articulated in the language of loss – the final fall of Muslim (also sometime conveniently portrayed as Islamic) rule in India. Khalīfa and Amīr constitute significant markers in the making of this ummah. The palpable anxiety over the submergence of Muslim identity and the desire to construct a body of Muslim ummah in post-colonial India are reflected in highlighting the 'serious challenges of Shuddhi Sangathan for deviating the Muslims from Islamic faith and re-conversion to Hinduism'.[44] Reference to colonial period Shuddhi Sangathan of the Arya Samaj[45] is significant to show continuity in the form of ghar-wapsi endeavours by Hindu Right.[46]

The Board too constructs a Muslim legal subject around the idea of dār-ul-qaza in a non-Muslim country. Outlining the need for dār-ul-qaza, the Board states:

> It is the duty of Muslim to establish dār-ul-qaza in non-Muslim countries to resolve their disputes and accept the decision of the qāzi wholeheartedly. Muslims should spread the network of dār-ul-qaza to resolve their personal related problems, so that poor and oppressed classes particularly women could get justice easily and inexpensively.[47]

So, in criminal matters ground is clearly ceded to constitutional law, but the Board asks the state to adhere to the constitutional provisions for religious minority rights in matters of personal law. At the same time, taqlīd is practised and protected with open declaration that the qāzi's decisions 'should be accepted wholeheartedly' without any question. However, dār-ul-qaza is not an Islamic court in the strict sense of the term in contemporary India, but simply 'arbitration councils with no real or claimed judicial powers or authority and their adjudication are recommendations and advice'.[48] But significantly, Indian courts, including the Supreme Court in a judgment in 2014, have always refrained from declaring dār-ul-qaza illegal.[49]

Contemporary shari'a reform practices in India

Organizations such as the Board, Imārat, Shia Personal Law Board, Tablīghī Jama'at, Jama'at-e-Islami, Ahl-e-Hadīs and certain localized personal law dispute resolution organizations such as Muhalla Committee of elders in Kerala are the conformist ones engaged in shari'a-related activities. However, the field of shari'a politics is also prominently peopled by reformists of broadly two types: the traditional reformists and the radical reformists.

The first of these, the traditional reformists, represent the dominant trend within India. Drawn largely from urban and urban-oriented middle-upper middle class, the reformists of this type are educated, non-ʿulamā, non-expert and predominantly Muslim women. They operate within the alternative-shari'a-interpretation-framework and challenge ʿulamā by claiming to project an authentic Islam according to their alternative interpretation of shari'a in matters of Muslim personal law-related issues. They believe that the ʿulamā belonging to dominant sections are promoting patriarchal values; are oblivious of changing time; and are not 'modern'. They complain that dār-ul-qaza practices archaic rules besides being inefficient. As a result, they do not mind going to constitutional courts for marriage- and divorce-related disputes, which is contrary to the position of ʿulamā. They are not only dared and tested by the expert ʿulamā but also projected as part of the hideous design of the local–global 'enemies of Islam'. Such reform endeavours have also largely been not very successful as 'reform' in matters of religion has traditionally been perceived as part of colonialist and 'modernist' agenda among ʿulamā and literate and semi-literate Muslim masses, to which reformists do not have a studied response. Their endeavours also become further suspect due to aggressively pursued Hindutva demand for the 'reform' in Muslim personal law.

We have labelled them 'traditional' reformists as that they operate within the long established subcontinental urban-educated-high-caste-elite modernist framework, and are confined to cultural and ritual symbolism. The modernist ideological locations of these 'traditional' reformists have rendered them incapable of engaging with religion and religious people. Dismissive of all things religious, they rely largely on the state to bring about changes through legislations. Organizations such as Bharatiya Muslim Mahila Andolan fall under this category.

The Radical Reformists: They too are reformists as they act within the alternative-shari'a-interpretation-framework – but with a difference as they have radically gone a step ahead of the traditional reformists. The best example of this type is the Tamil Nadu Muslim Women Jamaat, which is a rural, semi-urban Muslim women interest-pressure group, yet to take the shape of a movement. They are radical for they not only resolve disputes but also adjudicate talāq themselves according to Islamic tenets refusing to be dependent on dār-ul-qaza. Unlike the traditional reformists the women's Jamaat links the issues of gender discrimination, violence within marriage, talāq and triple talāq with the generic questions of poverty, adverse existence and women's constitutional and religious rights, in short with the larger political and economic structures of inequality. For example, their activities include acquiring joint ownership of land (patta) rights for women and organizing working women (including Dalit women) for obtaining ownership rights in quarries and sand mining. This approach has enabled them to situate the Muslim women's question within the broader context of democracy, justice, freedom, and governance. Jamaat's motto, 'Self-Respect is the first step of women's Liberation', appears to be inspired by the Dravidian self-respect movement. Their idea of freedom and democracy has resulted in their efforts to construct a women's mosque, despite strong opposition from dominant Muslim organizations. They act in the name of Islam to protect their faith, which according them has been corrupted by male ʿulamā.[50]

Predicament of the secular-shari'a-Hindutva divide

Despite these reformist endeavours, it is the Board and the ʿulamā who form the most representative body for the protection of shari'a. Although the shari'a and dār-ul-qaza are outside the constitutional law, the Board draws upon the constitutional principles to ensure the sustenance of the Muslim personal law and their own authority. As a part of their continued struggle to protect the Muslim personal law as a constitutional guarantee, the Board and ʿulamā have recently launched a Deen-Bachao, Dastoor-Bachao Tahreek (Save Faith, Save Constitution Movement) in March 2015 in order to 'save faith and constitution from the Brahmanic onslaught, and to emancipate all the minorities from atrocities, injustice, oppression, tyranny and violence'.[51] Significantly, ʿulamā have succeeded in bringing certain Dalit organizations and leaders in this movement.

It appears that the extreme adversity, communal hostility, the state's anti-Muslim discriminatory policies and practices have additionally forced people to adopt an atavistic position with regard to shari'a. The Board has emerged as the dominant arbiter between the state and the Muslims, and shari'a as a platform to forge unity of all Muslims to counter the 'common enemies', eliding the vertical divide among Muslims particularly along the caste lines. Thus, the highly communalized situation appears to be advantageous to the Board and taqlīdī ʿulamā to reinforce their authority over Muslim masses.

Despite the dominance of taqlīdī conservatives and conformists in the field of shari'a politics, Muslim laity particularly has not remained a passive consumer and recipient of shari'a normativity. Indeed, Muslim laity has learnt to devise ways and means to manoeuvre inventively the unbending shari'a normativity in their favour, circumventing the authority of the taqlīdī ʿulamā. It is these ways and means that we turn now to.

The field of conviviality: everyday laity ijtihād, justice and democracy

In the face of shari'a normativity, there is something else too taking place – the field of conviviality – which may not be an immediate threat to the power and authority of the Board and ʿulamā, but is certainly introducing new dimensions in the field of shari'a practice, particularly when this is being crafted mostly by women. Significantly, it is not only outside the Board but also outside the reformist framework.

The realm of everyday laity ijtihād constitutes the field of conviviality. Based on independent reasoning of lay Muslims of all sections, as distinct from the ʿulamā or experts/professionals, it is primarily not propelled by faith but by the contingencies of life and its counter-intuitive comprehension. Though not driven by faith, it does not involve the abandoning of their Muslim, or even Islamic identity. The laity, through the field of conviviality, subverts the normativity of taqlīdi shari'a and dār-ul-qaza by ingeniously devised ways and means. Importantly, they do not theologically disturb the ʿulamā as they do not at all have any alternative-shari'a-interpretation project. It is an everyday convivial field of the laity's idea of justice and accessible, immediate democracy, which breaks free of normative fiqh. It is characterized by a spirit of camaraderie and bonhomie, a sort of sardonic rendering of the high literalist shari'a into earthly, human form, devoid of awe, fascination and fear. Thus, everyday shari'a-related laity ijtihād practices are mechanisms to grapple with the chaos in existence with a strategy of conviviality and have the last laugh at the high literalist shari'a.

As noted above, the field of conviviality does not refer to complete break from the religion/religious and Muslim/Islamic ethos and identity, but creating spaces within the given structured spaces of shari'a normativity, where every day experiences of existence and convivial sociability subvert the fixed shari'a normativity.

Impious women performing conviviality

This field of conviviality is inhabited predominantly by women. These Muslim women are free and autonomous, but not in the manner of the 'pious' Salafi Muslim women of Cairo in the 1990s, who have been presented by Saba Mahmood[52] as a case to develop some kind of generic Islamic organizing principle to counter western secular-modernist feminism or western political machinations. These convivial Muslim women did not need any high Islamic ideological project to counter Indian traditional reformists, secularist-modernists or taqlīdi ʿulamā. They are mundane and earthly; not guided by any high Islamic ideology but by the contingencies of everyday life; guided by the Social not by the Faith, and therefore termed here *impious*.

The Muslim personal law covers matters related to marriage, divorce, child custody, inheritance and endowment, but it is the triple talāq question which has currently come to be politically fore-grounded to the extent that the whole personal law question has been reduced to this. However, it is the steadily increasing cases of khul'a and faskh-e nikah (women initiated divorce and annulment of marriage process) in dār-ul-qaza that have become a cause of great concern for 'ulama and many Muslim men heralding a restorational shari'a politics led by the dominant sections of 'ulama.

Khul'a, dār-ul-qaza, ʿulamā, qāzi, laity, 'sensible' wives and undesirable husbands are the elements that make the stage where conviviality is performed.

Khul'a and dār-ul-qaza: towards a convivial theology

Khul'a has come in handy for these Muslim women faced with acutely adverse marital life within the equally undesirable larger everyday social existence.[53] Through khul'a, these 'sensible' women seek to avail the theologically obtainable but socially denied redemption and emancipation from the undesirable situation with convivial defiance. In the process, they actually pave the way for a convivial theology as opposed to that of normative taqlīdi theology. Not only the taqlīdi dār-ul-qaza but also the statist and 'reformist' political pressure in favour of regular court constitutes an obstacle. As a result, khul'a and dār-ul-qaza are now intrinsically intertwined. Thus, in the context of continuing heated debate over dār-ul-qaza vs. regular court, it has consistently been observed that most women prefer to go to dār-ul-qaza as it is accessible, affordable and less time consuming than formal courts. Activist and author Flavia Agnes in her written submissions to the Supreme Court of India recently in the Shayara Bano case has also argued that most Muslim women prefer to approach dār-ul-qaza for resolving their disputes as they find the procedure of formal courts expensive, long drawn and contentious, and its language and environment extremely alienating.[54]

Masājid Committee, Bhopal constituted by the government of the Madhya Pradesh province, India, has provided interesting data with regard to masālehat – reconciliation, for the year 2016–2017. It says, in 2016, a total of 386 and between January and March 2017, 80 men sought talāq out of which 20 disputes were resolved. For the same period, 459 and 131 women respectively sought khul'a – of which only 18 cases were resolved.[55]

Similarly, it has been reported – with some anxiety – from Hyderabad that more cases of khul'a have been witnessed than talāq (divorce by husband). According to the data from just one Sadr Qāzi area (out of seven Sadr Qāzis and two courts), only seven cases of talāq were registered during January to November 2015 as compared to 380 cases of khul'a during the same period. Similarly in 2014, 20 cases of talāq were registered compared to the 575 women who sought khul'a.[56] The same trend is reflected in the Nizamabad district headquarter (of Telangana province) where the total number of divorce cases registered with the qāzi under the old Waqf Board system between 2010 and 2014 were 497, out which significantly 338 (68%) cases were of khul'a.[57] According to a recent study by a leading law institute, percentages of cases filed by women are higher for khul'a (31.49%), annulment of marriage (faskh, 27.07%) and restitution of conjugal rights (20.43%). Though the study is based on limited responses from few Indian provinces, it reveals significant trend.[58] This seems to be a subcontinental trend.[59]

Distinct responses

This increasing trend of khul'a and faskh-e nikah has deeply disturbed not only the ʿulamā, but also many Muslim men. Typically, they blame jadidyat (modernism), maghrib-zadgi (adopting western life style), English education, higher education, co-education, fashion and consumerism, increasing urbanization, etc. for spurring women into challenging the traditional and Islamic authority of husband/men, reflected in the spike in khul'a;[60] attempt to deprive new generations of Muslims of their faith through polytheistic school curriculum is considered as the most dangerous of all for Muslims' un-Islamic practices.[61] A sharp response came from one Muslim man Nazeer who complained

> It is very bad. Educated women are forcing husband to give talāq. They don't want to take khul'a, even if the woman wants to end the marriage from her side. I have seen many cases like this. They are separating and forcing husband for talāq. Educated women in cities are troubling husbands and his family members very cleverly.[62]

In Nazeer's view, such a strategy was deployed to ensure that the woman's claim to alimony and other benefits did not end. On the contrary, there are many cases where Muslim men have preferred and pressured their wives to demand a khul'a so that they would be exempted from paying alimony and also get back the mahr and other gifts.[63]

But, convivial women it seems are not ready to endure silently any more the undesirable situation produced by the taqlīdi shari'a normativity. According to these women, khul'a is increasingly sought from extremely harsh marital existence, where husband is extremely strict; does not pay any attention to wife's views; is unable to provide for her financially, lack of love, affection and respect; commits physical or emotional violence; takes her for granted and considers her useless; is short-tempered; is always ready to find fault with his wife; has extra-marital relations; is jealous and suspicious of her fidelity; does not stand by her when required; neglects her requirements; would like to control her body and mind; expects her to be docile, obeying, tame and obedient like a cow. It is assumed that it is the wife's duty to serve her in-laws. She is expected to act as a 24 hours' maid servant.[64] But sometime it can also be just general unhappiness and detestation for the husband, dislike for his physical appearance, or falling in love with other man, which are also very much within the shari'a grounds for khul'a[65] but disapproved generally as immoral and immodest.[66]

Husbands and in-laws are emboldened by the taqlīdi ʿulamā in several ways. For example, the Board's current nikāhnāma (an Islamic marriage contract) charts the duties of wife among others as she cannot visit anyone without her husband's permission; she must safeguard her modesty and look after the children; the visits of the wife to her parents and mahram (unmarriageable kin) is allowed only if 'necessary'. But importantly, this nikāhnāma mentions only husband's right of talāq in the sense that wife alone is at fault by default; there is no mention of khul'a, and that husband too can be at fault; neither is there any mention of delegation to the wife of the power of divorce (talāq-etafwīz).[67] However, this nikāhnāma does address the question of domestic violence suggesting that the wife should be treated justly by the husband and that violence should be 'avoided', but it is too vague, which may be interpreted to mean that violence is permissible but better avoided – as limited beating is allowed.[68] A nikāhnāma in use by Andhra Pradesh State Waqf Board outlines similar duties for wife.[69]

Convivially towards accessible shari'a

It is obvious that khul'a has become one of the mechanisms for the Muslim women to defy normative shari'a expectations. In the following, we present certain select cases from contemporary India to explicate the laity ijtihād propelled by the field of conviviality, which the ʿulamā, expectedly have described as ignorance and misuse of shari'a. The laity practitioners are simultaneously in and out of the domain of faith.

The bazaar qāzi, the bazaar shari'a

One of the key figures in the field of conviviality is the bazaar qāzi. 'Bazaar' and 'bazaari' (of bazaar) are employed by people of elite, high textual tradition with disdain to denote common, ordinary thus inauthentic, low, vulgar and untrustworthy. Here, however, it refers to accessibility, and bazaar qāzi is employed to describe a situation of bazaar justice and democracy, which lies outside shari'a normativity.

Conviviality, in practical terms, includes not only the idea and will to defy, but more importantly to mould shari'a restrictions to one's advantage, which is markedly different from 'reform the shari'a' endeavours. This is reflected in the ways in which in everyday life, laity imaginatively manoeuvres the muftis[70] and qāzis to get a decision in their favour, and there are qāzis/muftis to oblige readily by interpreting a shari'a as per the requirements. They may be called bazaar qāzis/muftis.

Before the emergence of dār-ul-qaza as the institutionalized body promoted by the Board, Muslims would generally go to those local people 'regarded' as ʿālim (the learned one; scholar of Islam),moulvi,[71] qāzi and mufti for dispute resolution. Significantly, even after the advent of dār-ul-qaza, women are still 'making use of' local individual people ('hum unke paas bhi jaate hain', as one respondent said to me) as method of convivial practice. Even today, there is no national-level network of dār-ul-qaza, and in different places it works under different names, and in most places it is the individual bazaar qāzi who adjudicate the disputes.

Many pesh-imams (those who lead five-time prayers in a mosque) of small mosques, a simple hāfiz (a Muslim who knows the Quran 'by heart'), a local madrasa moulvi with little religious training; people associated with, or found around the places like dargāh (shrine of a Muslim saint), khānqāh (Islamic monastery), mazār of a pīr (grave of religious/spiritual revered person) qabristān (Muslim graveyard), can all act as mufti, qāzi, ʿulamā to give opinion in writing or orally on talāq, khul'a, etc. The symbolism of clothes, outfit, headgear, robes, appearance and beard plays an important role in the making of this bazaar qāzi.

This field represents the everyday convivial religious sociability and convivial theology. In the context of eroding legitimacy and authority of normative taqlīdi shari'a and dār-ul-qaza, this field of bazaar qāzi and justice acquires immense significance. The bazaar qazi also act as mediators between the client and certified dār-ul-qaza; and some of them quite defiantly have even tried to establish their own dār-ul-qaza. From the province of Karnataka, it has worrisomely been reported that:

> Everybody is establishing a dār-ul-qaza. There is neither any need to take permission from anybody, nor there is any organisation to control them. Decisions are also given in an arbitrary fashion; sometime under the influence of money power, sometime under the influence of local powerful people.[72]

I have not committed any sin. Bhopal has seen a surge in khul'a cases. The large number of khul'a cases is taking place in familial contexts where the husband has gone to the Gulf or other Arab country to earn a living, leaving behind wife and children. They are a kind of occasional visiting husband coming for short stays once in four to five years. Family bonds – emotional or otherwise – and control over family are weakened. Men complained that in the absence of their husbands, wives not only control the finances, even transferring property in their name, but also create all sorts of personal spaces independent of husbands, including having extra-marital affairs. Thereafter, they initiate the process for khul'a to dissolve marriage on the plea that the husband is neglecting his family and conjugal duties. Recently, it was quite talked about that husbands got together to protest against this and approached the prominent ʿulamā.[73]

The women on the other hand offer a different interpretation: As one woman who had sought annulment of her marriage told me:

> We are also human beings. We need support. Money is not the only thing, there are other needs. Emotional [could also be read as sexual] needs are more important. A guest type husband is of no use. I have not committed any sin. God has said taking care of your bodily needs is also 'ibādat (a religious act). I have taken care of household and children for so long, so what is wrong if I have kept some money for myself and my children. I am not asking for maintenance. You know, I had to go for faskh (annulment).

Significantly, while the men approached the 'ulamā to protest the rising tide of khul'a, this woman sought the intercession of a bazaar qāzi to annul her marriage.

Zohra bi. This is from a well-known North Indian city. Zohra Bi's husband is employed in another province, far away from her. Zohra Bi claimed that her husband telephonically pronounced triple talāq on her, and without wasting any time she married her paramour. Her husband, when he came to know of her second marriage, denied that he ever gave her triple talāq. He accused Zohra Bi of taking advantage of anti-triple talāq campaign in the country to justify her marriage with her paramour. He approached a local court, which advised him to seek assistance from the Superintendent of Police.[74]

Mampi of Bengal: reverse transference. This is a peculiar case of conviviality by practising reverse transference of triple talāq. A 16-year-old high school girl Mampi Khatoon, resident of a village 55 km from Kolkata, stunned the local community as she walked up to her husband and shouted talāq thrice to divorce him because he and her in-laws did not honour their promise that she can continue studies even after marriage in 2015 and ridiculed her resolve to study.[75]

Without any knowledge of shari'a but guided purely by the contingencies of her existence and emboldened by the much public talk about triple talāq, her idea of justice was based on the fact if men can pronounce triple talāq, so could she. Before this one Amreen Bano (24) of Meerut did the same to her husband who left her and two kids stranded one evening, saying 'Like a Muslim man gives talāq by saying it three times. I want to do the same.'[76] Mampi drew strength also from the convivial solidarity from her parents and others including a local woman social activist Miratun Nahar. Her neighbour Asma Bibi said, 'personally, I think it was very courageous of her to act the way she did.' Question whether according to shari'a it is right or wrong is of no significance; what is significant is that she did it convivially.

Southern conviviality.

This is from Sothern Indian state, but could easily be from anywhere in India. In this state, marital disputes are generally taken to local committees of elders, and which are run and controlled by different religious organizations belonging to different maslak. Each such committee has a dār-ul-qaza. People usually go to their maslak committee; however, they can go to other maslak committees according to their convenience. This is precisely such a case.

In a village a couple always quarrelled. And neighbours always complained. One day in a fit of anger the husband pronounced triple talāq, but when his wife created a ruckus and when his anger cooled off, he approached his maslak qāzi affiliated to a big organization. The qāzi asked him to repeat what he uttered, and having heard him, declared that talāq had indeed taken place. Disappointed with this verdict, the husband went to another qāzi of a small organization of another maslak, but did not tell him about his visit to the big qāzi. By this time he had discovered the importance of the words uttered at the time of pronouncing talāq and also the importance of intent. He decided to manoeuvre the situation. When asked by the second qāzi what words he had uttered, he described it in such a way that the second qāzi concluded that the talāq had not taken place.[77]

When the said husband had uttered the statement of talāq, no one but his wife had heard it. A neighbour had heard it only very hazily. Scholars in fiqh have classified commonly used words for divorce into two kinds: direct and indirect. The utterance of divorce using direct words is valid even without intention. In case of using indirect words, the divorce becomes valid only if the person says that he really meant to initiate divorce. The couple in this case admitted to the first qāzi the use of direct words; but to the second qāzi, they said that only indirect words had been used, and denied that there was any intention to divorce. Obviously, in concealing what he actually said, the couple refused to be guided by the taqlīdi shari'a.

Conclusion

Louis Althusser in his investigation into subject formation recognizes 'the ambiguity of the term subject', conveying the meaning of both 'a free subjectivity ... responsible for its actions' and 'a subjected being, who submits to a higher authority, and therefore stripped of all freedom'.[78] The process of subject formation in Althusser involves 'interpellation' and 'hailing'.

Within the context of this essay, we find that taqlīdi shari'a normativity hails Muslim women from the position of controlling authority. In Althusser, it is taken for granted that individual is a constituted subject and will always be there *within hail* and respond expectedly to the signals emanating from the authority above, which in our case is shari'a normativity and traditional and Islamic authority of husband/men. And yet humans have not just been a plaything in the hands of history or structures. Thus, the field of conviviality enables women/subject to exercise their subjectivity to tread in a zone of simultaneity of being in and outside the hail of shari'a normativity.

The convivial women, by being guided by the Social not by the Faith, attempted to re-constitute the field of shari'a normativity with a deep sense of defiance. The field of conviviality signifies a movement from the constituted subject to ontological self to defy the authority of the taqlidi shari'a legal monotheism. The convivial women did so by drawing upon the personal or collective convivial cultural resources without claiming to reinterpret shari'a. Thus, the field of conviviality decoded the occultated and petrified meanings in hermeneutics of taqlīdi shari'a with a hermeneutics of convivial suspicion. Ultimately, the convivial women move towards making a democratically accessible convivial theology as opposed to that of legal monotheism of normative taqlīdi theology.

Notes

1. Bourdieu uses the concept of field in a very rigid and structured sense where a social field 'exerts a force upon all those who come within its range' and those who come within its range are generally not aware of it, and its power is mysterious. See Terdiman, 'Introduction', 806. Bourdieu's concept of field is very much akin to his concept of habitus where primary predispositions constitute structuring principles to constitute human activities/practices. In this essay, a social field is characterized by people placed in a hierarchical social order. They gain knowledge of it in a process that generates critical reflections and enables them to exert influence upon the field in order to change it through a process of unravelling its mysteries by their defiant subjectivities. In other words, people are not just constituted by the field, but they constitute and re-constitute it as well.
2. Relating to Maslak. In Islamic scholarly writings on shari'a it is the term Mazhab which is employed to denote a school of Islamic jurisprudence. Therefore, Muslims claim to belong to the Hanafi, Shafi'i, Hanbali or Māliki mazhab, and only at times the word maslak is used as synonym for the term 'mazhab'. However, in Indian subcontinent since the term mazhab is widely used and understood for religion (such as mazhab-e Islam), thus the term maslak which is predominantly used for mazhab. But importantly, the term maslakin Indian subcontinent refers not only to the schools of Islamic jurisprudence, but also, and importantly, it refers to sects/denominations within a particular school of jurisprudence, such as Deobandi and Barēlwī, etc. within Hanafi school of thought. Therefore, maslak refers to a system of religious belief and worship based on a particular interpretation of Quran and hadith constituting a sectarian school of thought within an established school of Islamic jurisprudence, indicating at the existence of multiple maslak among Muslims beset with antagonistic relations.
3. Ijtihād in Islamic Shari'a and jurisprudence refers to independent reasoning by legal scholars in finding a solution to a legal question, not specifically provided in Qur'an and hadith, with creative reinterpretation in changed circumstances. But since long ijtihād is not practised that demanded taqlīd, which resulted in fiqh (Islamic jurisprudence) becoming ineffective in changed circumstances. The issue has since long been hotly debated and is central to any discussion on shari'a particularly with regard to Muslim personal law.

4. Taqlīd refers to imitating; conformity to legal precedents of earlier Islamic legal scholars; not applying any critical thinking in changed circumstances. Thus, taqlīd means: 'Acting on the opinion of another without knowing his evidence or demanding proof'. See Usmani, *Usul-al-Iftā waĀdābahu*. It is contrasted with ijtihād. Ijtihād and taqlīd have intensely been debated for long involving their historical, theological and jurisprudential dimensions and nuances, here we are using them in their essential sense.
5. The term of Hindutva was introduced by V. D. Savarkar in 1922–3. Ideology of Hindutva seeks to establish a Hindu Rashtra (Hindu Nation) and Hindu hegemony in India. It represents the predominant Hindu idea of nationalism and majoritarian communalism particularly against Muslims who are considered outsider, who ruled over Hindus by force and ultimately partitioned the sacred body of mother India. Hindutva ideology has found Muslim Personal Law an issue on which Muslims can be taught a lesson under the guise of implementing Common Civil Code.
6. Article 44 of the Directive Principles of the Indian Constitution says: 'The State shall endeavour to secure for citizens a uniform civil code throughout the territory of India.' The issue of uniform civil code has emerged a hotly and publically debated issue in post-colonial India, and is believed by Muslims as a means to curb personal laws, especially only of Muslims. The issue has further been complicated, as many Muslim women, affected adversely by the personal laws, have begun knocking on the doors of the Supreme Court beseeching it to uphold their fundamental rights to equality and liberty in keeping with constitutional provisions. The question of uniform civil code has acquired a distinct communal overtone after the famous Supreme Court of India judgement in 1985 on Shah Bano case. For general theoretical issues on UCC with reference to India, see Menski, 'The Uniform Civil Code Debate in Indian Law'; Mahmood, *Uniform Civil Code*; for a critique of Hindutva agenda of UCC, see Agnes, 'The Modi Government's Hindutva Ideology Could Stall Any Progress on the Uniform Civil Code'.
7. Ummah refers to a united community and brotherhood of Muslims independent of national boundaries with a shared history and bound by the tenets of Islam.
8. See Quaiser, "Choreographic Occultation and Petrification of Meaning."
9. Josselson, "The Hermeneutics of Faith."
10. For more on historical, social and political dimensions of shari'a, see Hallaq, *An Introduction to Islamic Law*; Safi, ed. *Progressive Muslims*; Abou El Fadl, *Reasoning with God*; Bennett, *Muslims and Modernity*; and Ziadeh, *Usul al-fiqh*.
11. These accounts led to the systematic articulation of the body of legal knowledge and rules in the eighth and ninth centuries by the great jurists such as Abu Hanifah, Mālik ibn Anas, Al-Shafi'i and Ahmad ibn Hanbal, the founders of the Hanafi, Māliki, Shafi'i and Hanbali schools of Sunni jurisprudence. A fifth school of Islamic jurisprudence is Fiqh-e Ja'faria named after the sixth Shiite Imam Jafar al-Sadiqfor Shia Muslims.
12. Schacht, *An Introduction to Islamic Law*, 70–71.
13. For an insightful discussion, see Bennett, *Muslims and Modernity*.
14. As is discussed below, this is very much true in case of India as well. For example, in March 2015, the secretary of the Islamic Fiqh Academy (India) stated that the principle of taqlīd has generally been accepted since the tenth-century AD onward, which is practised in India. See *Kalīdi Khutba*.
15. Hallaq, "Was the Gate of Ijtihād Closed?" 3–41.
16. Rabb, *Ijtihād*.
17. For discussion, see Milton-Edwards, *Islamic Fundamentalism since 1945*; and Gesink, "Chaos on the Earth."
18. Rahman and Moosa, *Revival and Reform in Islam*; An–Naim, *Toward an Islamic Reformation*; and Wadud, *Qur'an and Woman*. Although there is continuity, the nineteenth-century modernist notion of ijtihād was located strictly within an Islamic framework, while the contemporary modernist plea for ijtihād would like to draw not only upon shari'a but also upon critical perspectives of modern social sciences, see Taji–Farouki ed. *Modern Muslim Intellectuals and the Qur'an*.
19. *Otto, Shari'a and National Law in Muslim Countries: Tensions and Opportunities for Dutch and EU Policy.*
20. Mir-Hosseini, "Islamic Family Law and Social Practice," 23. In fact Mir-Hosseini is close to what Abou El Fadl states with reference to some earlier jurists – but ultimately stating that shari'a remains the Way and the Law of God, see Abou El Fadl, *Islam and the Challenge of Democracy*, 30–31.
21. For an intellectually powerful discussion on this question of contextualization of Islamic jurisprudence, see Coulson, *A History of Islamic Law*, especially 1–7 and 218–226.
22. Nasr, *Ideals and Realities of Islam*, 112.
23. For Ahl-e Hadīs view, see Fariwai, "Taqdeem"
24. For Shah Waliullah, see Dehlavi, *Hayat-e Wali*; and Nadvi, *Tārīkh D'awat wa 'Azīmat.*
25. Rahman, "Muslim Modernism in the Indo-Pakistan Sub-Continent;" and Esposito, *The Islamic Threat.*
26. Iqbal, *Reconstruction of Religious Thought in Islam.*
27. For how strong taqlīd as organizing principle is in Indian subcontinent, see Usmani, *Taqlīd ki Shari'yi Haisiyat*; and Thānvi, 'Letter'; and Thānvi, *Imdād-ul-Fatāwa.*
28. Amini, *Fiqh-e Islami kā Tārikhī Pas-Manzar*, 19–20.
29. See, for example: Khan, *Fatawa 'Alamgīrī Par Eik Nazar*; and Madani, *Fatawa Sanaullah Madani.*

30. Husain, *Administration of justice*, 13–16; and Ahmad, *The Administration of Justice in Medieval India.*
31. *The Hedaya, Or Guide.* Written in the twelfth century by the leading Muslim jurist Burhan al-Din al-Marghinani (1135–97), the original Arabic al-Hidayah remains a central text of Islamic personal law. It was translated into English by Charles Hamilton. Although since superseded, it remains a significant text in the history of colonial jurisprudence. Its significance can be gauged from the very fact that the four volumes of Hidayah continue to be one of the main texts taught in all the leading madrasa in India.
32. Gilmartin, *Anglo-Muhammadan Law*; and Kozlowski, *Muslim Endowments and Society in British India.*
33. Ali, *Principles of Mohammadan Law*; Fyzee, *Outlines of Muhammadan Law*; and Gilmartin, *Anglo-Muhammadan Law.*
34. Anderson, "Islamic Law and the Colonial Encounter."
35. Wilson, *An Introduction to the Study of Anglo-Muhammadan Law*, 2.
36. Jamiʿat-ul-ʿulamā-i-Hind founded in 1919 drew its inspiration from the eighteenth-century Muslim anti-European expressions. It claims that after the 1857 revolt ʿulamā were the main target of the British oppression and of the 200,000 people martyred during the revolt 51,200 were ʿulamā. During the anti-colonial struggle, Jamiʿat took the position that Hindu–Muslim unity was necessary for the country's freedom and it closely aligned with the Indian National Congress and had opposed the partition of India in 1947. See Rizvi, *Tārīkh Dār-ul-ʿUlum.*
37. Madani, *Muttahida Qawmiat Aur Islam.*
38. *All India Muslim Personal Law Board: Khidmāt aur Sargarmiyan.*
39. Shah Bano, a 73-year-old woman was divorced by her husband by triple talāq and denied maintenance. She approached the courts. Ultimately, the Supreme Court of India unanimously ruled in her favour in 1985. But it also passed some adverse remarks about Muslim personal laws and failure of parliament to legislate uniform civil code. Muslims accused the Government of imposing Hindu culture on minorities; and the Board vigorously campaigned for Muslim personal laws and identity. The Congress party led-Government finally passed The Muslim Women's (Protection of Rights on Divorce) Act (MWA) in 1986, which made Section 125 of the Criminal Procedure Code inapplicable to Muslim women. The Government was accused of 'minority appeasement' and as a result, perhaps to compensate the other side, magistrate in Ayodhya ordered opening of the gates of Babri masjid, which further produced the volatile communal politics in the days to come. See Mullally, "Feminism and Multiculturalism Dilemmas in India;" and Joseph and Sharma *Whose News?*
40. Though the Board has opposed UCC, but of late there seems to be some tension on the issue. For example, it has been reported that the present General Secretary of the Board has stated that if the Supreme Court of India implements the UCC, the Board would accept it. He may have made this statement with the view that the Supreme Court cannot do this, but another prominent Muslim organization has strongly condemned his statement (*Jadeed Khabar*, 27 December 2016).
41. Hallaq, *The Origin and Evolution of Islamic Law*; and Abualfaraj, *Evidence in Islamic Law.*
42. Qasmi, *Islāh-e Mu'ashra and Samaj kī Zimmedaariyan.*
43. *Imārat Shari'a: T'arruf, Khidmāt aur Sargarmiyan*, 5–6.
44. Ibid.
45. Arya Samaj, an Indian Hindu organization, was formed in 1875 for the revival of Vedic values and practices. It gained notoriety for its shuddhi (purification) activities for conversion to Hinduism creating communal passions.
46. Ghar Wapsi (Home Coming) is a series of religious conversion activities facilitated by extreme right wing communal Indian Hindu organizations, Vishva Hindu Parishad and Rashtriya Swayamsevak Sangh, to facilitate conversion of non-Hindus to Hinduism, particularly Muslims and Christians in contemporary India.
47. Bastavi, *Nizām-e Qaza ka Qyam: Ahmiyat aur Zarurat.*
48. "Petition against 'Shariat courts' is misguided." *The Milli Gazzette.*
49. *Vishwa Lochan Madan versus Union of India.*
50. http://www.stepswomenjamaat.org/; see also Deepa Dhanraj's perceptive documentary film on Jamaat, *Invoking Justice.* More generally on modernist, reformist, reconstructionist Islamic feminist thinking to bring about change in the status of women in general and in family law from secular perspective or from within the framework of the shari'a around the question of gender justice and equality, see Mahmood, *Muslim Personal Law*; Omvedt, *Violence against Women*; WRAG Report, *Aspects of Culture and Society*; Desai, ed. *Women's Liberation and Politics of Religious Laws in India*; Mernissi, *Women and Islam* as well as *Beyond the Veil*; Mir-Hosseini, *How the Door of Ijtihād Was Opened and Closed*; Haddad and Esposito ed. *Islam, Gender and Social Change*; and Ask and Tjomsland ed. *Women and Islamisation.*
51. *Deen Aur Destur Bachao Tahrik: Kya Aur Kyon*; and "*Board ki Sargarmiyon Kā Mukhtasar Khāka.*"
52. Mahmood, *Politics of Piety.*
53. Khul'a literally means to shed, as to shed clothes. Khul'a is taken to mean separation between spouses, for in Quran husband and wife are considered as one clothe (of each other); and through Khul'a they shed this

implied clothe. Thus, its extended implied meaning would be redemption, rescue, and emancipation. The situation in which the wife initiates divorce proceedings by mutual agreement is known as khul'a divorce (talāq-ul khul'a), with other related forms such as sulh, fidya and mubāra'a, having the same meaning, which is in order to obtain her divorce a woman pays compensation. But there are some differences in all the four forms. Khul'a means that the woman has to pay all that husband spent on her (mahr – dower, if it has been paid and any wedding gifts); in case of sulh, she will pay only part of it; fidya means paying more than what she got; and mubāra'a refers to her writing off a claim that she had against husband. Her right of fidya is considered to be at par with talāq.Any sensible woman can go for khul'a. If a woman is generally unhappy with her husband, even if she does not like his physical appearance, she herself can seek khul'a. If husband is at fault then it is prohibited for him to take any compensation. Khul'a can be decided by the spouses themselves and for this they need not go to court-'adālat-dār-ul-qaza. In case husband does not agree the wife can ask for the annulment of her marriage (Faskh-e-Nikah) and the qāzi is permitted to annul the marriage on valid grounds. However, sometime husbands are forced to agree by various means, but of course that is outside the shari'a. The issue has since long been intensely debated among the jurisprudents of various schools of jurisprudence.

54. Agnes, Written Submissions, 7.
55. Thanks to Urdu journalist Dr Mahtab Alam,Jamal Ayyub and Lamat Rahman for getting a copy of this statement. Copy on record.
56. *Siasat* Urdu daily, 27 February 2016.
57. Thanks to Irfan Muhammad for the Nizamabad figures.
58. Annexure A in Agnes, Written Submissions.
59. According to a report, numbers of women opting for khul'a are growing at an unprecedented rate in Pakistan's urban centres. On 31 December 2015, 12,733 cases of khul'a were still pending in family courts of four districts in Karachi. If 10 cases are resolved or disposed, 50 new ones are added, see *The Express Tribune*, 1 April 2016. In Pakistani Punjab, 13,299 khul'a cases were reported in 2012, which later rose to 14,243 in 2013, and in 2014, they went up to 16,942. In 2016, they have increased to 18,901, see *The Nation*, 27 June 2016. A report from Bangladesh reveals that Dhaka North City Corporation (DNCC) and Dhaka South City Corporation (DSCC) data show that around 67% of the divorce notices issued from 2011 to 2016 were by women, see *Dhaka Tribune*, 14 May 2017. In Bangladesh, Muslims in matters of personal law are governed by The Muslim Personal Law (Shariat) Application Act (1937). Qāzi, local Imam and mullā (here, a religious parson) solemnize Muslim marriage; there is no official qāzi court; qāzis are government servants only to maintain marriage and divorce records. Nikahnama has a column, which pertains to delegation to the wife of the power of divorce that by default means yes, unless otherwise written specifically.
60. Interviews; for general concern within the 'ulamā, see Qāsmi, *Islāh-e Mu'ashra and Samaj kī Zimmedaariyan*; and Qāsmi, *Muslim Personal Law Kā Mas'ala: T'arruf wa Tajziya.*
61. Nizamuddīn, "Shazrāt."
62. Personal communication.
63. *Dhaka Tribune*, 14 May 2017; Macfarlane, *Islamic Divorce in North America*, 195–6.
64. Author's interviews; Qāsmi, *Islāh-e Mu'ashra and Samaj kī Zimmedaariyan; Times of India*, 13 August 2015.
65. See Qāsmi, *Muslim Personal Law Kā Mas'ala.*
66. Based on personal interviews.
67. *Nikāhnāma – approved by All India Muslim Personal Law Board.* Office of the Board informs that it is the same Model Nikāhnāma that the Board had presented in 2005. Significantly, after 17 years of the model nikāhnāma, the Board in a Resolution passed in its Working Committee meeting held on 15–16 April 2017 stated that the wife can end marriage by khul'a, see *Guidelines & Advisory with Reference to Marriage and Divorce of Muslims in India.* Inclusion of talāq-e tafwīz perhaps may not take another 17 years.
68. See note 65 above.
69. Copy on record.
70. A Mufti is a person who is properly trained in the science of Fatwa literature and only then is entitled to issue a Fatwa, which is just a shari'a-based ruling/opinion, and which is not necessarily to be adhered to.
71. In high Islamic discourse, an honorific Islamic religious title was given to Muslim religious scholars, but in Indian subcontinent it refers to a low-level *madrasa* teacher, or pesh-imam (one who leads five-time prayers in a mosque), etc.
72. *Masarrat* Urdu weekly, 19 December 2016.
73. My conversation with several people has confirmed this. Some people close to dār-ul-qaza too have unofficially said so. Whatever the case, it is clear that rising cases of khul'a and strident shari'a-bashing over triple talāq have alarmed 'ulamā. In a seminar on khul'a and talāq, a Muslim personal law advocate expressed deep concern over the present 'lawlessness among Muslims in the matters of khul'a and talāq' (*Siasat* Urdu Daily, 15 May 2013). The Board has admitted that several steps have been taken to deal with this misuse (The Times of India, 13 August 2015). Msājid Committee, Bhopal has in 2017 organized training camps for nikāh-khwan (one who solemnizes the marriage), pesh-imams and muezzins (one who calls

Muslims to prayer from a mosque) at several tehsil level dār-ul-qazas and issued circulars in this regard (copies on record).

74. *Roznāma Rāshtriya Sahara*, Urdu Daily, 9 December 2016; conversations with local people. Allahabad High Court – Justice Suneet Kumar, 8 December 2016. Un-reportable items.
75. *Shongbad Pratidin*, 17 June 2017; *Doinik Nabodiganta*, 17 June 2017.
76. *India Today*, 4 May 2017.
77. Thanks to P. Majid and Mufti Aslam for interview. There is a great deal of debate on the question of intention (niyya) and uttering the word talāq among the established Islamic jurisprudents.
78. Althusser, "Ideology and Ideological State Apparatuses," 123.

Acknowledgements

Thanks to Michae Dusche who read the earlier draft presented in the conference organised by him in 2015. Thanks are also due to Muft Mushtaq Tejarvi for the occasional discussion and for readily sharing some material. Thanks to Manisha Sethi, who in the true spirit of a excavator-editor facilitated the writing of this essay. All the translations from Urdu are by the author.

Disclosure statement

No potential conflict of interest was reported by the author.

Bibliography

Abou El Fadl, Khaled. *Islam and the Challenge of Democracy*. Princeton: Princeton University Press, 2004.

Abou El Fadl, Khaled. *Reasoning with God: Reclaiming Shari'Ah in the Modern Age*. Lanham, Maryland: Rowman & Littlefield, 2014.

Abualfaraj, M. "Evidence in Islamic Law: Reforming the Islamic Evidence Law Based on the Federal Rules of Evidence." *Journal of Islamic Law and Culture* 13, no. 2–3 (2011): 140–165. doi:10.1080/1528817X.2012.733130.

Abul-Hasan Ali, N. *Tārīkh D'awat wa 'Azīmat*. Vol. 5. Lucknow: Majlis Tahqīqāt wa Nashriyat-e Islam, 1989.

Agnes, F. "The Modi Government's Hindutva Ideology Could Stall Any Progress on the Uniform Civil Code," Accessed May 2, 2017. https://thewire.in/49580/bjp-uniform-civil-code/.

Agnes, F., Written Submissions Filed on Behalf of the Majlis Manch in the Supreme Court of India, in the Matter of Shayara Bano, Petitioner Versus Union of India & Ors. May 17 2017.

Ahmad, M. B. *The Administration of Justice in Medieval India*. Allahabad: The Aligarh Historical Research Institute, 1941.

Ali, Syed, A. *Principles of Mohammadan Law*. Rev. Ed. Allahabad: Allahabad Law Emporium, 1983.

All India Muslim Personal Law Board: Khidmāt Aur Sargarmiyan. Delhi: All India Muslim Personal Law Board, 2010(2002).

Althusser, L. "Ideology and Ideological State Apparatuses." In *Lenin and Philosophy and Other Essays*. New York: Monthly Review Press, 1971

Amīni, T. *Fiqh-E Islami Ka Tārikhī Pas-Manzar [Historical Background of Islamic Jurisprudence]*. Delhi: Nadvat-ul-Musannifin, 1973 (1962).

Anderson, M. "Islamic Law and the Colonial Encounter in British India." In *Institutions and Ideologies*, edited by D. Arnold and P. Robb, 165–185. Richmond: Curzon Press, 1993.

An–Naim, A. *Toward an Islamic Reformation*. Syracuse: Syracuse University Press, 1990.

Ask, K., and M. Tjomsland, ed.. *Women and Islamisation: Contemporary Dimensions of Discourse on Gender Relations*. Oxford: Oxford International, 1998.

Bastavi, A. A. *Nizām-E Qaza Ka Qyam: Ahmiyat Aur Zarurat [Establishment of Islamic System of Adjudication: Importance and Need]*. Delhi: All India Muslim Personal Law Board, Undated.

Bennett, C. *Muslims and Modernity: An Introduction to the Issues and Debates*. London, New York: Continuum, 2005.

"Board Ki Sargarmiyon Kā Mukhtasar Khāka [Short Outline of Board's Activities]." *Khabanama [Newsletter], All India Muslim Personal Law Board* 9, no. 4 ((2015)).

Coulson, N. J. *A History of Islamic Law*. Edinburgh: Edinburgh University Press, 1964.

Deen Aur Dastur Bachao Tahrik: Kya Aur Kyon [Save Faith, Save Constitution Movement: How and Why]. Delhi: All India Muslim Personal Law Board, Undated.

Dehlavi, R. B. *Hayat-e Wali [Life of Wali]*. Delhi: Afzal-ul-Matāb'a, 1847.

Desai, A. R., ed. *Women's Liberation and Politics of Religious Laws in India*. Bombay: C. G. Shah Memorial Trust, 1986.

Dhaka Tribune, May 14, 2017.

Dhanraj, D. *Invoking Justice*. Documentary film, 2011. Directed and produced by Deepa Dhanraj for SAMA, Chennai.

Doinik Nabodiganta, June 17, 2017.

Esposito, J. L. *The Islamic Threat: Myth or Reality?* New York: Oxford University Press, 1993.

The Express Tribune, April 1, 2016.

Fariwai, A. "'Taqdeem' [The Presentation]." In Muhammad Muhaddis Gondalvi's book *Al-Islāh*. Gujranwala: Ummul-Qara Publications, 2011:85-111.

Fyzee, A. A. A. *Outlines of Muhammadan Law*. 3rd ed. London: Oxford University Press, 1964.

Gesink, I. F. "Chaos on the Earth: Subjective Truths versus Communal Unity in Islamic Law and the Rise of Militant Islam." *The American historical review* 108, no. 3 (2003): 710–733.

Gilmartin, D. *Anglo-Muhammadan Law*. Accessed April 12, 2015. http://islamicus.org/anglo-muhammadan-law/

Guidelines & Advisory with Reference to Marriage and Divorce of Muslims in India. Delhi: Issued by All India Muslim Personal Law Board, 2017.

Haddad, Yvonne Yazbeck and Esposito, JohnL, ed. *Islam, Gender and Social Change*. Oxford: Oxford University Press, 1998.

Hallaq, W. B. "Was the Gate of Ijtihād Closed?" *International journal of Middle East studies* 16, no. 1 (1984): 3–41. doi:10.1017/S0020743800027598.

Hallaq, W. B. *The Origin and Evolution of Islamic Law*. Cambridge: Cambridge University Press, 2005.

Hallaq, W. B. *An Introduction to Islamic Law*. Cambridge: Cambridge University Press, 2009.

The Hedaya, Or Guide. *A Commentary on the Mussulman Laws*. Tr. Charles Hamilton.London: W. H. Allen& Co.:1870

Husain, W. *Administration of Justice during the Muslim Rule in India*. Calcutta: University of Calcutta, 1934.

Imārat Shari'A: T'Arruf, Khidmāt Aur Sargarmiyan, [Imārat Shari'A: Introduction, Services and Activities] Accessed December 4, 2015. http://www.imaratShari'ah.org/introduction.html

India Today, May 4, 2017.

Iqbal, M. *Reconstruction of Religious Thought in Islam*. Lahore: Institute of Islamic Studies, 1999 (1930).

Jadeed Khabar, December 27, 2016.

Joseph, A., and K. Sharma. *Whose News? the Media and Women's Issues*. New Delhi: Sage, 1994.

Josselson, R. "The Hermeneutics of Faith and the Hermeneutics of Suspicion." *Narrative Inquiry* 14, no. 1 (2004): 1–28. doi:10.1075/ni.14.1.

Kalīdi Khutba (Key-note address delivered by Khalid Saifullah Rahmani): 24th Fiqhi Seminar. Delhi: Islamic Fiqh Academy, 2015.

Khan, U. *Mufti. Fatawa 'Alamgiri Par Eik Nazar [A Look at Fatawa' Alamgiri]*. Lahore: Maktaba-e Azīzīa, 1988.

Kozlowski, G. C. *Muslim Endowments and Society in British India*. Cambridge: Cambridge University Press, 1985.

Macfarlane, J. *Islamic Divorce in North America: A Shari'A Path in A Secular Society*. Oxford: Oxford University Press, 2012.

Madani, Hussain Ahmed *Muttahida Qawmiat Aur Islam [United nationhood and Islam]*. Delhi: Al-jami'at Book Depot, undated.

Madani, S. *Fatawa Sanaullah Madani [Fatwas of Sanaullah Madani]*. Lahore: Maktaba Ansarul-Sunniatul-Nabvia, 2016.

Mahmood, S. *Politics of Piety: The Islamic Revival and the Feminist Subject*. Princeton, New Jersey: Princeton University Press, 2005.

Mahmood, T. *Muslim Personal Law: Role of the State in the Subcontinent*. Delhi: Vikas Publishing House, 1977.

Mahmood, T. *Uniform Civil Code: Fictions and Facts*. New Delhi: Pharos Group, 2004.

Masarrat Urdu weekly, December 19, 2016.

Menski, W. "The Uniform Civil Code Debate in Indian Law: New Developments and Changing Agenda." *German Law Journal* 9, no. 3 (2008): 211–250. doi:10.1017/S2071832200006416.

Mernissi, F. *Beyond the Veil: Male- Female Dynamics in a Modern Muslim Society*. Cambridge, MA: Schenkman Publication Co., Inc., 1972.

Mernissi, F. *Women and Islam: An Historical and Theological Enquiry*. Oxford: Basil Blackwell, 1991.

Milton-Edwards, B. *Islamic Fundamentalism since 1945*. New York: Routledge, 2014.

Mir-Hosseini, Z. "How the Door of Ijtihād Was Opened and Closed: A Comparative Analysis of Recent Family Law Reforms in Iran and Morocco." *Washington and Lee Law Review* 64, no. 4 (2007): 1499–1511.

Mir-Hosseini, Z. "Islamic Family Law and Social Practice: Anthropological Reflections on the Terms of the Debate." In *Family, Law and Religion: Debate in the Muslim World and Europe and Their Implications for Co-Operation and Dialogue*, edited by S. Hass, 21–32. Vienna: Austrian Association for the Middle East Hammer-Purgstall, 2009.

Mullally, S. “Feminism and Multiculturalism Dilemmas in India: Revisiting the Shah Bano Case.” *Oxford Journal of Legal Studies* 2, no. 4 (2004): 671–692. doi:10.1093/ojls/24.4.671.

Nasr, S. H. *Ideals and Realities of Islam*. New Rev. Ed. Chicago: ABC International Group, Inc., 2000 (1966).

The Nation, June 27, 2016.

Nikāh-Nāma – Approved by All India Muslim Personal Law Board. Delhi: All India Muslim Personal Law Board, undated.

Nizamuddīn, S. “‘Shazrāt’ [Short Notes].” *Khabarnama [newsletter] – All India Muslim Personal Law Board* 9 (2015): 4.

Omvedt, G. *Violence against Women: New Movements and New Theories in India*. Delhi: Kali for Women, 1994.

Otto, J. M. *Shari‘A and National Law in Muslim Countries: Tensions and Opportunities for Dutch and EU Policy*. Amsterdam: Amsterdam University Press, 2008.

Qāsmi, A. *Islāh-E Mu‘Ashra and Samaj Kī Zimmedaariyan [Societal Reform and Society's Responsibilities]*. Sh'uba-e Nashr wa Isha'at, Imārat Shari'a Bihar, Orissa wa Jharkhand: Phulwari-Sharīf, 2012.

Qāsmi, Mujāhid-ul-Islām, Qāzi. *Muslim Personal Law Kā Mas'ala: T‘Arruf Wa Tajziya [Problems of Muslim Personal Law: Introduction and Analysis]*. Delhi: Muslim Personal Law Board, 1993 (1986).

Quaiser, N. “Choreographic Occultation and Petrification of Meaning: Post-Colonial Law and Alternative Subject.” *Society and Culture in South Asia* 2, no. 1 (2016): 79–102. doi:10.1177/2393861715609819.

Rabb, I. A. “Ijtihād.” In *The Oxford Encyclopaedia of the Islamic World*, edited by J. L. Esposito. Oxford: Oxford University Press, 2009. Accessed August 21, 2015 http://www.oxfordislamicstudies.com/article/opr/t236/e0354

Rahman, F. “Muslim Modernism in the Indo-Pakistan Sub-Continent.” *Bulletin of the School of Oriental and African Studies* 21, no. 2 (1958): 82–99. doi:10.1017/S0041977X00063242.

Rahman, F., and E. Moosa. *Revival and Reform in Islam*. London: Oneworld, 1999.

Rizvi, M. *Tārīkh Daar-ul-Ulum Deoband [History of Deoband's Seminary of Islamic Learning]*. Deoband: MaktabaDār-ul-Ulum, 1992.

Roznāma Rāshtriya Sahara, Urdu Daily, December 9, 2016

Safi, O., ed.. (2003). *Progressive Muslims: On Justice, Gender, and Pluralism*. Oxford: Oneworld Publications.

Schacht, J. *An Introduction to Islamic Law*. Oxford: Oxford University Press, 1982.

Shayara Bano versus Union of India. SCC Online SC 963, 2017.

Shongbad Pratidin, June 17, 2017.

Siasat Urdu Daily, May 15, 2013.

Siasat Urdu daily, February 27, 2016

Taji–Farouki, S. *Modern Muslim Intellectuals and the Qur'an*. New York: Oxford University Press, 2004.

Terdiman, R. “Introduction to Bourdieu, Pierre. The Force of Law: Toward Sociology of the Juridical Field [Translated by Richard Terdiman].” *The Hastings law journal* 38 (1987): 805–813.

Thānvi, A. A. *Imdad-ul-Fatawa [Assistance in Understanding of Fatwas]*. Vol. 5. Karachi: Maktaba Darul-ulum Karachi, 2004.

Thānvi, A. A. *“Letter” in ‘Ashiq Ilāhi. Tazkirat-ur-Rashīd [Biographical Descriptions of Rashīd]*. Meerut: Amiir-ul Matāb‘a, Undated.

The Times of India, Aug 13, 2015

Usmani, M., and T. Mufti. *Taqlīdki Shari‘Yi Haisiyat [Status of Conformity to Legal Precedents in Islamic Law]*. Karachi: Maktaba Dārul-ulum Karachi, 1985.

Usmani, M., and T. Mufti. *Usul-al-Iftāwa Ādābahu [Principles and Systems of Fatwa]*. Karachi: Maktaba Mua'rif-al-Qura'n, 2015.

Vishwa Lochan Madan versus Union of India. 7 SCC 707, 2014.

Wadud, A. *Qur'an and Woman: Rereading the Sacred Text from a Woman's Perspective*. Oxford: Oxford University Press,1999.

Wilson Sir, R. K., and G. G. Simm. *An Introduction to the Study of Anglo-Muhammadan Law*. London: W. Thacker, 1894.

WRAG Report. *Aspects of Culture and Society: Muslim Women in India*. Mumbai: Women Research and Action Group, 1997.

Ziadeh, F. J. “Usul al-fiqh.” In *The Oxford Encyclopaedia of the Islamic World*, edited by J. L. Esposito. Oxford: Oxford University Press, 2009. Accessed August 21, 2015http://www.oxfordislamicstudies.com/article/opr/t236/e0831

Part 3

Communities and Conflicts

Religion, law and state policing: accusations, inquests and arbitration of religious conflicts in colonial India

M. Raisur Rahman

ABSTRACT

While religious groups have recurrently approached the state and its institutions to rationalize their acts and selves, government taking recourse to referee religious concerns has had a long history. The colonial state in India was replete with specimens of the intermix of seemingly incompatible elements of the religious and the secular, in this case, religion and the legal network, avowedly one of modern state's key secular institutions. In the *qasbah* town of Amroha where in 1895 a dispute occurred between Shia and Sunni Muslims about the wording of *azan* (call to prayer), both sides lined up with petitions and memoranda to win over a verdict on their side. The British authorities played it well, to their own advantages and whims. Similarly, over a communal strife between some Muslims and Parsis of Bombay in 1874, a series of letters to newspapers invoked the British sense of justice and fairness. While 'a lover of peace' sought strict actions against the perpetrators of violence, a certain 'superior race' pledged their loyalty and law-abiding nature. Several arrests were made as a follow up but charges could not be proved against a large number of the captives. Disputes and lawlessness thus became an arena for the government to play a role in determining what was right or wrong and who could have the final word where laws and rulings, not scriptures, determined the course of religious destinies and identities. This essay explores the intermediary nature and significant interventions of the state in handling the tumultuous relationship between religion and law, rendering them even more volatile.

Introduction

E.E. Turner, the British Inspector-General of Police in Bombay stated the following in 1935:

> It is strange that while all the countries in the world from time immemorial have maintained their armies for protection from outside invasion, the question of efficient control of internal law and order, and supervision over criminals and crime in general, has never been tackled satisfactorily till comparatively recent times. Such was the case in India.[1]

He then continued to discredit the previous regimes and acclaimed the British government in India for the various efforts made in this direction; but added that even though multiple schemes had been tried, they were not very successful until 1860 when the British took the matter in their hand in a systematic fashion. The year 1860 must be noted as it marked the ascendancy of the formal British Empire in India as the British East India Company-run administration was transferred to the Crown with the passage of the Government of India Act 1858. In sum, Turner fully accredited the British Crown for its effective governance capabilities with regard to the police system – a claim too large to hold itself.

What is certain is that the police did exist as an instrument of colonial power and domination in India. The colonial character of the Police Act of 1861 shaped the organization of the police, which served British imperial interests at the expense of the society. In terms of its legacy in South Asia, the state continues to have a distraught relation with society. Under the colonial context of British metropolitan liberalism and the postcolonial context of a secular state, there should ideally be a separation of religion and law. But the state, in both cases, has stretched itself to manoeuvre religion in order to serve its imminent needs. Considering the intervening role of the colonial state and police allows us to better understand the anxious relationship between the state and its organs vis-à-vis religious matters in today's nation-state. India's colonial experience, as well as the role of religious communities in public sphere, enables us with unique insights into the complex and conflictual interface of state, religion and law.

This essay examines the role of the colonial government in arbitrating religious conflicts in India – a field laden with sentiments and consequent vulnerability – as a way to advance its own goals and tenacities. This paper shows the ways in which the colonial state and its legal system, as represented on ground by the law enforcement agencies such as the police and the local administration, handled or managed disputes among the native Indian population. In doing so, it offers a glimpse of the character of the colonial police, and in general of the colonial state and its institutional organs. Presiding over religious or sectarian groups and their disputes by way of regulations and authority allowed the colonial state to better control crowds, play favourites, keep groups lined up to the establishments as the ultimate arbiter of justice, and keep a check on all forms of disorderliness – or so they claimed. This essay develops this argument by considering two major examples of such incidents that took place in the second half of the nineteenth century in Bombay and in the *qasbah* or small town of Amroha – the Bombay riots of 1874 between some Muslims and Parsis and a Shia-Sunni dispute that took place in Amroha in 1895. Whereas the first case was interreligious in nature, the second rather sectarian or intrareligious; and similarly, while the first example draws upon a bursting, cosmopolitan colonial metropolis, the other focuses on a small town in the western part of the United Provinces in north India. This paper, thereby, departs from the traditional narrative of riots or violence essentially interreligious in nature and between Hindus and Muslims as monolithic groups. It also brings forward two unique sites, often viewed in isolation, to understand the phenomenon of religious disputes – a *qasbah* town usually treated as the hinterland, and a large metropolitan city of global import.

Both cases further depart from the characteristic understanding of religious conflicts in India as between two religious groups and stereotypically between Hindus and Muslims, briefly discussed towards the end of the essay. Having these examples permit us to move away from the dominant narrative that essentializes conflicts as primarily Hindu-Muslim, majority-minority phenomenon. While there is no denying the fact that a majority of riots have taken place between Hindu and Muslim groups, quite a few of them have had more than religious angles.[2] A case in point is the Mapilla or Moplah riots of 1921 in the Malabar region that borne out of agrarian conflicts between tenants and landlords in which case the former happened to be Muslims and the latter Hindus. K. N. Panikkar's complex study has shown how in many villages, Mapilla Muslims protected their Hindu rebel leaders from Muslim mobs coming from outside. Panikkar argues that the Malabar incidents that occurred in 1921 were more in line with the larger agrarian conflicts of the nineteenth century.[3] Besides, moving beyond Hindu-Muslim conflicts deepens our understanding of law-religion and state-community relationships. The more the colonial state had the opportunity of engaging with various combinations of communities, the better positioned the state was to crack open the multiple fissures in society and strengthen its own position vis-à-vis the native population. A further departure from Hindu-Muslim conflict model includes the occurrence of riots in other contexts, such as the Ramnad riots of 1957 among political workers, between Dalits and upper castes in the Worli riots of 1974, Kannadigas and Tamils after Cauvery water dispute in 1991, and the Hindu-Sikh riots following the assassination of Indira Gandhi in 1984. Riots or conflicts based on religious symbols and disputes are but one among many.

Whereas religious groups have recurrently approached the state and its administrative and legal bodies to rationalize their acts and selves, laws taking recourse to referee religious anxieties has had a long history. The colonial Indian state is replete with instances of the intermix of seemingly incompatible elements of the religious and the secular, in this case, the religious sentiment and the legal system, admittedly one of modern state's key secular institutions. Under the British rule, government bodies effortlessly found openings for intermediation when it came to disputes and mayhem. They played a critical role in determining what was right or wrong and who could have the final word where laws and rulings, not scriptures, determined the course of religious destinies and identities. As David Gilmartin has aptly summed up that even though 'the law was but one element in the structure of imperial authority, it provided a critical arena for the enunciation of the principles defining the state's relationship to society.'[4] Understanding the intermediary nature and significant interventions of the state in handling the tumultuous relationship between religion and law, rendering them even more volatile, is a key aspect that this paper deliberates upon.

Of state's manifestations, the way the colonial police positioned itself was no less than what Bernard S. Cohn has referred to as the 'theatrical display' of power pertaining to the premodern states in Europe and elsewhere.[5] Turner's exaggerated postulation, cited at the beginning of the essay that there lacked a widespread police system and that the British were the ones introducing it was both ahistorical and self-congratulatory.[6] There is ample evidence of internal security agencies and the police system existing throughout ancient, medieval, and early modern India. For one, Kautilya's *Arthasastra* provides for various officials directly or indirectly responsible for maintaining peace and security as well as guarding or overseeing of towns and cities across the Mauryan Empire during 321–185 BCE.[7] Similarly, the extensive system of policing in the Mughal state involved multiple officials and networks of intelligence and security.[8] But the British police officers such as Turner aggrandized for themselves a larger role in the colonial Indian public life, far more than the actual scenario. The claim that the notion of public security was the domain of the colonial police further loses ground for the simple fact that it was the army that largely conducted public order policing in India, even after the 1860s. Faced with a local disturbance, the police that mostly depended on their relationship to the social organization of the neighbourhood, feared that they could be overwhelmed by the mob and frequently resorted to interventions by the armed forces. Interestingly, as Rajnarayan Chandavarkar has analysed, the supposed 'coercive disposition' of the police force was inextricably linked to the nature of its daily relations in the street and the neighbourhood.[9] There is no doubt that this particular factor made them unpredictable and prone to local dynamics and politics, often playing off one or the other community. This allowed for the local parties or communities involved to reach out to the police authorities and seek intercessions in their favour against their opponents, in an attempt to place themselves as a key player in the local as well as larger domain. This paper, in part, shows this susceptibility of the police system that often failed to play its supposed neutral role in a matter of crisis wherein its focus remained on securing its own steadiness. In dealing with labour crises in Bombay mills, for instance, the police would suppress by arresting millworkers in large numbers while enlisting some measure of public sympathy in the blessings of the mill owners.[10]

No doubt, the colonial police, army, and bureaucracy were the prime movers of the might of the British Raj in India. The colonial police, in particular, aided by the local administration and interest groups remained a steadfast agency to bolster the British control and domination over India. One arena of its manifestation was in the field of religious conflicts of different kinds where the police coupled with the legal administration were inordinately aggressive in their approach in framing people or groups of people, conducting investigations – sometimes protracted in nature – and adjudicating conflicts and disputes, in many cases unnecessary and unwarranted. The primary concern of policing was the maintenance of public order and, in order to serve that, the police often assumed an overtly military character.[11] As Rajnarayan Chadavarkar says, the police force in India had military origins. Instead of dealing with law-breaking and ensuring the security of property and the person, the police were liable to understand crime in terms of rebellion and disorder.[12] In general, the colonial police was coercive, hegemonic, and an expression of the very nature of the colonial rule in India that was 'characteristically autocratic and repressive'.[13] Its interventions thereby reflected, and justifiably so, the core interest of the metropolis that it served. David Arnold, in his study of Madras police, has shown that the Indian constabulary, subordinated by the British officers was a model of colonial subjection. The political legacy of the Raj included an aggressive, militarized police aimed at subordination and service to the state.[14] So why were native people reaching out to the police that represented vertical exertion of colonial power and control? As indicated above and elaborated in the following pages, the answer lies in considering the various actors – including the police – entangled in a theatrical display of power, attempting to bolster their own positionalities within the colonial society.

Inter-religious arbitrations: the Bombay riots of 1874

The British colonial laws served the twin purpose of supporting the expanding commercial enterprise of Britain in India as well as keeping control over the colonial subjects intact. The latter in fact was a necessary precondition of serving the former. Laws, legal systems – civil and criminal, and arbitration of different kinds both inside and outside of the formal juridical structure were all instrumental in tending to the imperial interests. Regarding arbitration, police and magisterial interventions played key roles. Whenever such interventions were limited, the state's concern to conserve police, and judicial agencies was determined by 'its own priorities of rule.'[15] By the first decades of the nineteenth century, arbitration had come to be viewed as a potentially efficient and effective remedy to the delays and expenses of civil litigation in England.[16] But another aspect of this approach was that litigants were rarely represented by legal counsel. The government's emphasis to go for arbitration, which comes in heavily in the Indian Statutory Commission report, implied a lack of legal representation for the subjects involved. In early colonial South Kanara, for instance, arbitration was the most prevalent method of settling disputes.[17] This system certainly empowered the law and the police while undercutting the due process of law when looked at from the perspectives of the parties involved.

One example of such interventions is the Bombay riots that occurred in February 1874. Giving it ample coverage, *The Times of India* reported the occurrence of the riots and the subsequent developments very closely. These riots occurred between Muslims of 'the lower order', as the report would have it, whose 'religious fanaticism' was told to be unparalleled in nature since 1851. The pretext of this explosion was the criticism of the prophet of Islam by a Parsi man of letters – an identical cause that had instigated riots in 1851. Mr Rostumjee Hormusjee Jalbhoy, a Parsi, published in Gujarati a book on the renowned prophets and nations, comprising the lives of Zoroaster, Moses, Jesus and Mohammad and a comparative account of the creation of the world and a history of Muslims, Christians, Parsis and Jews. The section on Prophet Mohammad was for a large part a translation of Washington Irving's *Life of the Founder of Islam* (1850). Some Muslims argued that a sentence that began with the assertion that 'Mahomet had a son Ebrahim by a kept woman' provided a mortal offence to the followers of the faith.

A group of Muslim leaders approached the government and sought an intervention from the police on grounds that this work was provocative enough to cause riots. The Commissioner of Police heeded to this request, termed by *The Times of India* reporter as 'unfortunate' and an 'unwise step', especially as Muharram, the 10-day period at the start of the Islamic calendar to commemorate the martyrdom of Imam Husain ibn Ali, was around the corner. The newspaper reporter further asserted that by indulging in an act of censorship, the authorities instinctively vilified the Parsis as if the latter had indulged in vituperation deliberately. With the police interfering in the issue, circulation of the book was stifled. Some Muslims held a large meeting in the Byculla area of south Bombay, an area inhabited by all, but with substantial Muslim population. It is important to know that Muslims constituted a significant part of Bombay's expansive commercial and mercantile community holding significant position and eminence whereas a majority of them also worked in the emergent industrial network, mostly in labouring positions. While the Muslims, in general, seemed satisfied with the preventive actions that the government had taken, many hoped for the suppression of animosities between the two religious communities. But the following Friday morning, a group gathered outside the Jama Masjid (mosque) and engaged in a damaging spree. This led to the arrival of the police on the site. Although the situation came under control, sporadic incidents took place through Saturday and Sunday morning, resulting into the death of a Muslim and a Parsi. Of course, it enraged both groups. The Parsi community was not going to lie low, in particular as this small religious minority held a key segment of Bombay's wealth and several of its members were at the forefront of its business networks. By late nineteenth century, they had entered into a symbiotic patron–client relationship with the British.[18] Subsequently, a Parsi deputation under the leadership of Sir Jamshetjee Jejeebhoy (1783–1859), a prominent Parsi merchant and philanthropist, met with the Commissioner of Police Mr F. H. Souter who regretted the mischief done to the 'loyal' Parsi community.[19] But Souter refused to entertain the Parsi suggestion of implementing the martial law which he argued was meant for graver circumstances and the current disturbance did not warrant it.

What is interesting about the entire episode is the solicitation of interventions by respective communities as players and stakeholders to justify their respective stances and the administration's own positioning of what it needed to do. The administration obviously tried to defuse the Muslim backlash, around the time of Muharram. But the matter did not stop there. In a letter written on February 15, the Governor of Bombay, Sir Phillip Wodehouse, wrote to Sir Jamshetjee Jejeebhoy with a certain twist: 'As I write the military assistance for which you asked is in the town of Bombay, and the Government will be prepared to take such further action as may be necessary.'[20] He added that the Muslims were silenced with the arrest of some rioters and hoped that the Parsi gentlemen would refrain from any retaliation. What seemed to have aggrieved the government was the cause of provocation in the first place, the incitement among the Muslims, but more than that the Parsi attitude. In a special telegram to *The Times of India*, the Home Government stated that what it 'strongly disapprove of, was the subsequent attitude they [the Parsis] assumed towards the officers of the Government itself, and we are exceedingly sorry that the actions of these officers was not more prompt and decisive than it was.'[21] Since both religious communities approached the administration in quick succession, the authorities tried to placate both, not restricting the Muslims with a heavy hand as the Parsis would have wished, while attempting to keep the Parsis content with measures that the government had undertaken – all at the same time, geared towards finding a safe and lasting, if not amicable, solution. The situation would have been a little different had it been the Muslim elite and not the 'lower classes' who were involved.

An Anglo-Gujarati newspaper *Rast Goftar* which was started in 1851 by Dadabhai Naoroji and Kharshedji Cama, two highly regarded Parsi intellectuals, to promote social reform among the Parsis, applauded the *Pucka Bandubast* ('firm measures') that the Bombay police had undertaken and how those obstructing peace in the city had been dealt with a heavy hand. As an advisory piece of literature, it made several strong suggestions to the members of the community in order to deal with such situations more sternly and effectively in the time to come. It suggested that the Parsis should work on preparing themselves with better self-defence mechanisms. This sentiment prevails in a series of requests that several Bombay residents made with regard to the police-led inquests and charges. One Byramjee Jejeebhoy (1822–90), a wealthy Parsi businessman and founder of several educational institutions, disapproved of the way the police had dispersed the crowd during the riots. He argued that with such a method, the crowd could have re-gathered and the police should have been more efficient if they had attacked the rabble-rousers. As the discussion goes in *Rast Goftar*, the charges of inquests and arrests glare through the cases. A Parsi juryman on an inquest held at Jamshetjee Hospital asked for him to be relieved early, as he feared an assault by the Muslims since there were reports of similar attacks on Muslims in Parsi quarters.[22]

Given the nature of conflicts, both the communities approached to win favours from the British, the authorities played it well, to their own advantages and whims. Leaders and organizations made such requests for British interventions not only by way of direct, formal petitions but also in the form of public demands voiced in organized meetings or print media. A series of letters to newspapers invoked the British sense of justice and fair-mindedness. While an anonymous writer who called herself/himself 'a lover of peace' sought strict actions against the perpetrators of violence, another one self-labelled as 'superior race,' openly flaunting their Parsi identity and self-assigned racial superiority, pledged by the community's loyalty to the British and its law-abiding nature. In the aftermath of the riots, the police arrested several Muslims a majority of whom faced flimsy charges of committing riots and robbery. Of this, those arrested solely for the incidents linked to the riots that occurred on Friday numbered 62. Two of these, Dya Bahai and Banhau Dya, were later identified as persons involved in the assault. Most of the detainees were not verified with any direct links to the fracas.[23] This undoubtedly shows the arbitrary nature of interference and accusations of individuals, perhaps originating from the British stereotypical understanding of the Indian communities.

Looking at the Benaras Hindu-Muslim riots of 1809, Gyanendra Pandey convincingly shows how the colonial discourse reconstructed these riots. To the colonialist mind, Muharram or Holi meant above all 'frenzy or excitement' and the outbreak of violence, thus crystallizing the official view that occasions like Muharram lay at the root of the problem and Muslims, in particular of the weaver (*julaha*) caste, as 'bigoted' and the 'principal instigators' of these riots and some of the major upheavals of the revolt of 1857.[24] The actions and arbitrations that we have noted above in the case of Bombay could have likely resulted from such an understanding. In his perceptive study of the revolt of 1857 *Asbab-e-Baghawat-e-Hind* ('The Causes of the Indian Revolt'), Sayyid Ahmad Khan (1817–1898), the renowned Muslim reformer, educationist, and founder of the Muhammadan Anglo-Oriental College in Aligarh, observed:

> There is not the smallest doubt that all men, whether ignorant or well-informed, whether high or low, felt a firm conviction that the English Government was bent on interfering with their religion, and with their old-established customs. They believed that the Government intended to force the Christian religion and foreign customs upon Hindu and Mussulman alike. This was the chief among the secondary causes of rebellion.[25]

Although this statement needs a deeper contextualization within the 1857 revolt, Sayyid Ahmad Khan's reference to the British government's growing interventions in matters of religion is noteworthy.

Intra-religious intercessions: qasbah Amroha in 1895

Another example of governmental interference is from the small town of Amroha. Amroha is one of the oldest and most celebrated qasbahs located around 90 miles east of Delhi. A qasbah was an entity in between and a town and a village in size, population, and resources that the empires used, the Mughals and the British included, as an outpost for the ease of revenue collection from villages. By the late nineteenth century, these qasbahs had evolved on their own to become social, cultural, and intellectual hubs with a significant number of Muslims in high offices who defined the character of the place with its distinctive Islamicate culture.[26] With a significant Shia population at the helm of education and land revenue administration, the Shia community's presence in defining the Muslim culture was and still is writ large in this qasbah town. The colonial intervention in Amroha is rather unique where the government sought to mediate an intra-religious dispute between the Shia and Sunni residents, as the representatives of the two communities approached the administration. The interesting part of this interference is a theological debate rather than an episode pertaining to incitement of violence. The nature of conflicts aside, it is worth noting that in both the cases of Bombay and Amroha, hurt religious feelings of respective communities became the cause of disagreement. More interestingly, the parties seeking governmental interventions desired censorship to be imposed – a ban on a literary piece in Bombay and on the usage of a phrase in the *azan* (call to prayer) said in an Amroha mosque – as provocative enough to generate conflicts and even riots.

Regardless of shared grounds, occasional social tensions and conflicts between the Shia and the Sunni Muslims in northern India were commonplace.[27] Disagreements on issues ranging from theological self-definitions to ritual practices have often taken on forms of vehement mobilizations to open conflicts and even violence. Such fights could be over matters concerning the first four caliphs of Islam, often termed by the Sunnis as *khulafa al-rashidun* ('the righteous caliphs') the first three of whom – Abu Bakr, Umar, and Usman – in the Shia view are considered as the 'usurpers' of the office which should have gone in the first place to the fourth caliph, Ali. Several conflicts have taken place around an official pronouncement or shouting as a way of disassociation with the first three caliphs in a public Shia ceremony called *tabarra*, a practice in contrast to the Sunnis reciting a praise of the caliphs and the companions of the Prophet, *madh-e-sahaba*. But before such skirmishes took a form of public denouncement of each other and eventually turned into violent clashes in places such as the 1908 riots in Lucknow, a prominent seat of power for the Shia dynasty of Awadh, a rift between the two groups in full public view had already started. One grim example of such disputes took place in Amroha in 1895. The issue involved concerned the Islamic call to prayers or azan. In the neighbourhoods of Shafaat Potah and Darbar Kalan, the azan said in the Shia mosques contained a particular phrase, in addition to the regular verses common in practice with the Sunnis. Towards the end of azan, it added a phrase *khilafat-un-bila fasl*, which roughly translates as 'without intervening or connecting link,' meant to undercut the ascendancy of the first three caliphs as legitimate occupants of the sacred office of the caliph. It professed the Shia belief that considered Ali as the legitimate successor of the prophet in an unbroken chain with the Prophet. The Shias assert that the Prophet made his preference for the succession of Ali clear on many occasions, but Abu Bakr and his two successors impeded it, until Ali emerged as the fourth caliph. Insertion of this phrase in azan had occurred in larger urban areas such as Allahabad and Lucknow as well in other places where the Sunni counterparts had even taken the matter to the court.

In qasbah Amroha, the Sunni residents complained in a petition to the local authorities that since the insertion of the phrase *khilafat-un-bila fasl* was unnecessary and incongruous with their own belief, the government should act and proscribe its usage. To them, saying it in the azan was a denial of the rights of the first three caliphs as legitimate successors of the Prophet. Although such phrases were used in private Shia supplications, including it in azan was viewed as an attempt to universalize Shia belief in the larger public sphere, which was not shared by the Sunnis. One could construe this phrase as a pronouncement that Ali, the fourth caliph to the Sunnis, had directly succeeded the prophet, an issue that is at the base of the Shia-Sunni schism. Acting on the Sunni petition, Magistrate Mr. Hardy and the commissioner barred the use of the phrase at the end of the azan to which the Shias of Amroha promptly objected. The remainder of the story is one of intense mobilizations on both the sides. Shias and Sunnis not only organized their respective support groups around the cause but also made every effort to impress the administration with the finality of their respective versions, as revealed in a wide range of archival materials.

Both the Shias and Sunnis were eager to dominate the public sphere. In Amroha, the Shias had a significant presence and dominance in the local landholding network. For Sunnis, the foundation and growing influence of Deoband madrasa and Ahl-e Sunnat wa Jamaat movement out of Bareilly was a call to assert the community's presence in the region of Rohilkhand where Amroha was located. No wonder, both sides witnessed tremendous mobilizations. The Shia residents of other qasbahs, towns, and states rose in support of those in Amroha and submitted numerous petitions to the higher government officials of the region. Shias from the qasbah Jalali, the princely state of Patiala in Punjab, and from various districts including Ballia, Chhapra, Saran, Arrah, Champaran, Atrauli, Shikohabad, Bulandshahr, Moradabad, Aligarh, and Allahabad cutting cross the entire north India submitted petitions and memoranda to different officials, seeking to overturn the ban. Whereas Shia petitions attempted to bring to the notice of the administration 'the high handedness and defiant attitude of the Sunnis', they also highlighted 'the submissive and law-abiding spirit' of the Shias of Amroha to win the government over to their side.[28] Although not at a comparable scale, support poured in for the Sunni standpoint on the issue from outside Amroha as well. The prominent Sunni movement Ahl-e-Sunnat wa Jamaat submitted a petition to the government in favour of the ban. Such counter-mobilizations further fuelled the crisis while driving the colonial authorities at the helm of affairs.

In the midst of respective community mobilizations, the government apparently avowed to remain neutral. But it finally settled the score in favour of the Shias. The pretext was to ensure that the grimness of the situation led to 'no violence.' That aside, the government had its own reasoning behind this decision. It was enraged that the Sunnis of Amroha had 'sent telegrams to the Sultan of Turkey' regarding the question and had thereby demonstrated 'disloyal' tendencies. The politicking surrounding the azan and the incident itself highlighted a belief that alienated the two sects, engrossing people not only within the qasbah but also outside of it and inviting government intervention in a matter of theological disputation. The entire episode suggests that the conflicting religious groups, by deploying clever means and arguments, negotiated with colonial authorities, that is, the police and the local administration, to secure favourable solutions and outcomes for themselves. The colonial government's supposed neutrality on a matter of religious apprehension always gave way to interventions that at the end of the day served none but British interests. Overall, the entanglement of interests representing different groups determined the outcome.

Hindu-Muslim conflicts and British interventions

Let us also consider conflicts between Hindus and Muslims, which have remained the mainstay of conflict studies in India, especially communal in nature. Reflecting the larger political and social trends of the nation, Hindu-Muslim hostilities were a part of life in qasbahs as well. Chaudhary Muhammad Ali (1882–1956) of qasbah Rudauli, a landlord, writer, intellectual, and a highly active member of the Progressive Writers' Association, fervently wrote in 1948 how the Hindu-Muslim tensions remained a part of life. His statement that 'a conflict over Baqr Eid is old news' is quite telling in this context.[29] The issue of cow slaughter was a major bone of contention between the two communities and *Baqr Eid*, or *Eid al-Adha*, as a festival that required Muslims to perform annual animal sacrifice was an occasion that regularly generated discord between Hindu and Muslim groups. The formation of separate communal identity among both Hindus and Muslims of qasbahs was quite entrenched and not always grounded in religious symbolism. It is interesting to note that qasbahs such as Badaun and Bijnor saw Hindu-Muslim rivalry for control over municipal boards,[30] and the Muslim demand for separate electorates, an issue of great dissonance between Hindu and Muslim leaders of late colonial India, was raised in places such as Rampur and adjoining qasbahs. Community interests here too attested to the needs of rallying behind colonial authorities and seeking support for their own respective causes as players in the fray. This allowed the government agencies to play an intermediary role and tend to their own needs and policies.

In his study on communal riots in Bengal, Suranjan Das writes about the British partiality for one religious group over the other. His analysis shows how the police kept mum when the lower-class Hindus suffered several attacks at the hands of the Muslim crowd in Kishoreganj. A section of contemporary opinion blamed 'the inertness of the local police' for the outbreak, thereby allowing the riots to unfold in the first place. A Hindu member of the Legislative Assembly alleged that the superior officers deliberately chose to ignore the warnings. Some Hindu newspapers contested that there was no reason why the police could not have controlled the riots spurred by a handful of mullahs. As if this was not enough, the government replaced G. S. Dutt, a Hindu, with Burrows, an Englishman as the District Magistrate. This administrative change led to the rumour that the new officer was there was to teach the Hindus a lesson for their anti-government acts and to fan Muslim communal interests.[31] Such administrative instances have continued to exist in post-colonial India and can be seen in what Paul R. Brass has termed as 'the dynamic process of riot production,' an analysis that focuses on how riots are produced rather than on why they happen.[32] Continuing his analyses, Brass further adds: 'riots persist because they are functionally useful to a wide variety of individuals, groups, parties, and the state authorities.'[33]

Regarding Hindu-Muslim tensions in Bombay, the Indian Statutory Commission, a commission that arrived in India from Britain in 1928 to study constitutional reform, conveyed that there was a need for the two communities to find a way out of hostilities. It also stated the government's neutrality and inability as well as how the adoption of a new policy provision would help it address some underlying causes. The Commission's report ran several iterations of the need that the two communities should themselves find a mutual way out and 'work earnestly towards creating a new atmosphere of trust and a better understanding between the Hindus and the Muhammadans [sic.].' It also mentioned the passing of the new section 295-A[34] of the Indian Penal Code that had 'greatly strengthened Government's hands and has had the effect of putting a stop for the time being to writings and speeches of a more scurrilous nature.'[35] The report went on to re-emphasize that the Governor in his address to the Bombay Legislative Council in August 1926 as well as in his tours had referred to the matter frequently and had appealed for 'mutual tolerance and a spirit of give and take'. What this give and take entailed is entirely unclear. The report also claimed that the 'government has all along adopted a neutral attitude in these disputes'. But Article 295-A was open to multiple interpretations and one wonders how a government could claim to have remained neutral while also harping on its role as the principal regulatory agency on these issues.

Additionally, the Indian Statutory Commission report added:

> While sympathizing with the natural desire of each party to perform their religious obligations without interference or annoyance, Government have, where the demand of religion come in conflict with civil rights, aimed primarily at upholding the common rights of the individual, compatibly with the maintenance of law and order.

This aligned very well with the government's desire to keep options open and arrive at any decisions as it would please, given its own interests and compulsions. The report also privileged the local police authorities who acted on behalf of the government. In most cases the authorities must have exercised discretionary powers but, as the report expanded, they had always striven to 'uphold the customary and common law rights, but when the preservation of law and order – which is their primary function – demands it, these rights are temporarily suspended by orders under the emergency powers.'[36] What it could further imply is that the local officers did work in tandem with the parties involved upon being approached but were no less prone to multiple influences and backgrounds.

Concluding remarks

Gyanendra Pandey charts out the role of the colonialist discourse in painting religious groups in a particular light with fundamental antagonisms such as those between 'Hindus' and 'Muslims' as some sort of monolithic categories.[37] The primary role, in his analyses, of the colonial construction of communalism was to essentialize violent outbreaks to specific religious groups or gatherings. He shows this by studying how the colonial officials viewed and characterized the Benaras riots of 1809 over the next one hundred years. In addition, the police maintained a list of 'bad characters' who were rounded up in times of disturbances.[38] While there was a need among the officials to pass the burden on to the natives for violent clashes and disturbances as they were trying to firm up their presence in the Indian subcontinent, the British presence was solidified by the end of the nineteenth century. As they had crushed the revolt of 1857 with a heavy hand, the British confidence had grown manifold, as witnessed in the examples discussed above. I would add that the colonial state could act on their impulses to further solidify their grip post-1857. In the larger schema of conflicted interests and contenders, they could play one native group against the other and could favour one or the other, depending on what suited their immediate, local, larger, short- or long-term needs.

What we have noticed in the cases of Bombay and Amroha is that the parties that were least irksome and exhibited greater faith in the colonial state without overtly challenging it – the Muslims in Bombay and the Shias in Amroha–finally had their way. The Muslims of Bombay and the Shias of Amroha successfully worked their way through the colonial law and order machinery to triumph over their respective rivals, namely the Parsis and the Sunnis. By deploying clever means and arguments, these groups negotiated with the colonial authority – the police and the local administration – to secure favourable outcomes for themselves. The colonial state, in turn, ruled in favour of a religious group only if such an action served its own purpose of consolidation of political power. Whereas the Bombay incident did not require mobilization from outside as the city itself was the hub for the influential Parsi community, the Amroha episode radiated out to other qasbahs, towns, and cities for the fact that the bone of contention was part of a larger theological debate and the small size of qasbahs allowed for inevitable cross-qasbah alliances and allegiances.

By considering the way law, rulings and the police operated in cases of religious disputes, this article expands on the idea that state mediation via local bodies pertaining to law and order was a prototype or a step short of law-making. As situations arose, the government meddled into the crises as well as determined and executed its newly minted policies and rulings. The broader contexts of the colonial law existed, but the local agencies could tweak them to suit their existing understanding and imminent needs. At a historical moment of relationships where things were centred around the dualities of the colonizer-colonized, individual-society, victim-offender and where the multiplicity of identities and the government's own needs and impulsiveness to win one over the other mattered, religion and religious practices became fertile grounds to operate on. With a firm understanding that certain issues were not bound to be solved through mutual negotiation, the colonial state emerged as an interceding agency – even in unwarranted areas – adjudicating cases and assuming greater powers over its subject population.

Notes

1. He further commented: 'Under the Mughal Emperors a semblance to a Police system existed only in the big towns – the rural population being left to look after themselves. Ordinary crime received practically no attention, and it would appear that Police activities were limited to intervening with Military force only on such occasions as widespread violence or actual rebellion.' *Typescript lectures on the police in India by E. E. Turner.*
2. Such an argument has been made by Gyanendra Pandey. See Pandey, *The Construction of Communalism.*
3. Panikkar, *Against Lord and State.*
4. Gilmartin, *Empire and Islam*, 13.
5. Cohn, *Colonialism and its Forms of Knowledge*, 3.
6. The statement itself underestimates the well-organized nature of the police system in India prior to 1860 such as under the Mughal Empire where perhaps, no city or town 'was without a *kotwal* [who] was responsible for the safety and protection of the people living in a city or town. He would hunt down thieves, punish criminals, imprison delinquents and keep a record of all people living in the various quarters of town (*muhalla*).' These were only a few of the many tasks that were bestowed on a *kotwal.* For details, see Hasan, *State and Locality in Mughal India*, 39.
7. Olivelle and McClish, *The Arthasastra.*
8. For a glimpse into the kind of network that engaged the Mughal *kotwal*, see Singha, *A Despotism of Law*, 6, 8.
9. Chandavarkar, *Imperial Power and Popular Politics*, 183.
10. Ibid., 164–8.
11. Gooptu, *The Politics of the Urban Poor*, 113.
12. Chandavarkar, *Imperial Power and Popular Politics*, 182.
13. Gooptu, *The Politics of the Urban Poor*, 180.
14. Arnold, *Police Power and Colonial Rule.*
15. Singha, *A Despotism of Law*, 125.
16. Jaffe, *The Ironies of Colonial Governance*, 189.
17. Bhat, *Judiciary and the Police*, 73.
18. Luhrmann, *The Good Parsi*, 88.

19. The term 'loyal' as applied to the Parsi community is to be noted. Since this event occurred in 1874 when Muslims continued to be seen by the British government as the instigators of the revolt of 1857. The Muslim social reformer Sayyid Ahmad Khan (1817–1898) through his writings and actions was active during this time to prove that Muslims too were loyal to the British and it was in the interests of the Muslims to ally with the British and adopt Western learning.
20. *The Bombay Riots of February 1874*, 11.
21. *The Times of India* (Bombay), July 28, 1874.
22. Ibid., 14–15, 18.
23. Ibid., 29.
24. Pandey, *The Construction of Communalism*, 32–7, 66–108.
25. Graham, *The Life and Work of Syed Ahmed Khan*, 39–40.
26. For a flavour of the wide-ranging intellectual contributions of qasbah Amroha and what set it apart from other places, see Rahman, *Locale, Everyday Islam, and Modernity*, 52–65.
27. For a detailed account on communal conflicts and religious disputations in Amroha between Shia and Sunni Muslims, see: Jones, 'The Local Experiences of Reformist Islam in a "Muslim" Town in Colonial India: The Case of Amroha', 896–905. Imtiaz Ahmad has noted widespread Shia-Sunni conflicts and tensions of varying intensity but confines them mainly to Bombay and Lucknow and further qualifies that Shia-Sunni riots were not longstanding in Lucknow and did not occur until 1908. See, Ahmad, "Perspectives on the Communal Problem," 144–9.
28. *Dispute between Shias and Sunnis of Amroha, Moradabad District.*
29. In a letter to his daughter Hima written in November 1948, Chaudhary Muhammad Ali mentions about a murder in the village of Jafar Mehdi on the occasion of Baqr Eid, Hindu outrage in Wazirganj over slaughter of goats, and Hindu insistence in Saiyidanpur that Muslims should not slaughter goats, leave aside cows. For details, see: Rudaulvi, *Goya Dabistan Khul Gaya*, 83–4.
30. Robinson, *Separatism among Indian Muslims*, 82.
31. Das, *Communal Riots in Bengal*, 126–7.
32. Brass, *The Production of Hindu-Muslim Violence*, 16.
33. Ibid., 34.
34. Article 295A of the Indian Penal Code contains the following: 'Deliberate and malicious acts, intended to outrage religious feelings or any class by insulting its religion or religious beliefs. – Whoever, with deliberate and malicious intention of outraging the religious feelings of any class of citizens of India, by words, either spoken or written, or by signs or by visible representations or otherwise, insults or attempts to insult the religion or the religious beliefs of that class, shall be punished with imprisonment of either description for a term which may extend to three years, or with fine, or with both.'
35. *Indian Statutory Commission*, 13.
36. Ibid., 14.
37. Pandey, *The Construction of Communalism*, 23–6.
38. Chandavarkar, *Imperial Power and Popular Politics*, 162.

Disclosure statement

No potential conflict of interest was reported by the author.

Bibliography

Ahmad, I. "Perspectives on the Communal Problem." In *Communal Riots in Post-Independence India*, edited by A. A. Engineer, 130–155. Hyderabad: Sangam Books, 1984.

Arnold, D. *Police Power and Colonial Rule, 1859-1947.* Delhi: Oxford University Press, 1986.

Bhat, N. S. *Judiciary and the Police and Early Colonial South Kanara.* New Delhi: Mittal Publication, 2001.

Brass, P. R. *The Production of Hindu-Muslim Violence in Contemporary India.* Seattle and London: University of Washington Press, 2003.

Chandavarkar, R. *Imperial Power and Popular Politics: Class, Resistance and the State in India, C. 1850-1950.* Cambridge: Cambridge University Press, 1998.

Cohn, B. S. *Colonialism and Its Forms of Knowledge: The British in India.* Princeton, NJ: Princeton University Press, 1996.

Das, S. *Communal Riots in Bengal, 1905-194.* Delhi: Oxford University Press, 1991.

Dispute between Shias and Sunnis of Amroha, Moradabad District, File no. 106C, General Administration Department. Lucknow: Uttar Pradesh State Archives, 1896.

Gilmartin, D. *Empire and Islam: Punjab and the Making of Pakistan.* Berkeley and Los Angeles: University of California Press, 1988.

Gooptu, N. *The Politics of the Urban Poor in Early Twentieth-Century India*. Cambridge: Cambridge University Press, 2004.

Graham, G. F. I. *The Life and Work of Syed Ahmed Khan*. Delhi: Idarah-I Adabiyat-I Delli, 1974.

Hasan, F. *State and Locality in Mughal India: Power Relations in Western India, C. 1572-1730*. Cambridge: Cambridge University Press, 2004.

Indian Statutory Commission: Hindu-Muslim Relation, File No. 143-K (b), Home Department, Special Branch. Mumbai: Maharashtra State Archives, 1928.

Jaffe, J. *The Ironies of Colonial Governance: Law, Custom, and Justice in Colonial India*. Cambridge: Cambridge University Press, 2015.

Jones, J. "The Local Experiences of Reformist Islam in a 'Muslim' Town in Colonial India: The Case of Amroha." *Modern Asian Studies* 43, no. 4 (2009): 871–908. doi:10.1017/S0026749X08003582.

Luhrmann, T. M. *The Good Parsi: The Fate of a Colonial Elite in a Postcolonial Society*. Cambridge, MA: Harvard University Press, 1996.

Olivelle, P., and M. McClish. *The Arthasastra: Selections from the Classic Indian Work on Statecraft*. Translated and edited by Patrick Olivelle and Mark McClish. Indianapolis: Hackett Publishing Company, 2012.

Pandey, G. *The Construction of Communalism in Colonial North India*. Delhi: Oxford University Press, 1990.

Panikkar, K. N. *Against Lord and State: Religion and Peasant Uprisings in Malabar, 1836-1921*. Delhi and New York: Oxford University Press, 1989.

Rahman, M. R. *Locale, Everyday Islam, and Modernity: Qasbah Towns and Muslim Life in Colonial India*. New Delhi: Oxford University Press, 2015.

Robinson, F. *Separatism among Indian Muslims: The Politics of the United Provinces' Muslims, 1860-1923*. Cambridge: Cambridge University Press, 1974.

Rudaulvi, C. M. A. *Goya Dabistan Khul Gaya*. Lahore: Punjab Academy, 1956.

Singha, R. *A Despotism of Law: Crime and Justice in Early Colonial India*. Delhi: Oxford University Press, 1998.

The Bombay Riots of February 1874: Reprinted from the Times of India. Bombay: The Times of India Printing Works, n.d.

The Times of India. Bombay.

Typescript lectures on the police in India by E. E. Turner, Inspector-General of Police in Bombay: The Organization and Work of the Police in India. Oxford: Bodleian Library, 1935.

The mosque as juristic person: law, public order and inter-religious disputes in India

Tanweer Fazal

ABSTRACT

The dispute between Muslims and Sikhs over the Shahidganj mosque in Lahore in the early 1930s served as the prelude to the Punjabi Muslims' decisive shift in favour of the Pakistan movement. The competing political campaigns, religious polarization and intermittent spells of violence that it triggered has attracted the attention of historians interested in the development of communitarian mass politics and partition. However, the dispute also played out in the colonial courts and became the site on which some of the knottiest questions of colonial jurisprudence were debated. The present essay looks at this ignored aspect of the Shahidganj conflict. Could the mosque, like a Hindu deity, be designated a juristic person? What laws would apply in an inter-religious dispute of this nature? And whether in such matters, the state law enjoyed preeminence over religious laws. Despite the unanimity over the building's antecedents as a mosque, the courts – all the way from the Sikh tribunal, to the High Court to the Privy Council – ruled in favour of the Sikhs. The essay seeks to understand how these competing claims were adjudicated and what were the imperatives of the colonial government that resulted in such a judicial outcome. It then proceeds to examine the Ram Janmabhoomi-Babri Masjid case in order to understand the continuities as well as departures in the exigencies of the post-colonial state, and the resolutions it offered thereof in such disputes.

In the early 1930s, in undivided Punjab, the dispute between Muslims and Sikhs over the ownership of, and access to the Shahidganj mosque, occasioned competing political campaigns, religious polarization and intermittent spells of violence. The dispute threatened to further embitter the Sikh-Muslim inter-communal relations, that were already very perilous. Certainly, the conflict set the context for the re-ordering of politics in the 1930s Punjab prompting the rise of communitarian mass politics amongst both Sikhs and Muslims. For instance, it has been argued that the campaign around Shahidganj mosque helped the Muslim League to gain a foothold in provincial politics. A parallel process among the Sikhs leading to the consolidation of Akali politics, could be discerned. The Shahidganj dispute put the non-denominational and pro-Zamindar Unionists to test, paving the way for their eventual decline.

Historical accounts of the Shahidganj crisis have typically focused on the politics surrounding it: the deployment and manipulation of religious symbols, the role of Akalis, the Muslim League and other communitarian organisations, and its implications for the course of politics in the province. M. Khurshid and M.A. Malik document the turn of events and map the role of the Unionists and different Muslim organisations.[1] David Gilmartin's essay studies the different modes of mobilization of Muslims, each articulating the idea of an Islamic community, and a concomitant conception of politics. The incident thus served as a prelude to the Punjabi Muslims shift in favour of Pakistan movement.[2] Sana Haroon gives us an insight into the different 'real and prospective' custodial interests in the Shahidganj site: the Sikh mahant Jiwan Das, the SGPC that wrested control over it, the Anjuman-Islamia whose claim got spurned, and the organization of 'collective communal interest' in the site.[3]

Despite its evident centrality in the political imaginary of colonial Punjab, the legal dispute and the events surrounding it – ranging from the case in the district court, adjudication in the Sikh tribunal, the contestation in the Lahore High Court and the final verdict in the privy council – have received only scarce attention in modern Indian history. In particular, the adjudication and the long legal battle that involved some profound and foundational questions of modern jurisprudence, including the pre-eminence of colonial law over the divinely ordained, whether a religious deity or an institution could be juridical person (represented by the next friend), or the subject of adverse possession or limitation – has not prompted sufficient scrutiny by legal historians.

In recent years, though, a renewed interest in the dispute and the arbitration can be noticed amongst those seeking to draw parallels with the Ramjanambhumi-Babri Masjid property dispute.[4] In many ways, the origins and historical trajectory of the two conflicts seemed drawn on quite similar lines. In both cases, local conflict acquired supra-local proportions, with both the public and the legal arena drawn in, and its outcome, it may be argued, served to redefine not only the past, but the future course of political history. As was Babri razed in 1992, the Sikhs had demolished the mosque in Lahore in the year 1935. There are, however some critical points of departure that ought not to be missed. First, the fact that the mosque at Shahidganj, the plug of Muslim grievance, was demolished by the Sikhs only *after* having won the legal battle over possession warrants attention. Second, the demolition was not a brute demonstration of majoritarian aggression, but in fact, in contrast to it, it were the minority Sikhs who finally had the upper hand through a sustained legal defence.

The dispute and its contours

The mosque stood in the Shahidganj Gurudwara complex located in the Landa Bazar area of Lahore city. It was widely believed and also adhered to by the parties in conflict that the mosque was built by the Mughal governor of Punjab during the reign of emperor Shahjahan some 250 years ago. The entire complex was spread over a vast area, where over the years, especially during the Sikh reign in Punjab, a gurudwara came to be constructed. According to the Sikh claim, it commemorated the memory of several of their co-religionists who were martyred by the 'tyrannous' Mughal governor. As Punjab came under British rule in 1849, Nur Mohammad, a descendant of the *mutawali* sought possession of the Mosque but failed to convince the Court. In 1925, the Sikh Gurudwara Act was promulgated and Shahidganj came to be listed amongst the Gurudwaras to be governed by the Act. This prompted a renewed fervour among the Muslims of Lahore, and Anjuman Islamia, claiming to be representing the opinion of all believing Muslims petitioned the Sikh Gurudwara Tribunal. The tribunal decided in favour of the Sikhs on grounds that the mosque had since long ceased to be a place of worship for the Muslims. All property attached to the Shahidganj complex, including the mosque, was transferred to the newly formed Sikh Gurudwara Prabhandhak Committee (SGPC) of Lahore. Having secured its possession, the SGPC soon undertook to renovate the complex, and demolish all 'non-Sikh structures', including the mosque.

The demolition of the mosque in June 1935, undertaken after the verdict favouring the Sikh case, drew angry protests from Muslim religious and political groups. Very frequently, such protests turned into riots, police firings and arrests. Legal appeal challenging the decisions of the Tribunal and the district judge appeared the only course left open to the agitators. In this essay, I explore the ways in which the high Court verdict on Shahidganj affair sought to address some seemingly complex and conflicting concerns. At the level of ideas, the conflict centred on sources of law, the ascendancy of the modern jurisprudence over the divine, whether the religious code will prevail when the plaintiffs and the defendants belong to different religions, the question of religious endowments and ownership of donated property, its custody and alienation, but above all, the supremacy of the colonial state and its authority.

The Shahidganj dispute in the high court

The suit challenging the decision of the Sikh Tribunal was dismissed by the district court in 1936, and subsequently, an appeal was made in the High Court of Lahore. The plaint did not make claim for either the possession of the property or the eviction of the Sikhs – nor did it seek that the mosque be handed over to the hereditary *mutawali*. In the main it sought a declaration that the building was a mosque in which all followers of Islam had a right to worship.[5] In addition, it asked for a mandatory injunction to reconstruct the building. It was argued, on behalf of the plaintiffs, that the defendants had no right to use the Mosque for purposes, which according to Mohammedan Law, was opposed to the purposes of a mosque.

Interestingly, while the petitioners were a motley mix of men, women and children claiming right to use the Mosque, a wakf property, dedicated to God,[6] plaintiff number 1 was the Mosque itself, which immediately prompted a series of question, the most central being whether the Mosque could be a juristic person represented by the next friend. Inhering in this key question were a number of claims. First, the mosque owing to its sacredness had a perpetual existence; second, the property in a mosque belonged to God alone and nothing ('except, perhaps an Act of the Legislature') could deprive God of his property; following from this, the mosque could not be conceived of as an ordinary piece of immoveable property on which the Limitation Act would apply. The burden of the appellants' argument was thus to demonstrate that the mosque being a juristic person with sacredness as its defining feature could not attract secular state laws – such as the law of limitation – and instead ought to be administered by Mohammedan law that governed Wakf. Moreover, even if the Limitation Act was held to be applied, a new period of limitation began with the demolition of the mosque, because 'when the property is dedicated to sacred uses, it is the duty of the owner, to maintain the sacred character of the land or the building so dedicated'.[7]

In the High Court, there was unanimity between all sides on the history of the building of the mosque and its subsequent takeover by the Sikhs. The majority decision – led by Chief Justice Young and seconded by Justice Khede – however, dismissed the plea. It is worth reading the grounds on which the Muslim case found little support in the High Court. More significant, in our opinion is the differing opinion of Justice Din Mohammad who relied upon the same foundational principles and procedures of British jurisprudence to find merit in the suit. What could be the reasons within and outside the court that finally prevailed and justified the adverse possession and demolition of the mosque? Since the two differing opinions operated within the same codes and techniques of adjudication, are we to conclude that modern legal rationality is limited by the subject location of those delivering justice? And finally, what insight does the case offer us into colonial statecraft and its rationalizing principles?

The mosque as a juristic person

Drawing upon case law on Hindu deities, the Muslim plaintiffs asserted that since the Mosque itself was dedicated to God and maintained its sacred character in perpetuity, it could not be owned nor could its ownership be transferred to any mortal being. Consequently, it could not be subjected to adverse possession.

The respondents in the suit, the SGPC and other, conceded the status of juristic person to the mosque, but this concession, quite ingeniously was granted to 'mosque as an institution', and not to any building 'consisting of stones, bricks and mortars'. SGPC too marshalled case law in support of its position. In the first case, *Shankar Das v. Said Ahmad (1884) 153 PR 1884*, the caretaker of a mosque, on behalf of and for the benefit of the mosque, purchased a house adjoining the mosque. A Hindu man, Shankar Das, whose house adjoined the purchased house, filed a suit of pre-emption arguing that the neither the mosque nor its guardian had any right on the ground of the said mosque's vicinage as it was the property of the deity and not of any earthly owner. The Judges decreed that though 'theoretically wakf property belongs to no human owner, nevertheless mosque was an institution, and its possession is maintained by its lawful guardian.' In the judges' opinion, a mosque was 'as much an estate as a house owned by a private owner'.[8] In another case, *Jindu Ram v. Hussain AIR (1914) Lah 444*, it was held that the mosque – in contrast to a *dharamshala* or temple – was not a juristic person, could not hold property, and therefore, the *mutawali* had no right of pre-emption.

Both the cases mentioned above lent support to the respondents' case that the mosque was 'immovable property' and could not escape the provisions of limitation. The majority opinion tended to concur with the respondents and insisted on maintaining a distinction between mosque as an institution and as a mere building. For Chief Justice Young, the analogy with the Hindu deities appeared to be contrived: a 'mosque is the house of the God, but is not the deity'.[9] Regardless that it belonged to God, the mosque had all the attributes of any temporal property; it could be owned by 'the institution (juristic person) or by anyone else who may acquire adverse possession over it', he stressed. Mindful that such a separation could potentially strengthen the Muslim case too for it could be argued that what was possessed by the Sikhs was only the building and not the juristic person as a sacred entity – the learned Judge clarified, albeit incongruously:

> A "juristic person" cannot exist apart from property or right. All property in the mosque and all rights having been lost to the Muslims and to the juristic person 12 years' adverse possession, the juristic person – a legal fiction – ceases also to exist. It owns nothing and represents nothing.[10]

The Muslim claim in the High Court went beyond the question of ownership of the mosque, and centred instead on its maintenance and use. It drew strength from an earlier adjudication, *Balabh Das v. Nur Mohammad* (AIR 1936 PC 83), which held – invoking the principle of 'extra-commercium' i.e., the sacred character of such land is not lost even after the property is sold out – that it was the obligation of the new proprietors, whether atheists or infidels, to maintain its sacred character. Judge Young, however, remained unimpressed. The principle of extra commercium could be applied only if the dispute involved only Muslims, and not 'Muslims and third parties'.[11] Justice Bhide, who concurred with fellow judge Young, further clarified that 'extra-commercium' as a feature of Wakf property was not typical to Mohammedan law, but remained unaltered even under Hindu law'. However, when it came to the title of 'dedicated property', it rested not on Mohammedan or Hindu law but on law of limitation as it prevailed in British India.[12]

The High Court had to consider too the petitioner's claim that the razing of the mosque attracted criminal liability under section 297 IPC (destruction of sacred edifices with the purpose of offending religious sentiments).[13] In their defence, the Sikh parties refuted the Muslim claim that the building demolished had continued to be a mosque. They asserted that since 1762, when the Sikhs secured the possession of the building in question, Muslims had never been allowed to offer prayers. The structure itself was used partly as a residential quarter, and partly to store fodder. Rather than maintaining it as a mosque, one of the rooms was used for the recital of the Sikh religious scripture, Granth Sahib. And in accordance with the Limitation Act, the defendant's title had matured into full ownership long before the advent of British rule in Punjab. Therefore, the use of the building in violation of its original character constituted no wrong and accordingly no new cause of action arose even after the demolition of the building. They claimed that the suit was barred by the principle of *res judicata*, the provisions of Sikh Gurudwara Act and the decision of the Sikh Gurudwara Tribunal. In other words, what had been demolished was in law not a mosque at all.

In dismissing the criminal case on Sikhs for hurting Muslim sentiments through their act of demolition, Judge Young drew analogies and symbols that were typical of the communal politics of the time. A criminal liability for the demolition of the Mosque, would, according to the learned Judge, be tantamount to Hindus demanding that Muslim owners of cows maintain its sacredness forever and refrain from slaughtering it. He also sought to caution the Muslims that such a proposition could turn against them. It would become incumbent upon the Muslims to maintain the sacred character of temples wherever they had taken possession, demolished or erected mosques over them.[14]

There can be no distinction in law...between different forms of land dedicated to God, for instance, there is no distinction between a mosque and its site dedicated to God and land dedicated to God for the use of that mosque. The same would apply to Hindu temples and the land dedicated thereto.[15]

Eternal sacredness and continuous wrong: the minority view of justice Din

Differing with both the respondents' position and majority opinion, Justice Din Mohammad insisted that the issue of ownership in relation to the mosque was distinctive from ordinary cases. Even the two cases cited by the respondents, he observed, clearly acknowledged the mosque to be an institution and not simply any other immoveable property. In *Jindu Ram v. Hussain* for instance, the judges recognized the mosque as a juristic person, whose ownership was not held by any person. Thus, the caretaker 'was not the proprietor of the mosque in the same sense' in which he could be the owner of his own private dwelling. However, for the purpose of valid exercise of right of pre-emption, he alone was the 'sole guardian and manager' of the mosque.[16] He also held that in the case of dedicated property, particularly wakf, law recognized certain rights which did not dissolve with the 'extinguishment of the original owner's title', even when the legal titled had passed to an adverse possessor.[17] Thus, for instance, in *Ram Rao v. Rustum Khan* (1902) 26 Bom 198, the Courts restricted the new possessor of the Muslim graveyard, Ram Rao, from constructing a house over it. The judges held that the plaintiffs, whose relatives were buried in the graveyard retained the right to perform all worship and ceremonies in accordance with Islamic culture.[18]

Thus for him, it was not simply a matter of adverse possession of the Shahidganj mosque by the Sikhs beyond the period of Limitation. What needed to be determined was whether the acquisition of the mosque was a single act of wrong, or a series of wrongs committed by the respondents. The Muslim case was of course that the mosque never ceased being a mosque, and its possession and use – whether to store fodder, or to recite the Guru Granth Sahib – by the Sikhs violated its original object. This, and its ultimate demolition constituted egregious continuing wrongs inflicted upon them.

Justice Din Mohammed found merit in the appellants' case as he sought support from a series of judgments that involved dedicated properties such as a Muslim graveyard, a Hindu temple or a church. Citing cases from India as well as those from Britain, he observed that even an adverse possessor is bound 'by those obligations by which the property adversely possessed by him is bound'. For him, therefore, 'the rights of a mosque to be treated as such as well as the rights of the worshippers to use it as such are rights not only incidental, but, ... paramount to the estate'. Such rights continue to stick to the mosque even when it passes into the hands of a non-Muslim.'[19]

Justice Din Mohammad found that various judgments[20] gave strength to the appellants argument that the use of the mosque by the Sikhs in a manner 'inconsistent with its sacred character' was a 'continuing wrong'.[21]

> When the act of the defendant is a continuing injury, its continuance after the date of first action is a new cause of action for which a second action can be brought, and so from time to time until the injury is discontinued. An injury is said to be a continuing one so long as it is still in the course of being committed and is not wholly past. Thus the wrong of false imprisonment continues so long as the plaintiff is kept in confinement and a trespass continues so long as the defendant remains present upon the plaintiff's land.[22]

Justice Din Mohammad's conclusions stood remarkably at variance from the other two judges on the bench. The difference was profound and touched upon the fundamental principles and assumptions of British jurisprudence. Thus, in case of deciding the dispute over a mosque, the

Mohammedan law held pre-eminence, which was applicable even when one of the parties to the dispute was a non-Muslim. Adhering to the Mohammedan law therefore, a mosque was a place of Islamic worship and would remain so till eternity. In the legal parlance, the mosque was a juristic person and not an ordinary immovable property. It is placed extra commercium and thus not touched by the Limitation Act. The sacred character of the mosque is never lost by any act of desecration, he held. Thus, an adverse possessor of a religious institution continues to remain under 'heavy burden' of using it for the purpose for which it was built failing which any potential beneficiary could seek relief in a court of law. This was because, so long as the 'original shape and form' of the mosque remained intact, the trespass by a wrongdoer was a continuing injury. More emphatically, the judgment stressed that the 'quantity and quality of the rights of an adverse possessor could not exceed that of the original possessor'.

The dispute in the privy council: religion and the sovereign

The contrary view taken by Justice Din Mohammad had little effect on the outcome in the High Court. The case, *The Mosque, Masjid Shahidganj and others v. SGPC, Amritsar and another*, reached the Privy Council in 1938 on appeal from the High Court of Lahore. A five judge judicial committee of the Privy Council examined the appeal but offered no relief to the plaintiffs. However, some of the principles that the Privy Council invoked had a bearing on the colonial courts' approach towards questions of religion and its interface with the British law, in particular, some of the knottiest questions such as the sources of religious law, the parity between Hindu deities and the mosque as holders of immoveable, property, the essence of religion and its peripherals, the preeminence of the colonial law over the personal law of religious groups and so on.

The judicial committee of the Privy Council vetoed the lower court's decision to recognize the mosque as a juristic person that could hold property. It thus rejected the analogy between the 'individual deities of Hindu religion' that in jurisprudence were recognized as juristic person and the 'mosque as an institution'. The question whether a mosque would be accorded *locus standi in judicio* by a British Indian Court was a matter of procedure, and in the case of Hindu idols, the procedure took account of the 'polytheistic' features of Hindu religion and recognized certain doctrines of Hindu law as 'essential' to conclude that an idol could be the owner of property. The considerations mentioned above were specific to Hindu law and Hindu deities from which 'no general license could be derived for the invention of fictitious persons', it was concluded.[23]

The courts were not only defining what was sacred and what merely temporal – in doing so, they were also trying to determine what sort of laws were in operation in the dispute. While the colonial legal system recognized Hindu and Mohammedan personal laws in matters of succession, betrothal, wills, marriage, divorce, adoption, legacies, gifts or any other religious issues – the Shahidganj case was an intricate one. Though it involved two different faith communities, the religious structure in dispute was originally a mosque and was indisputably established and agreed upon. The Muslim case depended upon the applicability of the Mohammedan law regarding wakf property and its inalienability.

In the High Court, the minority view of Justice Din Mohammad had held that the authority of personal law was not obliterated when the parties in dispute belonged to two different faiths. The solution to this complexity was rather straightforward: 'Muslims when... they deal with the property of the Hindus', are faced with Hindu law. Similarly, when Hindus seek to acquire the property of the Muslims, they 'have to contend with the Mohammedan law'.[24] The majority view, as can be surmised that 'Mohammedan law' did not 'necessarily' govern even in cases in which 'Mohammedans alone were interested', leave aside cases where the conflicting parties belonged to two different religions. In holding this, the chief justice sought authority from section 5 of the Punjab Laws Act (1872), which allowed modifications in the personal laws of Mohammedans and Hindus through legislative enactments or customary practices. Furthermore, he also reminded the petitioners that the Limitation Act in India being equivalent to the Act of Parliament enjoyed authority over the Mohammedan law.

On the question of preeminence of state law over religious law, the Privy Council was even more unequivocal. The Council members expressed their dismay over the practice of relying on witnesses, usually a cleric, to interpret religious scriptures. It forcefully argued that the 'system of expert advisors (muftis, maulvis or in the case of Hindu law, pandits)' that was once in use, had long been abandoned.[25] Denying divine origins to the personal laws, the council stressed that Muslim or Hindu laws were 'legislative enactments' applied by the courts to 'certain classes of matters and certain classes of people'.[26] In a sense, they were part of the law of the land which the British Indian courts were expected to administer in terms of their own knowledge and competence.

As the Mohammedan law was essentially a British legislative enactment, its citation by the plaintiffs for the period preceding the English annexation of Punjab was oxymoronic, their lordships in the judicial committee felt. The onus was thus squarely on the appellants to establish whether the property in dispute was vested in the Sikh Gurudwara in accordance with the then prevailing law of the land. 'Who, immediately prior to the British annexation was the local sovereign of Lahore'? What law was applicable in that State? Who was recognized by the local sovereign...as the owner of the property now in dispute?',[27] were questions that were germane to the case but had not attended to by the appellants throughout the case history. Thus, history, documented as much as anecdotal and conjectural, was at play in the decision of the Privy Council.

> By a tradition which cannot be ignored (though their lordships are thankful to be free of any duty to investigate its truth) the land adjacent to the building was regarded by the Sikhs as a place of martyrs, it being commonly held among them that Bhai Taru Singh had on this spot suffered for his religion at the hands of Muslim rulers and that many others including women and children had been executed here...Its history after 1760 is summarised in the...language of Bhide J. that "it is scarcely likely that the Muhammadans would have been allowed to have access to the building for any purpose whatever during this period (1760 to 1853).[28]

In colonial jurisprudence, therefore, what emerged as sacrosanct were the procedures established by the British Courts and laws enacted by the legislature. No exemption could be sought on subjects covered under personal laws on the plea that they had their origins in the revelations, scriptures or tradition. As personal laws too were human enactments, they needed to conform to the authority of principles and procedures of the British Indian Courts. While procedures were critical and served to undermine the aura of divinity associated with religious laws, it was in their encounter with the general law of the land that their eminence came to be tested. Irrespective of the case citations and historical documents that the Muslims of Lahore marshalled in favour of their position, the colonial courts upheld the ascendancy of the Limitation Act of 1908, Punjab Laws Act (1872) or the Sikh Gurudwara Act (1925). In the final analysis, it was the sovereignty of the state and jurisprudence that was reinforced.

What is remarkable is the Court's caginess in according to the mosque a legal status similar to the Hindu deities. In fact in any dispute over the ownership of sacred property, Hinduism and other religious forms that observed deity worship had a distinct edge over others. Curiously, even when the lower courts were amenable to accepting the mosque as a juristic person, a careful distinction between person and institution was introduced to suggest how the mosque was also an immovable property and therefore bound by the limitation act. Similarly, despite sufficient case law (as highlighted by the plaintiffs and the minority verdict) regarding the sacredness of the mosque and the demolition being a continuous wrong, the majority opinion in the Lahore High Court was disinclined to offer any relief to the appellants. In what ways do we then read the approach of the colonial courts on Shahidganj controversy? Was it the independent moral authority of the courts, the logic of modern law (which placed itself above the religiously ordained legal systems), and the emphasis on the procedure that finally came to determine the outcome? Or was it the colonial statecraft – a combination of concerns regarding public order, a reward for the allegiance of Sikhs during 1857, a fear on the part of the colonial state that a decision in favour of Muslims would open up a Pandora's box of conflicts over the demolition and annexation of sacred sites in the medieval past.

Whether the legal domain is autonomous of the exigencies of the colonial bureaucracy and its political interests is a question that requires much deeper probing. Julia Stephens, in her essay on the promulgation of section 295 A which criminalized insults to religion, found that rather than a strict separation between sentiments/emotions and modern jurisprudence, an entanglement between the two could be noticed. Stephens argues that between the Court and the public arenas, there seemed to be continuity in this regard. The Court itself became a powerful space for making complex arguments about devotion and empathy, and the politics of the street fostered alliances in defence of injury and grief.[29] We can see a similar process at work here: the conflicts of the street, the rioting and the violence, the claims, entitlements and wrongs, all being transferred to the courtly arena. And how does the court respond? Analysing the Allahabad High Court verdict on cow slaughter, Mathew Groves argues that loyalty to the Crown could improve a community's chances of eliciting a favourable judgment. Thus, in *Queen Empress v. Imam Ali and others (1887)*, it was the British leaning towards the Muslims, a pay off for their loyalty, that resulted in the verdict rebuffing the arguments favouring cows as sacred to Hindus.[30]

Maintenance of public order does appear to be the determining factor in most such conflicts. In the Shahidganj dispute over the ownership of mosque too, colonial administrators and the courts seemed to have adopted the least precarious course–uphold the status quo. Indeed, a change of ownership after more than 150 years of its possession with the Sikhs could further complicate the law and order situation, an immediate worry for the administrators. This seemed to be the leitmotif of colonial governmentality, a key mechanism in the imperial conflict resolution. An unstated policy of 'no change' adopted whilst dealing with religious disputes of the natives helped the imperial courts and administrators to circumvent re-opening the wounds of the past, or triggering new resentments. The Chief Justice Young spelt it out so unequivocally:

> One thing is clear that if the general proposition was established–greatly to the detriment of the maintenance of law and order–that there could be no adverse possession of land dedicated to God and the Limitation Act did not apply, there is no mosque in this country built on the site of a Hindu temple which could not now be recovered by the Hindus.[31]

In a somewhat similar case in neighbouring Sindh, in the controversy regarding the ownership of the *Manzilgah mosque*, the British administrators as well as the Sindh provincial government relied on indecision, procrastination as well as incarceration to quell the Muslim outcry against government occupation of a mosque building and its premises. In this case though, while it was the government itself which was the occupant, it refused any quarter to the Muslim agitationists demanding a return of the mosque under pressure from the dominant Hindus of the town who threatened action if any concession was granted to the Muslims.[32] As yet another illustration, the dispute over the ownership of the Mahabodhi temple in Bodh Gaya is instructive. Though the temple was itself of old vintage, over time, the proprietorship as well as management of the temple, its premises, and the revered Bodhi tree had passed into the hands of the Shaivite mahants. The Mahabodhi Society comprising Buddhist activists staking a claim over its ownership and management, offered a challenge to the existing arrangement. Though the viceroy Lord Curzon and other British officials expressed their keenness to restore Buddhist ownership, it was the fear of public outcry, reaction of the Hindu press and adverse judgment from Calcutta High Court that aborted their plans. The status quo continued until a legislation by the Bihar government in 1949 made Buddhists the co-managers of the Mahabodhi temple.[33]

Non-interference and status quo – emerging from the fear of disturbing public order – appears to be the hallmark of imperial decision-making when faced with dispute between communities. This often led to indecision and inaction evident as it is in the two cases cited above – Masjid Manzilgah and Mahabodhi temple. Irrespective of the merits of the case, maintenance of status quo of more than 150 years, ultimately, appears to be the guiding spirit behind the judgments in the lower court, the high court as well as the Privy Council in the Shahidganj dispute. Despite avowed adherence to the established principles of modern legal rationality – precedence, equivalence, universality, and procedure – the courts and various arms of the state arrogated to themselves the task of dispute resolution, the exigencies of which in fact often forced them to depart from legal norms.

A postcolonial postscript

Did the post-colonial situation throw up similar exigencies? To certain extent, such an imperative continues to inform the decisions of the courts in post-colonial context too. A case in point is the Allahabad High Court's decision on the title case in the Ramjanambhumi-Babari Masjid dispute.

Mirroring the Shahidganj case, the Ayodhya dispute is not only long-drawn in history but is also principally a dispute over the reading of history itself. What is known as the Babari mosque is held to be built by Mir Baqi, Mughal emperor Babar's governor in the year 1528. The Hindu case has ranged between suits denying the existence of the mosque to those who argue that the mosque was built after the demolition of an ancient temple dating to Maharaja Vikramaditya's time. The site in dispute is claimed by the Hindus as the birthplace of Lord Rama. Since the middle of the nineteenth century, it was admitted that Hindus had been worshipping in a chabootara of 39.6 square yards. Earlier in 1855, following Hindu-Muslim violence in the town over possession and control of the premises, a bifurcation mutually arrived at divided the premises into two parts, outer and inner courtyards. The inner courtyard adjacent to the mosque was accessible to the Muslims, while the outer portion was left to the use of the Hindus. The dispute came into judicial notice in 1885 when Baba Raghubar Das of Nirmohi Akhara petitioned for permission to build a temple of Ram Lalla on the Chabootara. The court of the sub-judge refused to disturb the status quo on grounds that such permission would incite violence between communities. Appeals against this order in the courts of district judge and judicial commissioner too fell. The judgment of the judicial commissioner (1886) unequivocally stated that there was nothing on record that could prove the proprietorship of the plaintiff.

All through the colonial period, both the executive and the judiciary displayed remarkable unanimity in sticking to the principle of status quo when faced with intractable disputes between communities. However, chinks appeared in this consensus post-Independence. From the Mahabodhi case, Ian Copland concludes that the weak foundations of colonial authority prevented it from intervening effectively in such disputes[34]; in contrast, the legitimacy of popular government allowed the post-independence Indian state to enact legislation and effect alteration in the existing situation in favour of the Buddhists.

However, it could also be argued that the acquisition of popular legitimacy rendered the state and its functionaries even more vulnerable to the vicissitudes of everyday politics. Thus, soon after independence, on the night of 23 December 1949, a Hindu mob managed to enter the inner courtyard of the Babari mosque and install an idol of Ram Lalla right below the central dome. Since then, the inner premises of the mosque, so far under Muslim use, became inaccessible to them. The persistent Muslim demand for the removal of the idol was not heeded to by the local authorities who frequently took the plea that this would incite Hindu sentiments. A new status quo was congealed. It allowed rituals to continue with access provided to a limited number of Hindu priests. This status continued until 1986, when an order from the district judge of Faizabad, allowed the Babari Mosque to be opened to the general Hindus for *divya darshan*. The opening of the locks unleashed a series of events involving massive campaigns and counter mobilisations, culminating ultimately in the demolition of the mosque in December 1992.

Between 1949 to early 1990s, several suits pertaining to the title of the complex were filed by parties which were clubbed together and attended to by a three-judge bench of the Allahabad High Court in 2010. Broadly, the various defendants and the plaintiffs belonged to two religious groups, the Hindu and the Muslim. However, both sides were marked by internal fractiousness. There was no unanimity either over the historicity of the temple or the dispute, the existence of the mosque or the proprietorship of the temple. While defendant 1 and 2, Gopal Singh Visharad and Ramchandra Das argued that

Muslims were never in possession of the Ramjanambhumi and if ever they did so, it ceased since 1934. The Nirmohi Akhara and its Mahant, Raghubar Das (Defendants 3 and 4) denied that Babar had ever constructed a mosque in the place, denied the existence of the graveyard as well, and argued that what was demolished on 6 December 1992 was not the mosque but some small temples of the Akhara. Defendant number 13 and 14, Baba Abhiram Das and Pundrik Mishra (replaced by his chela, Dharam Das) held that the temple did not belong to any individual, math, sect, mahant or Akhara. Britishers reclaimed the entire land in the state after the British annexation of Awadh. Thus, rights of Muslims, if any, stood lost. The Hindus, by default, could not be held guilty of installing the deity as in any case, Mir Baqi built the mosque after demolishing the ancient temple of lord Rama built by Maharaja Vikramaditya. Defendant number 17, Ramesh Chandra Tripathy insisted that the idols were not placed by the mob, but existed from time immemorial. In fact, what was demolished in 1992 was not a legitimate mosque, as emperor Babar was an invader had not legal authority to construct a mosque. In suit no. 5, the plaintiff was Bhagwan Sri Ram Birajman represented by the next friend. It argued that since the place itself was worshipped as the birthplace of Lord Ram and the presiding deity was Lord Ram, both the deity and his birthplace were juristic persons. The petition denied the existence of any mosque as there was no minaret, nor a wazukhana (place for ablution). Further, after the riots of 1934, there was no record of any namaz being offered at the site, and the graves of Muslims that were present inside its precincts had been flattened long back.

Interestingly, in the Ayodhya case, it was the turn of the Muslims to invoke 'adverse possession' and '*res judicata*', so as to ensure their title. As per the Sunni Wakf Board, the mosque was built by Babar more than four centuries ago, and by virtue of their 'long, exclusive and continuous possession', the Muslims perfected their title by 'adverse possession'. The act of the installation of the deities within the inner premises of the mosque was an obstruction in the rights of Muslims to offer their prayers – a 'continuing injury'. The mosque, in accordance with the Islamic law, continued to exist even after its demolition, as the performance of namaz did not depend on the existence of concrete structures, the Board argued.

In the Ayodhya case, one could see a clear leaning of the state executives towards majority popular opinion. In the episode of the deity being installed under the central dome of the mosque, the district administration of Faizabad was far from neutral. The Allahabad High Court judgment took note of the partisan role-played by the then Deputy Commissioner, K. K. Nayyar in this regard. Similarly, in 1986 when the locks of the mosque were opened for the general public on the orders of the district judge, J. Khan in the High Court, noticed many anomalies in the procedure adopted by the then district judge. He also took exception to the fact that the district magistrate and the superintendent of police played a supportive role in ensuring that the appeal to open the locks succeeded.

Ultimately, the title suit came to be decided, less on the basis of evidence as much of the historical evidence marshalled was anecdotal and conjectural. Aware of the fact that the judgment itself was of historical importance whose repercussions could be far and wide, the judges looked for a solution that could assuage the feelings of all the parties in dispute. J. Khan's judgment, which became part of the majority judgment, upheld that the structure in dispute was primarily a mosque, and no temple was demolished to construct the mosque. However, it could have been built over the ruins of ancient temples. It was held by the Hindus that somewhere in the area – and not exactly where the mosque was built – was the birthplace of Lord Ram. It was only after the construction of the mosque that such a view gained currency. Ram chabootara and Sita's Rasoi, the two Hindu sacred sites within the premises were in existence prior to 1855; however, it was 'unique and absolutely unprecedented' that inside the compound of the mosque, Hindus were worshipping their deity and Muslims offering their namaz. As both the parties failed to prove the commencement of their title, 'by virtue of joint possession, they could be joint owners' without having any formal partition. Finally, the judicial order divided the premises into three equal parts among the three disputants – the Nirmohi Akhara, the deity Ram Birajman and the Sunni Wakf Board. Aware of the complexities involved, J. Khan, in his ruling, decreed that place under the central dome be retained with the deity, and the chabootara and Sita's rasoi with the Nirmohi Akhara. Was this a just resolution or an unequal compromise?[35]

It is important to note that the colonial state, deficient of popular sovereignty, took refuge in principles of non-interference, preferring the maintenance of status quo when faced with disputes of such nature. This dimension of colonial technique of governance informed and guided the actions of both, the executive and the legislature. Consensus over adherence to this principle and practice seems to fall apart in the post-colonial times as state officials pandered or succumbed to majority opinions. It is the courts then that are tasked upon to offer a dispute mitigation mechanism. And in assuming the role of the arbiter in such disputes, the courts, like their colonial predecessors, hold out the path of least possible conflict as the resolution. The principles cardinal to modern jurisprudence–evidence, procedure, precedence–are often overlooked.

Notes

1. Khurshid and Malik, "Shahidganj Mosque Issue and the Muslim Response."
2. Gilmartin, "The Shahidganj Mosque Incident."
3. Haroon, "Custodianship of Shahidganj in Colonial Lahore."
4. Mukul, "Lessons for Ayodhya from Lahore Gurudwara"; Chhibber, "1940 Verdict in Lahore Gurdwara Case"; and Sachar, 'The Impending Ayodhya Verdict."
5. *Masjid Shahidganj Mosque vs Shiromani Gurdwara Parbandhak* (1940) 42 BOMLR 1100 para 6.
6. Anjuman-i-Islamia had stopped pursuing the case after the defeat in the Tribunal.
7. *Mosque Known as Masjid Shahidganj v. Shromani Gurdwara Prabandhak Committee* (Lahore) 1938 AIR (Lah) 369, para 4.
8. Ibid., para 136.
9. 1938 AIR (Lah) para 11. Ritu Birla has shown how in the run up to the passage of the Hindu Endowment Act of 1890, a series of judgments established the deity as a legal subject capable of holding property, filing suits, and being sued. This reflected not necessarily the precise ritual convention but indeed the 'transformation of the Hindu endowment into a form of contractual private property'. Birla, *Stages of Capital*, 80–86.
10. 1938 AIR (Lah).
11. Ibid., para 12.
12. Ibid., para 27.
13. Ibid., para 13.
14. Ibid.
15. Ibid.
16. Ibid., para 137.
17. Ibid., para 106.
18. Ibid., para 99.
19. Ibid., para 12.
20. Among others, the judge referred to *Muhammad Ahmad v. Muhammad Fazul AIR (1917) Lah 160, Sarat Chandra v. Nerode Chandra, AIR 1935 Calcutta 405* and *Hukum Chand v. Maharaj Bahadur Singh AIR (1933) PC 193.* In *Muhammad Ahmad v. Muhammad Fazul*, the dispute was regarding a mosque in which the defendants were residing with their families. The plaintiffs challenged the defendants right to reside within the mosque premises and sought perpetual injunction restraining the defendants from living there. The lower court dismissed the suit on the ground that the defendants continuous staying within the premises for more than 6 years was protected by limitation. The division bench of the Punjab chief Court however overruled the lower court arguing that the occupation by the defendants of the mosque premises for the purpose of residence was an 'act of desecration' of a place of worship which amounted to a 'continuing wrong'. And going by section 28 of the Limitation Act, 'a fresh period of Limitation' began to run in favour of the plaintiffs 'at every moment of the time" during which the defendants occupation of the mosque premises continued. The judges clarified that the occupation of the premises was an actionable wrong which could be objected to by any person who had the right to use the mosque as a place of worship. Ibid., para 110.
21. Ibid., para 111.
22. Ibid., para 113.
23. Masjid Shahid Ganj vs Shiromani Gurdwara Parbandhak (1940) 42 BOMLR 1100, para 14.
24. J. Din Mohammed, 1938, AIR (Lah) 369, para 69.
25. 42 BOMLR 1100, para 9.
26. Ibid., para 9.

27. Ibid., para 10.
28. Ibid., para 3.
29. Stephens, "The Politics of Muslim Rage."
30. In 1887, a five-judge bench refused to penalize Imam Ali and his brother for slaughtering a cow, and thus hurting the religious feeling of the Hindus under section s. 295 of IPC. The judges ruled that the cow was not a religious object whose protection s. 295 afforded. It went on to conclude that cow worship was not an essential part of Hindu religion. Groves, 'Law, Religion and Public Order in Colonial India: Contextualising the 1887 Allahabad High Court Case on "Sacred" Cows'.
31. 1938 AIR (Lah) 369, para 13.
32. Masjid Manzilgah was the name popularly given to a complex of buildings on the banks of the Indus at Sukkur', Sindh. It consisted of a serai (inn) and a mosque believed to be built by the Governor of Sind during Akbar's reign. The buildings were taken over by the British at the time of the conquest during the middle of the nineteenth century and used as a residence by its military and political officers. Since the year 1920, Muslims of Sukkur had been demanding the return of the buildings to the community which in the 1930s was taken up by the Sindh Muslim League. On the part of the British authorities and the provincial government, the reason for their reluctance in acceding to the demand was a powerful Hindu opposition that was against any concession to the Muslims of Sukkur. See Khuhro, "Masjid Manzilgah, 1939–40."
33. Copland, "Managing Religion in British India."
34. Ibid.
35. Social science reflections on Ayodhya judgment appear torn between broadly two approaches: one saw it as an instance of inter-faith mutuality and negotiated peace and the other, deplored the trumping of secularism and imposition of majoritarianism. For the first approach see Nandy, "The Judges Have Been Injudicious Enough to Create a Space"; Mani, "Where Angels Fear to Tread". For the second, see Menon, "Ayodhya Judgment'; Gupta, "Dissecting the Ayodhya Judgment"; and Teltumbde, "Whither the faith of Indians." Interestingly, even those who agreed with the settlement recognized that the judgment did not meet the high standards of modern jurisprudence. For instance, Lata Mani writes: 'Was the judgment fair? If one thinks of history and law as the primary means of just recompense it was clearly not ... If however one asks whether it may facilitate peace understood as negotiated compromise..things look more hopeful and less bleak'. Mani, "Where Angels Fear to Tread," 12.

Disclosure statement

No potential conflict of interest was reported by the author.

Bibliography

Birla, R. *Stages of Capital: Law, Culture, and Market Governance in Late Colonial India*. Durham and London: Duke University Press, 2009.

Chhibber, M. 2010. "1940 Verdict in Lahore Gurdwara Case May Play Key Role in Deciding Ayodhya Dispute." *Indian Express*, October 2.

Copland, I. "Managing Religion in British India: The British Raj and the Bodh Gaya Temple Dispute." *Journal of Church and State* 46, no. 3 (Summer 2004): 527–559. doi:10.1093/jcs/46.3.527.

Gilmartin, D. "The Shahidganj Mosque Incident: A Prelude to Pakistan." In *Islam, Politics and Social Movements*, edited by E. Burke and I. M. Lapidus. London: I. B Tauris, 1988: 146–168.

Groves, M. "Law, Religion and Public Order in Colonial India: Contextualising the 1887 Allahabad High Court Case on 'Sacred' Cows." *South Asia: Journal of South Asian Studies* 33, no. 1 (2010): 87–121. doi:10.1080/00856401003592495.

Gupta, A. "Dissecting the Ayodhya Judgment." *Economic & Political Weekly* 45, no. 11 (December 2010).

Haroon, S. "Custodianship of Shahidganj in Colonial Lahore: Land, Land Use and the Formation of Religious Community, 1850–1936." *Indian Economic and Social History Review* 54, no. 2 (2017): 183–220. doi:10.1177/0019464617695678.

Khuhro, H. "Masjid Manzilgah, 1939-40: Test Case for Hindu-Muslim Relations in Sind." *Modern Asian Studies* 32, no. 1 (February 1998): 49–89. doi:10.1017/S0026749X98002613.

Khurshid, M., and M. A. Malik. "Shahidganj Mosque Issue and the Muslim Response: 1935-36." *Pakistan Vision* 12, no. 1 (2011): 125–142.

Mani, L. "Where Angels Fear to Tread: The Ayodhya Verdict." *Economic and Political Weekly* 45, no. 42 (October 16–22, 2010): 10–12.

Menon, N. "Ayodhya Judgment: What Next?" *Economic and Political weekly* 46, no. 31 (July 30, 2011): 81–89.

Mukul, A. 2003. "Lessons for Ayodhya from Lahaore Gurudwara." *Times of India*, April 4.

Nandy, A. 2010. "The Judges Have Been Injudicious Enough to Create a Space for Compassion and Human Sentiments." *Tehelka*, November 6.

Sachar, R. "The Impending Ayodhya Verdict." *Mainstream* XLVIII, no. 40 (September 25, 2010). http://www.mainstreamweekly.net/article2343.html. (accessed July 15, 2017).

Stephens, J. "The Politics of Muslim Rage: Secular Law and Religious Sentiment in Late Colonial India." *History Workshop Journal* 77, (Spring 2014): 45–64. doi:10.1093/hwj/dbt032.

Teltumbde, A. "Whither the Faith of Indians, Your Lordships?" *Economic and Political Weekly* 46, no. 46 (November 13, 2010): 12–13.

Cases

Masjid Shahidganj Mosque vs Shiromani Gurdwara Parbandhak (1940) 42 BOMLR 1100.

Mosque Known as Masjid Shahidganj v. Shromani Gurdwara Prabandhak Committee (Lahore) 1938 AIR (Lah) 369.

Art, law and the violence of offence taking

Malvika Maheshwari

ABSTRACT
Since the end of the 1980s in India, groups associated with various political parties, religions, regions and castes have come to regularly attack artists and damage artworks. Straining relations between religious communities concomitant with the decline of secularism – as a practice if not as a norm – in Indian politics provides the context for such competitive and violent proclamations of 'hurt sentiments.' However, this paper focuses on the complementary explanations of how the rule of law has also come to not appear as a straightforward 'solution' to this 'problem.' It shows the fragility of the fundamental right of free speech and expression in India today, where the shifting legal regime is hardly an assurance against the concrete alternatives of lethal threats and violence, which have legitimized, over time, as Pratap Bhanu Mehta has argued, 'the insidious idea that it was not the state's job to protect freedom, but to discipline that freedom in the name of some conception of propriety' (Mehta, 2012). To be sure, the focus of this paper is not to slam vigilant, and even, as many would argue, necessary laws and regulatory bodies, but to explore how the legal reasoning and workings might have actually come to be a rational choice for offence-takers, to develop theoretically and apply practically in their endeavours.

On 12 August 1993, at a town hall in Faizabad, the city bordering Ayodhya, about 15 to 20 men belonging to the Bajrang Dal vandalized an exhibition titled *Hum Sab Ayodhya* (We are all Ayodhya), tearing down the displayed photographs and text panels.[1] Put together by Sahmat – which had after theatre artist Safdar Hashmi's death in 1989 emerged as a vitalizing platform of solidarity and resistance for artists and intellectuals[2] – the extensively researched exhibit was their attempt to highlight Ayodhya's 'composite history, geography, and culture' in a bid to 'neutralize the image of vandalism and intolerance that had begun to be associated with the city' in the wake of Hindu nationalist siege of the Babri Masjid/Ramjanmabhoomi.[3] On the third day of the display, while Sahmat's volunteers were out to lunch, Bajrang Dal led the attack – in the presence of the local police – ostensibly as a way to show its disapproval of one panel titled *Ram Katha* among the eighty-three archaeological, art historical, and photographic materials that were on display; accusing Sahmat of 'insulting Hindu sentiments' by displaying a 'poster' depicting Hindu deities Rama and Sita as siblings instead of husband and wife.[4]

As word spread – to the extent of Sahmat's denouncement by 'professedly secular writers and critics' for being 'insensitive' to popular feelings, for the timing of its activities in the midst of heightened communal tensions,[5] and for 'taking money from a government run by Safdar [Hashmi's] murderers'[6] – its organizers repeatedly emphasized that there was no such 'poster' with any visual reference that the Bajrang Dal claimed to be offended by. Instead, the 'poster' they referred to was two lines of a text panel, which synoptically mentioned the Buddhist *Dasratha Jataka* – one variation among numerous religious, nonreligious, and regional stories of Lord Rama – different from the more popular versions of Tulsi

Das's *Ramcharitmanas* (which formed the basis of Doordarshan's epic TV serial *Ramayana*) and 'probably older' than the other well-known version by Valmiki.[7] But the victimhood-generating capacity of this misinformation was indeed the critical rationale for Bajrang Dal to justify its attack in the name of protecting the interests of Hindus, and decreasing the likelihood of its own members being penalized.

As a result, within two days of this attack, another of Sahmat's event *Muktnaad* (Free Expression) – to be held a few days later, on August 14 and 15 in Ayodhya, marking the anniversary of India's independence – came under the shadow of controversy, this time for artists allegedly causing a 'breach of the peace,'[8] so did the *Hum Sab Ayodhya* exhibition in New Delhi, which was still being shown at the state-administered Teen Murti House.[9] While *Muktnaad* withstood Bajrang Dal's disruptive tactics[10] and the threats of violence[11] – in that the performances went on without any incident of disruption being reported – primarily on account of increased security arrangements for Human Resource Development minister and senior congressman Arjun Singh's visit. In Delhi, however, on the afternoon of August 21, the police seized the 'objectionable' *Ram Katha* 'posters' from the exhibition at Teen Murti, without providing the organizers a copy of the seizure memorandum, issued by the lieutenant governor, or even informing them of it. Moreover, in the seizure notification, which the police left with the museum staff, not only was the forfeited material incorrectly mentioned as 'posters,' it also did not identify reasons for the forfeiture, as is mandated by law. When Sahmat registered these concerns in a letter to the governor, they did not receive a reply from him. Evidence suggests instead that the orders of the seizure were given 'without the application of mind by the concerned authority,'[12] but on whose insistence remains unclear. Whatever the governor's reasons for acting as a 'rubber stamp,' it was inconsistent with Arjun Singh's support to Sahmat, but aligned with the Speaker's suggestion in the Lok Sabha five days earlier to the government's 'concerned ministry to take note of the objections' raised by BJP members: that Sahmat's 'posters which arouse passions and hurt sentiments should be removed.'[13] As my interviews show, Prime Minister Rao himself was against his HRD minister funding Sahmat's event and 'did not want the artists to go to Ayodhya in the first place.'[14] The Uttar Pradesh Congress Committee had backed Rao in this, boycotting the events in Ayodhya and Faizabad, despite Singh's much-publicized visit from Delhi.[15]

BJP leaders like L. K. Advani and A. B. Vajpayee, who was also the leader of the Opposition at the time, went on to blame Singh in the Parliament for 'tensions in the country,' while conveying their disagreement (*asahamati*) with Sahmat's 'posters.' In this case, like in various other instances that followed, BJP's support to the Bajrang Dal, based on their ideological and organizational intimacy, only partially explains their stance. The bottom line was that the faction-riven Congress party had lost face over its double game with no alternatives to offer and BJP aimed to use this opportunity for political gains, too. Thus, instead of dwelling on acceptable versions of the Rama story, as Bajrang Dal had, and appear as a party only for Hindus, BJP launched an offensive in the Parliament against Congress by foregrounding questions of fairness in politics, to which Congress or any of its allies had no reasonable defence. Politically, it would be easier to dislodge the Congress this way, and disable its own supporters from crossing over, who may not have agreed with Bajrang Dal's violence especially in the wake of the backlash the party faced after the demolition of the Babri Masjid. Congress's record of the 1980s – of playing the religion card in matters of free speech, especially its decision to ban *The Satanic Verses* after objections from Muslim members in the Parliament like Syed Shahabuddin – came in handy for the BJP. This was best illustrated by Advani's statement in Lok Sahba:

> You cannot have double standards about this poster and different about Salman Rushdie's book. After all, Salmam Rushdie's book hurts some sections. I can say that I differ with it, but this Government went to the extent of banning it, without even reading it ...You have one standard for that and another standard for Sahmat, which publishes this objectionable poster and is given a government grant ... It is because of this that people everywhere are expressing their fury [rosh].[16]

Despite Singh's patronage, and Bajrang Dal's vandalism, it was Sahmat that ended up with criminal cases registered under Sections 153A and 295A of the Indian Penal Code against it in the two Congress-administered states – Uttar Pradesh and Delhi – without the attackers being penalized in any way. To not fully realize the government's contribution in the rise of Hindu nationalism in general, and in the attacks on artists in particular, especially 1993 onward is to misjudge the extent to which artists, already by early 1990s, had become pawns in this game of competitive communal politics. It is not altogether surprising, therefore, that after the entire brouhaha, when parliamentarian Gurudas Das Gupta, a member of the Communist Party of India in the Rajya Sabha, asked whether the government was 'aware' or 'believes' that 'of late the right of artists is being tampered with,' Congressman and Minister of State Rajesh Pilot could simply get away by 'assur[ing]' the House that 'there is no threat to the freedom of artists in the country.'[17]

One need not overlook the irony that Sahmat was backed by the Congress to see that what the Sangh Parivar's attack on its exhibition did was not necessarily reveal some hidden Hindu nationalist ideology or its preferred modus operandi of resorting to brute force, which the destruction of Babri Masjid or even Sahmat's various public initiatives to resist the rise of Hindutva had already managed to show (*Artists Against Communalism* 1991; *Images and Words* 1992; *Anhad Garje* 1993 among others). Instead, Hindu nationalists' (and subsequently others') growing obsession to mobilize brute physical violence against artists can be understood only when we recognize the all-importance of the 'institutional fabric' affecting and informing this behavior.

While the rigmarole of electoral politics and the rise of Hindutva, as seen above, remains the most stubborn aspect of the rise in the attacks against artists in India, in this paper, I turn attention to the complementary question of how the rule of law also failed to appear as a straightforward 'solution' to this 'problem,' especially when religion is involved. To push the argument further, the specific development of the administrative and the regulatory state in India has in fact had a decisive influence in triggering not less but more protests against artistic expression: not simply in the sense of 'state-sanctioned violence' – made possible by 'weak' communalized and criminalized institutions offering 'carte blanche' to the 'mob' – or in the way that Lawrence Liang, following Annette Kuhn, regards censorship mechanisms employed by the state as 'being formative or constitutive.'[18] But one has to also take into account the inconclusive character of state institutions – and especially the higher judiciary – whose frequent endeavours to be on the side of free speech through frustrating procedural delays and rising costs of litigation, through a lack of consistency and expertise, and through what Pratap Bhanu Mehta has called 'its own excessive moralism' has had dampening effects: both containing but also stimulating the fracas over free speech.[19]

It was not before eight years, in July 2001, that the Delhi High Court invalidated the notification 'approved' by the lieutenant governor that proscribed the 'posters' from the *Hum Sab Ayodhya* exhibition, by which time not only did the precariousness of artists' security and the right to free speech in India been firmly established through numerous similar instances of vandalism across the country, but also the impact of the now-allowed 'posters' was less decisive, wrested from their original context. Similarly, while endorsing Sahmat's objection to the vagueness of the notification (not indicating, for instance, what was 'considered objectionable' or not revealing the 'community whose religious behalf is offended') the judgment – decided by a bench of three judges – was practically silent with regard to the pernicious effect itself of such 'official' notifications accompanying the outburst of brute, criminal violence. In other words, by focusing, even if usefully, on the merits of due processes in the invocation of the IPC or in the issuing of notifications for such forfeiture, and remaining silent about the underlying substantive issues of free speech, the judgment seemed to inadvertently suggest that however insidious, as long as the processes were not violated at the time of litigation, legal sanctity was maintained.

As it were, the more violent and unruly offence taking got over the years (to only name a few: M. F. Husain 1996 onwards; Deepa Mehta 1998 and 2000; Taslima Nasreen 2003; Chandramohan/MSU 2007) the more pronounced and fastidious the presence of the legal in the felonious became. This aspect has been the underhand of the authority that is wielded by the offence-takers, augmenting their ability to threaten and inflict physical damage and pain, and making it seems possible for them to appear on the side of law. It is true that by mastering street style agitations, or destroying the Babri Masjid, Hindutva wielding militias like the Bajrang Dal had already by early

1990s emerged as the 'champion of Hindus.' However, if Hindu nationalists continued to only foist their command through the streets, how could they hold sway over the streets? To borrow from Stephen Homes' analysis of law and democracy, in what way could they establish dominance over its own domination-imposing apparatus? Sangh Parivar's politics of violence to control artists would not amount to much if the law continued to accommodate the artists. If force was the only source of authority, Sangh Parivar could itself has never gotten off the ground. Favourably for them, there was another way to assert control: legal. Offence-takers reigned in over artists by the manipulating the law, the very apparatus that artists could eventually rely on. While the law might not always come to their aid, it could, given its loopholes and ambiguities, be indirectly channelled and abused. This is precisely why when parties like the BJP or the Shiv Sena came to power to form the government by mid-1990s, their violence did not simply translate into uncontrollable, violent conflagrations but a far more enduring malediction for artists.[20] By turning to the police, the judiciary and other regulatory bodies, the attackers not merely 'precipitated the taking of offence' as Kajri Jain has argued, as much as this manoeuvre showed the cunning pragmatism of violent offence taking: that weakening the law could be far worse for artists than mere spurts of outrage, as it weakens the deterrent power of violent damnation.[21]

The paper is divided into six parts that show not so much the history of censorship in India by focusing on any specific regulatory institution, or even to chronicle instances of violent attacks on artists. Rather, to show the fragility of the fundamental right of free speech and expression in India today, where the shifting legal foundations are no longer an assurance against the concrete alternatives of lethal threats and violence. I borrow the analytical framework here from Anupama Rao's work on the constitution of Dalit atrocity through law, not simply for the methodological direction it offers, but also to reinforce the pervading violent proclivities of India's democracy, which run far deeper, and alongside the eruptions of violent offence-taking.[22] Like Rao, the idea here is not simply to 'critique' vigilant, and even, as many would argue, necessary laws and regulatory bodies. Neither do I plainly suggest a causal relation between the escalation of violence against artists and the complacency of the legal regime. The widespread and dramatic increase in the criminalized competitive and communal electoral politics, the onslaught of globalized media and economic liberalization of the 1990s, the rise and radicalization of Hindu nationalism since the mid-1980s, the politically creative and deepening bargaining capacity of hitherto disadvantaged groups – all played a part in the definitive increase in the anxieties around free speech and the attacks against artists. However, if the violence of offence taking steadily came to not so much dislocate, but relocate itself in the courts, it remains also one critical element among many others that contributed to the precariousness of free speech, with law itself emerging as a medium of harassment. As Akeel Bilgrami writes in the context of academic freedom: 'the opposite of freedom is not necessarily always coercive agents and policies and institutions but the presence of much less easily identifiable tendencies.'[23]

'What comes first: the law or the offence?

The Indian Penal Code of 1860 ushered in institutionalized regulatory mechanisms for speech that arose from the creation of the Common Law. Having its basis in the draft of Criminal Law prepared by Thomas Macaulay in 1837, it contains detailed provisions relating to offences against the state and the community. There are, for example, sections on public safety, public decency, morality, religious harmony, defamation and intimidation, insult and annoyance. In the matter of targeting artists, one of the most abused sections of the IPC is 153A (invoked against Sahmat, for instance), which restricts speech that 'promotes enmity between different groups on grounds of religion, race, place of birth, residence, language, etc., and doing acts prejudicial to maintenance of harmony.' Another is Section 295A, punishing those who act with 'deliberate and malicious intention' to insult religious beliefs. These explicit laws did not only arm the colonial rulers with an assortment of coercive strategies that set the trap around legally acceptable speech norms to eliminate offences, but it also for the first time formalized the contours of different kinds of speech, creating, in Foucauldian sense 'a differential administration of illegalities.' For the colonial regime, this embedding of offences within the structure of law, aided mobilizations to curtail speech, administer justice, caste prejudice, and hunt down offenders but also to unsettle the diverse social and religious divisions.

One implication of this language of the law, analogous to institutional arrangements, has been that the 'group' or person claiming this 'enmity' are required to justly prove it, even if this means causing further obstruction of harmony, which ironically is then justified for the maintenance of harmony. Another implication has been that the settlement of such a dispute, as Pratap Bhanu Mehta has highlighted, 'necessitated the government to appear to side with one party against the other,'[24] which also only precipitates further resentment and group enmity. However, if Congressmen like P. Ananda Charlu, as early as 1886 warned of the section's potential 'to accentuate evil. . .encouraging insidious men to do mischief,' there were at the same time Indian leaders who also embraced this regime of law, circumventing speech to prevent the virulent and competitive spread of religious passions, revealing their belief as much as their superiority that India's masses were not ready to manage the demands and responsibilities related to free speech, particularly in dealing with religion.[25] The faith of India's elite in the utility of these laws is indicated from the fact that the independence movement though significantly struggled against the often-excessive and brutal censorship regime of the British government, precipitated by the IPC, this colonial framework of laws, instead of being rejected was 'preserved, sustained and expanded' for governance in independent India.[26] While indeed prohibiting speech, 153A or other similar sections like 295A have equally offered a convenience to those who are intent on aggrandizing communal tensions.

British officers since the late eighteenth century onwards began to articulate speech as a category of governance of 'native' Indians, as widely indicative of a language of colonial domination. The colonial state, thus, justifying its presence as its moral obligation to civilize backward societies began to identify its radical political and moral opposition. This imperative established a basis for intervening in Indian law, politics, society, culture and religion – initially through deportation of faltering journalists and trials for libel but eventually establishing mechanisms of direct and pre-censorship regulations for curtailing freedom of cinema, press, and theatre as well as instituting stricter laws against sedition, defamation, public decency, morality and offences relating to religion. These provisions, as is widely acknowledged, were not merely disabling for speech rights, but also enabling, playing a critical role in the creation and the official recognition of an *Other* – a community of offended, sensitive, and hurt. 'Rather than reflecting primordial religious attachments' or merely establishing legal codes over an already existing grid of social norms and forbiddance, Asad Ali Ahmed has shown that 'the cases before the colonial courts were not only enabled by the law but largely constituted by it.'[27] This indeterminate legacy of speech laws was amplified by evidences that neither did progressive judgments in a straightforward manner remodel existing social practices, nor did legal intervention become the ultimate benchmark for acceptable practice; court judgments often remained without consequence. But on purely practical grounds, what legal precedents did was to convey to artists – first as subjects and then citizens – that the state was not averse to ally on the side of those who claimed to be offended and stoked up mobilizations. If legal provisions enhance offence, then claims of being offended will be forthcoming, justified through a glossary of distinct terminology of insult, hurt, harm, and outrage among others.

Art as offence

The Constituent Assembly's discussions from 1946 to 1949 – that birthed both freedom of speech as a fundamental right and restrictions fundamental to that right in the Constitution of independent India – were largely unconcerned with outlining the differences of and limits for various forms of speech (such as commercial, press, artistic, religious, scientific,). Yet, the pursuit of a sovereign state's various considerations – 'security', 'public order', 'morality' and the like – required different forms of speech to be regulated differently, and at different times. The obvious implication of this for the administration of a newly independent nation, itself in the throes of instability and crisis, was the continuation of specific legislations introduced by the colonial government that included regulations that affected the freedom of artists more than others: the Dramatics Performance Act of 1876, the Cinematograph Act of 1918, or sections of the IPC.

These regulations notwithstanding, acknowledging the efficacy of artistic expression and the transformative power of the arts (and thus the need for specific regulations), as opposed to other forms of speech, in the years immediately after independence artists as a community were explicitly sought out by the Indian state, as art critic Geeta Kapur writes, in its efforts to 'stage an honorable transition from the feudal to a modern, democratic, secular, moderate version of socialist society.'[28] If art practice was supported for 'educating public taste,' 'preserving and innovating culture,' and even 'boosting foreign relations,'[29] the Nehruvian government's (India's first and longest) practice of appointing them as representatives in the Parliament, bestowing national honours, and patronage in no small way contributed to artists being regarded as 'honorary members of the national elite,'[30] partaking in the state's progressive agenda of honouring modernity, democracy and freedom.

These extraordinary, perhaps even unfair and lofty, expectations from the artistic community, alongside the political symbology of the romantic myth surrounding them – 'citizen-subjects with enhanced sovereignty'[31] – not surprisingly impacted the jurisprudence of free speech, however, without consistency or any exemplary clarity. On the one hand was a straightforward narrative that considered artistic expression to is the same as any other form of speech, subject to the age-old belief that offensive expression simply needed to be suppressed, demonstrating, which after Anupama Rao I borrow from Ernesto Laclau's idea of political commensuration.[32] On the other hand, there were at least two notable implications of discriminating artistic expressions from other kinds of speech. First, regulatory practices of the state routinely prompted the idea that aesthetic purpose can provide a reliable basis to judge art, in that artists were regarded as gifted and extraordinary, worthy of not being 'subjected to same constraints imposed on other members of the society,'[33] just like the arguments in the judgment of acquittal given by Justice Nasrullah on a charge of obscenity against painter Akbar Padamsee in 1954, independent India's foremost trial involving an artist.[34] This raises obvious tensions: when, and if at all, is discriminating between speech and artistic expression possible? On what basis do judges ascertain these differences? Moreover, how is this inconsistency in jurisprudence to be resolved? The irresolution of these questions has proved to be critical in selectively inciting mobilizations against artists, with statements of Hindu nationalist attackers like 'if the courts cannot touch them, we can?' Or 'who do the artists think they are? Some kind of god?'[35]

The second issue in part contradicts this idea, and is linked to the expectation of national gain from art practice. This is something with which various other kinds of speech are hardly burdened, implying some sort of binding notion that the value of artistic expression can be judged objectively and not for its own sake, as something instrumental or strategic, based on the purposes it fulfils, and therefore rightfully challenged when it fails to achieve these. The implications of this are even worse: it reduces artistic expression to being merely functional; its protection highly precarious, dependent on the utility it serves.

The problems with these inconsistencies can be observed in two broad but distinct spheres: In the state's role as an allocator: funding certain art forms and artists (depending on the calculation of purposes to be fulfilled) through the institution of National Akademis, art circles (*mandals*), schools (*vidyalayas*), museums, and fellowships and state awards. This kind of institutional backing in the production of art itself makes certain speech possible and ensures the silencing of others. And in the state's role as a regulator: instituting specific institutions and legislation against speech excesses to protect not just itself, but also communities and individuals, from issues it disapproves of, such as obscenity, blasphemy, immorality, and communal strife, among others.

This latter point is critical – explored in the following pages – for precisely how it has, over time, had the contrasting outcome of not necessarily lessening, but inciting mobilizations of offence-taking and conflicts related to artists.

To define or not to define

Section 292 of the Indian Penal Code relating to obscenity, which was invoked to incriminate Padamsee, as thousands of other artists, extends to 'any book, pamphlet, paper, writing, drawing, painting, representation, figure or any other object.' Section 153 of 'promoting enmity between different groups' specifies 'words, either spoken or written, or by signs or by visible representation or otherwise.' Laws of prior restraints – on theatre, the Dramatics Performance Act 1876 and the Cinematograph Act of 1952 for cinema – describe the mediums as 'words spoken' as opposed to 'written words' for the former and the latter as a 'combination of act, speech, sight and sound.' Customs Act 1962, wherein by an administrative order the import of books, films, music and the like can be banned, refers to these as 'goods.' Following Howard Becker, it appears, with regard to framing laws, the state shows 'no direct interest in the works of art themselves; its interest is confined to keeping peace among its citizens and by enforcing the rules of the game.'[36]

However, the banality of these words, visual representations, or signs disappears when they appear in courtrooms as 'art works,' and their creators are referred to as artists. Akbar Padamsee, M. F. Husain or even Sahmat for instance in the courtroom was not considered merely as 'accused;' they were artists or a group of artists. But under what conditions these spoken words, images, writing, and drawings merit the definition as art, and thus deserve a certain leeway in judicial and legislative processes, as we have seen, remains unclear. On the one hand, outlining 'certain standard' has been considered essential to ensure that not 'everything and anything and everywhere' in the name of art is allowed. For many artists themselves as early as the 1950s, when dancer Rukmini Devi Arundale spoke in the Rajya Sabha as a nominated member, not determining the boundaries to decipher not just art from other speech, but also 'good' and 'bad' art would be much the same as 'violence masquerading as brotherhood.'[37] On the other hand, laws and judgments against offensive or hurtful expressions have consistently operated without *defining* something as art, since that in itself is restrictive, as it is commonly acknowledged. Indeed, in the years since independence, in some of the landmark trials involving artists at the higher judiciary, judges have been generally sympathetic to the latter view. Yet, there is no escaping the fact that even if they distance themselves from making glaring aesthetic judgments, judges remain, to paraphrase Lawrence Liang, the principal editors, critics and censors, shaping aesthetic tastes and normalizing techniques they themselves employ to arrive at the judgment.

In doing so, the judiciary has recurrently sought refuge in questions of artistic purpose and its instrumental value: for the purpose of x, how do we evaluate y? Phrases like 'provides a sense of fulfillment which makes like meaningful,'[38] or 'has redeeming social value,' 'achieves the objectives of the state,'[39] and 'carry within themselves, a comprehensive view of social life,'[40] have been typical responses in judgments concerning regulation of artistic expression, focusing on what it is making happen or leading to.

This emphasis on purpose may itself be an aesthetic judgment, however, even if philosophy of art and its purposes are brought together, for the most part law is interested in asking more specific questions than philosophy does. As Justice Krishnaiyer, quoting American legal scholar M. R. Cohen, noted: 'the law is not a homeless wandering ghost. It is a phase of human life located in time and space.'[41] In other words, the courts have essentially put forth the ideas that: (a) you know it is art when you see it[42]; and (b) 'social purposes' it fulfills is a reasonable basis of determining its limits. Enduring over time, these legal logics have provided plenty of leeway to both, governments and groups like the Bajrang Dal to similarly identify and subvert artistic expression.

Incomprehensibility and offence

In *Raj Kapoor and ors. v. State and others* (1980), the president of a youth organization complained against the producers of a Hindi film *Satyam Shivam Sundaram*, alleging that the film was obscene and indecent, making the producers liable to an offence under Section 292 of the IPC, despite the fact that the Central Board of Film Censors (since renamed as Central Board of Film Certification) had cleared the film for exhibition with 'adult' certification. The producers approached the High Court with a petition that the obscenity notice was an abuse of the judicial process, brought about due to ulterior considerations and that no prosecution could be legally sustained since the film was already cleared by the film board, governed by the Cinematograph Act 1952. After the High Court dismissed the petition, the producers approached the Supreme Court where its judgment, penned by Justice Krishnaiyer, clarified that while a clearance from the Film Censor Board is of relevance, it does not hinder the courts from deciding if a film is obscene or not. It allowed the appeal and sent back the case to the High Court for a fresh disposal, cautioning 'inexpert criminal courts' against 'rushing in… lest the judicial process become a footpath for any highwayman wearing a moral mask holding up a film-maker who has traveled the expensive and perilous journey to the exhibition of his certified picture.'[43]

But more importantly, the judgment contained an elaborate discussion on the sensitive nature of art appreciation where artistic freedom relied heavily on the active participation of the 'enlightened society… in the administration of justice to aesthetics.' The Supreme Court put forth an argument that demands for censorship or restraints on artistic speech, like the controversy over *Satyam Shivam Sunadaram* were born out of the 'narrow mindedness of the society' and their 'lack of comprehension.' In the past, such precedents can be traced all the way back to Padamsee's acquittal when the judgment stressed that those who 'do not understand the art about such pictures' could not hold artistic liberties to ransom. Even most recently, in 2008 Delhi High Court's Justice Sanjay Kishan Kaul, in an otherwise critical defence of painter M. F. Husain's right to freedom of speech and expression noted that those who objected to the artist's works were 'not the types who would go to art galleries or have an interest in contemporary art.' Quoting Picasso, the judgment stated that [art] 'ought to be forbidden to ignorant innocents, never allowed into contact with those not sufficiently prepared.'[44]

As supportive of free speech as these judgments may be, they perpetuate the idea of art being an incomprehensible 'mystery,' a mystery that excludes the vast masses.[45] The courts have time and again, however inconsistently, interpreted art as a 'specialized language' that the 'ordinary' citizen might find it difficult to 'comprehend.' Such a discourse contributes not so much to the debates on the role of art in a democracy per se, as much as towards the impossibility of democratizing the arts, widening the gap between the 'arts' and the 'people:' heightening the suspicion behind artistic intent, and transforming the idea of creativity into a form of incomprehensibility and elitism. As violent mobilizations against artists and interactions with the attackers reveal, the fundamental source of distrust – diluting even the clamour of 'hurt sentiments' or communal animosity – was the pathos of different kinds of inequality, of the imagined wealth, fame or skill, felt by the attackers between themselves and the artist. It is not that these inequalities did not exist before, rather the anxiety and the despair over it thickened through the processes of economic liberalization at the end of the 1980s. The eagerness to destroy the image, and the artist was partly also eagerness to see the imagined and actual privileges (like security) of the elite (that particular artist but also the elite, 'ameer log' in abstraction) be impaired by the ordinary.

Bureaucracy matters

The complications of regulating the limits of artistic expression are intensified by a complicated division of specialized tasks related to it: framing of laws, their interpretation, and their effective implementation, among others. Ultimately, a robust free speech regime needs the willing cooperation of an efficient bureaucracy. For instance, under the Dramatics Performance Act 1876,

> The government is empowered to prohibit a play if the performance is deemed scandalous or defamatory in nature; if it is likely to excite feelings of disaffection towards the government or to deprave and corrupt the audience. It gives police the power to enter a house with a warrant and seize material that is suspected of having been used, or is intended to be used for a performance. The act gives state governments the power to prohibit dramatic performances within an area unless a copy of the script is furnished to a designated officer at least three days before it is staged.[46]

While the DPA as a 'preventive measure' against 'inflammable spoken words' (which, unlike the 'finality about the written word,' can be 'disputed and denied') has been upheld consistently by the parliament and the judiciary in the 'interests of public order and security,' critics of the Act have focused their attention on the inconsistent and uninformed ways of its implementation, especially with the ill-informed police 'masquerading as professors of culture.' If the Act has been explicitly listed as a State matter,[47] making inherently inconsistent in implementation – dependent on the practices of local police under different state governments – artists, researchers and even parliamentarians have highlighted common challenges obstructing the fair implementation of the Act across the country. While the DPA in most states require senior police officials like the deputy commissioner, the traffic police commissioner, or even the district magistrate, to read the script in order to clear or deny it for a performance, in reality, however, 'the district magistrate does not find any time to go into it. It is not even seen by the inspector. It goes to the head constable and it is he who reads the script and it is he who is supposed to hold whether it is in order or so on.'[48] The absurdity magnifies as a natural by-product of this hierarchal system, since the often-poorly educated constable, entrusted with determining the value, and therefore the permissibility, of the drama script, is not even required to be either interested or trained in the task. Legal scholar Siddharth Narrain describes the idea of police as theatre critics as having a 'near Borgesian quality, bordering on the fantastic but real enough to be used extensively.' A similar story can to told about the fate of 'goods' under the Customs Act (1962). Its most (in)famous instance occurred in 1988 when novelist Salman Rushdie wrote an open letter to Prime Minister Rajiv Gandhi pointing out the 'strangeness' of the decision that the ban on his English literary novel *The Satanic Verses* was in fact issued by the Ministry of Finance under Section 11 of the Act.

But the sphere in which the bureaucracy, in alliance with the government, probably exerts its power in the widest and most perceptible manner is the regulation of cinema. Only a cursory glance at the workings of the Central Board of Film Certification, in pursuance of the Cinematograph Act,[49] can frustrate even the most conservative of the supporters of free expression. Various past and presently serving members of the board emphatically concur.[50] But unlike, DPA or the Customs Act, the central dilemma with film censorship and certification is not so much the presence of a 'competent authority.' In fact, the central government, under whose mandate lies the CBFC, but not DPA – since films are exhibited all over the country while theatre's reach in limited – has attempted to show some preference for appointing members on the Board with at least a minimum interest, experience and knowledge of films. Instead, the major challenge film-makers and cinema-related artists face with the CBFC is that the allocation of 'permissions' to screen the films tends to comply with the wishes and interests of the ruling government, in blatantly unfair ways. The assortment of ways in which the government wields its influence includes the following: the appointment of members to the Board and their longevity in the office is at 'the pleasure of the government;' it has also repeatedly ignored or refused to incorporate and implement suggestions of numerous independent and ministry-appointed committees that involve reduction of government control, restructuring of the board, allowances for greater artistic leeway, etc.; arbitrary and time-consuming procedures for application of certificates; excessive corruption in granting certificates to film producers; general institutional mismanagement and apathy, including instances wherein positions on the board, even that of the chairman and advisory panels, remains vacant for long periods of time; and not to mention, the lack of clarity within the government and the Board about the role and validity of such an intervention: to judge taste, or permissibility, or setting moral standards remains unclear.[51]

There are two unmistakable implications of the phantom threat of such tactics of control and intimidation: first, the Board's decisions have increasingly relied on the demands of various pressure groups that the government wishes to keep in good humour for its own political interests; and second, it has ensconced itself beyond criticism, seldom allowing 'political films' to see the light of the day. To give one example of a film-maker's concern: 'they'll nab you at the slightest and there is nothing you can do. I think it is a major reason why even our best known filmmakers rarely broach political themes boldly.'[52] CBFC's lack of autonomy has not only led to it being widely associated with the wishes of the 'establishment,' but its sharpest critics, like legal scholar A. G. Noorani has gone so far as to call such a system unconstitutional since it cannot be called independent or quasi-judicial.[53]

The religion of offence

For centuries religious texts and stories have provided material for artistic representations, which in turn have not only impacted discourses surrounding religion, but they have also sparked controversies by offending conventional piety. In independent India, books like *The True Furqan, Ayesha, Rama Retold, What has Religion Done for Mankind*, and more recently novels like *The Satanic Verses, Dharmakaarana*, and countless others on all kinds of gods, goddesses, religions and faiths have been routinely proscribed on grounds of public order, provoking enmity between groups and for offending sentiments. An even greater number of films on similar subjects are routinely refused permission from being shown. Attacks on M. F. Husain's paintings of Hindu goddesses Saraswati and Durga, ban on drama productions like *Last Temptation of the Christ* in Kerala and disruption of *Shakespeare ki Ramlila* at the Prithvi Theatre in Mumbai and the vandalism of Sahmat's *Hum Sab Ayodhya* exhibition – all bear the brunt of allegedly outraging someone's religious sentiments. If these are condemned as offensive artworks, their theme indeed remains religion. Then, in Rao's sense, must not their proscription be also underlined as religious censorship? Would it not be, in its more exaggerated form, a carrying forward of, to use Margaret Bald's phrase, 'a specter from the distant past of the Inquisition and the burning of heretics'?[54]

Many cases of censoring artistic speech involve offending religious sentiments, provisions for which are specifically indicated in law, like noted above, IPC's Sections 153 (promoting enmity, disharmony, hatred, ill will between different groups on grounds of religion) and 295 (deliberate and malicious acts intended to outrage religious feelings of any class by insulting its religion or religious beliefs). The guidelines for the regulation of cinema warns specifically against 'visuals or words contemptuous of racial, religious or other groups,' although under the DPA performances at religious festivals are specifically excluded from it. How have the courts articulated the divide between a constitutional commitment to free speech and these provisions of law, which are broad enough to outlaw a lot of speech, and also not curb communal enmity? How have they read the difference between artistic works and religious idioms since so much of religion is channelled through art and vice versa?

French philosopher Bruno Latour in his book *Iconoclash* argues that like art, if you show that religion too is man-made 'you nullify the transcendence of the divinities, you empty the claims of a salvation from above.' He further writes, 'the critical mind is one that shows the hands of humans at work everywhere…the more the human hand can be seen as having worked on an image, the weaker is the image's claim to offer truth. The trick to uncover the trick is always to show the lowly origin of the work, the manipulator, the counterfeiter, the fraud behind the scenes who is caught red- handed.'[55] To rationally resolve the tensions between artistic and religious expression, judicial institutions in India lay at heart of uncovering this trick, and Pratap Bhanu Mehta's critique of the court's attitude to religion and jurisprudence on free speech is most instructive here. His argument is threefold: first, that the 'practice of Indian constitutionalism not only outlines the public values that ought to be authoritative constraints on behavior, it also seeks to regulate the meaning of religion.' It intervenes to regulate religion since 'constitutional practice requires religion be made subordinate to public purposes,' while at the same time claim that these 'public purposes do not impinge upon religious freedom.' This is his second claim. Finally, the only way to resolve this is by precisely 'controlling the meaning of religious doctrine.'[56]

While Mehta's account is not a historical study of how courts in India came to position themselves as authorities on religion and interpreters of religious texts, it fleshes out moments whereby (a) court's handling of religion became such that nothing about it could warrant interrogation, altercation or criticism (in the name of public order, 'mental stress' of a community, etc.) or be offensive (the court's own interpretation of religious doctrines and a stress of its moral authority). And (b) argued elsewhere, is that by putting aside the focus on the principle of clear and present danger to curtail speech, the courts have pushed back the limits of speech about religion to a point whereby even its criticism, through forms like ridiculing and lampooning, has fallen beyond the purview of legitimate speech acts.[57] Therefore, instead of championing a robust free speech regime than political calculations would allow, the courts are precisely becoming instruments subverting the 'critical minds' that Latour refers to. In other words, instead of allowing the possibility of 'human hands' to be shown in the making of religion, the courts in India are doing the opposite – extending the transcendence of the divine to the sphere of artistic expressions, that is, tucking even art away from the realms of its lowly origins to that of the sacred.

Conclusion

Much of the discussion around the striking escalation of brute violence against artists and the vandalism of art seen in India since the early 1990s is focused on the advancement of the Hindu nationalist movement and the concomitant decline of secularism, in practice, if not as a norm. However, these attacks are equally, if not more, an outcome of extensive metamorphosis in the country's regulatory institutional regime, as we have seen above. The equilibrium levelling the administration of free speech, though always tense and delicate, has increasingly been fractured over time: while the tactics and rhetoric of competitive communal politics have progressively challenged the commonly held assumptions about state authority – through ideologies and atrocities – state mediation itself has been all the more inconclusive. The communalized and criminalized public institutions, the costs and delays in the deliverance of justice, the dissemination of authority and anxiety with the deregulation of the mass media have only heightened overtime – these are anyway tendencies that have a potential to trigger obstructing violence, even independent of any actual ideological apparatus. Although the situation of regulatory affairs in India seems to be embellished with whatever 'weak [democratic] state' imagery that conjures up – even what Stephen Holmes describes as a 'sovereignless' condition where 'rights can be imagined but not experienced'[58] – it remains a working democracy, functioning within levelling constraints. If judiciary's independence, though ridden with complexity, or the stunning obsession with electoral politics, however imperfect, bespeaks of the rights-enabling functions of a liberal democracy, the capacity for reassertion of constitutional representative governance, or a regeneration of neutrality, fairness and temperateness – what Thomas Blom Hansen refers to as the 'sublime' dimensions of state power[59] – remain robust, particularly through vibrant civil society initiatives, like Sahmat's. To address the complexities of the attacks on free speech even more, it is equally crucial to understand that such violence of offence-taking is not simply 'anti-democratic,' in the sense that the attackers and the offence-takers, in fact, have depended far more than ever, and in perverse ways, on the very logics of democracy's functioning: both to justify and carry out their attacks. It is precisely this aspect that underlines how the field of law emerged a strategic battleground overtime, and the legal discourse became appealing even to the most unlawful among the offence-takers. That is, greater were the flaws and cracks in the institutional arrangements, easier it became for offence takers to exploit them; and the more the culture of legality thrived, the more the security for artists depreciated. In other words, the characteristic contribution of the violence of offence taking in contemporary India has been to leave unresolved what it set out to do: to transform legal into the lethal, or the lethal into legal?

Notes

1. The range denotes the discrepancies in media's reporting and interviews with members of Sahmat.
2. Analogous to the magnitude of its opposition, Arindum Datta described these interventions as 'signaling a shift' in Sahmat's workings, underlined by a slant toward a 'more liberally defined cultural politics' – 'from a suspicion of mainstream culture and media to an attempt to address the mainstream.' Sahmat opened this exhibition in Faizabad, in addition to taking it to 17 other cities across the country, including Delhi and riot-hit areas like Bombay, Surat, and Ahmedabad among others. See Datta, *Sahmat, 1989–2004*, 201.
3. See Muralidharan, "Against Cultural Hegemonism."
4. The exhibition did not face any such objection in any of the 17 other cities it was exhibited in. Written by historian Romilla Thapar, the text on the panel read, 'in this version Sita is not the wife but the sister of Rama. At the end of the exile when Rama returns to Ayodhya, Sita is made queen consort of Rama and they rule jointly for sixteen thousand years.'
5. See Rajagopal, *Politics After Television*, 185–6.
6. See Deshpande, *Sahmat and Politics of Cultural Intervention*, 1589.
7. For Sahmat to bring out these often-contradictory, little-known aspects of Rama's stories was the most crucial aspect of mounting the exhibition, to reinforce 'India's cultural and religious pluralism,' contradicting Sangh Parivar's claims of religious homogeneity. But unfamiliarity, in general, makes acceptance difficult, just as the televised *Ramayan* had accustomed audiences to standardized images of Rama and Sita.
8. Beginning at the 'stroke of midnight,' *Muktnaad* was a nightlong 10-h performance by singers, musicians, dancers, and poets assembled from across the country on the banks of the river Sarayu. The preparations for the event were affected by the spread of a bitter lie: that *Muktnaad* was 'a front for an attempt by Muslim fanatics to sneak into the disputed site under cover of darkness and reconstruct the Babri Masjid after blowing up the temporary Rama temple.' Added to that, the increased police deployment in the city during the days leading up to the event because of Intelligence Bureau reports that 'martyrdom brigades' (*shaheedi jathas)* were converging on Ayodhya, only magnified the suspicious murmurs about Sahmat's intentions. A testament to Sangh Parivar's formidable local network, these distractions created an occasion for the governor of Uttar Pradesh (the state was under President's Rule after the demolition of the mosque) to withhold permission for organizing Muktnaad until the final week. Even when Sahmat received the green light, local residents mostly stayed away from the event for fear of trouble due to hearsay that riots might break out again, for instance.
9. Like Chinese whispers, misinformation about Sahmat's activities in Ayodhya thereafter emerged as reports in national newspapers where BJP leaders in New Delhi accused Congress's Arjun Singh, as Sahmat's ally, for 'compelling' the Kendriya Vidyalaya Sangathan, a system of central government-run schools, to purchase copies of the 'offensive Rama poster' for a sum of rupees two lakhs.
10. For example, asking Sahmat volunteers why they were 'celebrating Pakistan day'.
11. Sangh parivar members roamed the streets that led to the riverbank, carrying lathis and knives.
12. *Trustees of Safdar Hashmi Memorial Trust v. Govt. of NCT of Delhi*, 2001, 852.
13. After the Speaker's intervention, Sahmat decided to call off the exhibition, before the police seized the panels.
14. Interview, August 2008.
15. Singh projected himself as secularism's main defender in Congress (apparently to make a bid as the future prime minister), uncovering factions within the party over this issue.
16. *Lok Sabha Debates*, 1993, 7580–86.
17. *Rajya Sabha Debates*, 403, 18–22.
18. Liang, "Sense and Censorbility," 28–34.
19. Mehta, "The Crooked Lives of Free Speech," *Open Magazine*, January 30, 2015.
20. See Holmes, *Passions and Constraint.*
21. Jain, *Taking and Making Offence*, 200.
22. Rao, Violence and Humanity: Or, Vulnerability as Political Subjectivity, *Social Research* 607–32.
23. Bilgrami and Cole, *Who's Afraid of Academic Freedom*, Introduction, xi.
24. Mehta, "Our Scissorland," *Indian Express* (New Delhi), January19, 2012.
25. See Nair, "Beyond the 'communal' 1920s," 317–40.
26. See Dhavan, *Publish and Be Damned*, 11.
27. Ahmed, "Blasphemy, the Indian Penal Code," 173.
28. Kapur, "Secular Artist, Citizen Artist," 422–39.
29. Objectives spelt out at the time of the creation of the National Akademies of Art (Lalit Kala, Sangeet Natak, and Sahitya Akademi) in the 1950s.
30. Kapur, "Secular Artist, Citizen Artist," 424.
31. Ibid., 425.

32. Laclau explains this as procedures that produce equality by creating equivalence between unlike persons, discourses, forms of speech, etc..
33. See Becker, *Art Worlds*, 14.
34. *State at the instance of S.H.J. Kanga v. Akbar Padamsee*; 249 of 1954.
35. The two quotes are from interviews conducted with two members: one each from the Bajrang Dal and the Vishwa Hindu Parishad, August–September 2008.
36. Becker, *Art Worlds*, 177.
37. *Rajya Sabha Debates*, March 1955.
38. *Anand Chintamani Dighe v State of Maharashtra*, 2002 (1) BomCR 57.
39. *K. A. Abbas v. The Union of India*, 1971 AIR 481.
40. *T. Kannan v. M/S. Liberty Creations Ltd.* Madras High Court, 2007.
41. *Raj Kapoor and Ors v. State and Others*, 1980 AIR 258.
42. Rao, Violence and Humanity: Or, Vulnerability as Political Subjectivity, *Social Research*, 11.
43. See note above 41. 258.
44. *M. F. Husain v. Raj Kumar Pandey*, Delhi High Court, 2008.
45. Berger, *Ways of Seeing*, 2008.
46. Narrain, "Censorship and the Law," 49–52.
47. Entry 3 in the State list II reads 'theaters and dramatic performances; cinemas subject to provision of entry 60 of list I; sports, entertainment and amusements.'
48. *Lok Sabha Debates*, April-May 1958. However, this remains a common practice in many states, which continues until this day; corroborated through interviews with numerous theatre artists.
49. Pre-censorship for cinema is governed by the Cinematograph Act 1952 under which it is stated that a 'film shall not be certified for public exhibition, if, in the opinion of the authority competent to grant the certificate, the film or any part of it is against the interests of the sovereignty and integrity of India, the security of the States, friendly relations with foreign States, public order, decency or morality or involves defamation or contempt of court or is likely to incite the commission of any offence.' In *Khwaja Ahmad Abbas vs Union of India* (1968) Supreme Court upheld the 'necessity' of prior restraint since a 'combination of act and speech, sight and sound in semi darkness of the theatre with elimination of all distracting ideas have a strong impact on the minds of the viewers and can affect emotions.'
50. Interviews conducted with former members of the CBFC board, New Delhi and Mumbai, August 2008 and March 2009, respectively.
51. CBFC has generally been maligned for its extra sensitivity to concerns of 'decency and morality,' along with religion. Most recently it circulated a list of 25 'objectionable words' that included: 'bastard,' 'screw,' 'masturbating,' which would not be allowed in any category of the certificate. Lawrence Liang noted of this decision: 'one of the hallmarks of absurdity – especially as manifested by government policies-is its ability to confuse our reactions, provoking umbrage when it ought to provoke raucous laughter.' Liang, 'Thanks to CBFC, we need to come up with better abuses today,' *www.dailyo.in*; 15 February 2015, accessed on 20 February 2015.
52. Quoted in Sethi et al. "Who's afraid of censorship!" *India Today*, January 7, 2014.
53. Noorani, "The Constitution and Censorship of Plays," 31–33.
54. Bald, *Literature Suppressed on Religious Grounds*, ix.
55. Latour and Weibel, "Introduction," *Iconoclash: Beyond Image Wars in Science, Religion and Art*, 2004.
56. Mehta, *Passion and Constraint*, 313.
57. Mehta, "Freedom's our defense," *Indian Express* (New Delhi), March 4, 2010.
58. Holmes, *Passions and Constraint*, 19.
59. Hansen, *Violence in Urban India*, 144.

Disclosure statement

A slightly different version of this paper was previously published in Malvika Maheshwari, '*Art Attacks: Violence and Offence-taking in India*, New Delhi: Oxford University Press, 2019. No potential conflict of interest was reported by the author.

Bibliography

Ahmed, A. A. "Blasphemy, the Indian Penal Code, and Pakistan's Postcolonial Predicament." In *Censorship in South Asia: Regulation from Sedition to Seduction*, edited by W. Mazarella and R. Kaur, 172–205. Bloomington: Indiana University Press, 2009.

Bald, M. *Literature Suppressed on Religious Grounds*. New York: Facts on File Inc, 2006.

Becker, H. S. *Art Worlds*. Berkeley: University of California Press, 2008.

Berger, J. *Ways of Seeing*. London: BBC & Penguin Books, 2008.

Deshpande, S. "Sahmat and the Politics of Cultural Intervention." *Economic and political weekly* 31, no. 25 (June 22 1996): 1586–1590.

Hansen, T. B. *Violence in Urban India: Identity Politics, 'Mumbai,' and the Postcolonial City*. Delhi: Permanent Black, 2001.

Holmes, S. *Passions and Constraint: On the Theory of Liberal Democracy*. Chicago and London: University of Chicago Press, 1995.

Kapur, G. "Secular Artist, Citizen Artist." In *Art and Social Change: A Critical Reader*, edited by W. Bradely and C. Esche, 422–439. London: Tate Publishing, 2007.

Latour, B., and P. Weibel, eds. *Iconoclash: Beyond Image Wars in Science, Religion and Art*. Germany: MIT Press and ZKM Karisruhe, 2004.

Liang, L. "Sense and Censorbility." *Art India* (Special Issue on Censorship) 12 (3) Quarter III) (2007).

Lok Sabha Debates. New Delhi: Lok Sabha Secretariat, 1958.

Mehta, P. B. "Passion and Constraint." In *Politics and Ethics of the Indian Constitution*, edited by R. Bhargava, 311–338. New Delhi: Oxford University Press, 2008.

Muralidharan, "Against Cultural Hegemonism" *Frontline*. 18, no. 16 (August 2001): 4–17.

Nair, N. "Beyond the 'Communal' 1920s: The Problem of Intention, Legislative Pragmatism, and the Making of Section 295A of the Indian Penal Code." *Indian Economic Social History Review* 50, no. 3 (2013): 317–340. doi:10.1177/0019464613494622.

Noorani, A. G. "The Constitution and Censorship of Plays." *Economic and political weekly* 43, no. 10 (March 8 2008): 31–33.

Rajya Sabha Debates. New Delhi: Rajya Sabha Secretariat, 1955.

Rao, A. "Violence and Humanity: Or, Vulnerability as Political Subjectivity." *Social research* 78, no. 2 (Part 1, Summer, 2011): 607–632.

Secular moral/legal commitments revisited: an interlude by way of afterword

Sasheej Hegde

ABSTRACT
The effort here is to problematize the conceptual and analytical resources developed in the study of both 'secularity' as a normative object and the associated question of the interface of religion and law in the context of modern secularism. Working off a division and/or antinomy central to the essays that comprise this special number, I attempt to complicate the terrain of debate by setting in course a complex series of questions about the very nature and scope of a revitalized *analytics* of secularism. In doing so, for the most part, our reflection juxtaposes the claims of an anthropology and history of secularism with the demands of a normative order of construal given over to instituting 'secularism' as a foundational socio-political norm. The main contention is that this juxtaposing can change the way in which we approach the very question of secular moral/legal commitments. Built into the structure of this appraisal overall is a framework seeking to redeem the idea of normative secularity from the genealogical and diagnostic constrictions that define and frame the order of its commitments. The afterword also implicates a thought about normativity as performative, one that could re-orient our reflections about contentious socio-political norms and ideals such as secularism.

Normative, in philosophy, means every judgment which evaluates or qualifies a fact in relation to a norm, but this mode of judgment is essentially subordinate to that which establishes norms. Normative, in the fullest sense of the word, is that which establishes norms.[1]

1. A movement across: a little (scholarly?) genealogy

Not least since the anthropologist-historian Talal Asad formulated his important distinction between the '*secular*' as a domain of historically constituted and variably related behaviours, sensibilities and ways of knowing, and '*secularism*' as a doctrine and political arrangement within the modern state,[2] the study of both secularity as an object of analysis and the question of the interface of religion and law in the context of modern secularism has been divided into two often fractious halves – the 'moral psychology' of religion (as indeed of the secular) and the politics of secularism. Of course, it is certainly true that not all ranged across the terms of this divide need to accept or follow Asad's expansive reading of the genealogy of the secular; and also, what is more, Asad himself, in instituting the distinction that he did – between the 'secular' and 'secularism' – never saw the two as ever fully separable, even taking the secular as 'conceptually prior', and asking how its concepts, assumptions, sensibilities and practices work to support or undermine secularism as a modern political arrangement.[3]

But the division between the 'fact' of the religious and/or of the secular – even as enacted across 'phenomenological' registers which do not privilege statements of belief over experience, but instead are open to the evidence supplied by experience as it is lived and embodied in practices – and the 'instrumental' use of religion and/or of secularism persists. I would like to think that the essays that comprise this special number – '*Communities and Courts: Religion and Law in Modern India*' – situate themselves in this general (should we say, scholarly?) genealogy, even as they work off it in confounding ways setting in course a complex series of questions about the very nature and scope of 'secular moral/legal commitments' specifically. I will turn to this latter axis in course, but for the moment let us listen to the essays that comprise this special number.

2. A measure of the papers

As the chief architect of this collection Manisha Sethi pithily formulates in her elaborate and remarkably erudite introduction to the number:

> Whether fixated on privatised belief as in Europe, or the increasing public support to religion by the state, law can be understood as one of the key discourses through which religion is constituted in our times. This gives rise to several distinct but interrelated questions: first, in this time of increasing judicialization of religion, who can approach the courts for redress, on whose behalf and to what end?; second, what happens when faith and law confront each other, and relatedly, do we see faith and law as contested sovereignties; and finally, what does secular law do when one faith confronts another? (in this volume)

Pointing in the direction of 'bundled religio-legal subjectivities [which] are produced in and through multiple modes of governance and law', she is explicit that the 'fraught relationship between religion and law cannot be understood by focusing on the courts alone without placing each of these cases in a wider social and political canvas' (in this volume). The aspiration of '*Communities and Courts*', accordingly, is to map out the diverse situations and transactions wrought upon the contemporary diffused and dispersed politics of secularism (as reflected in the management and governance of religion in the context of the modern state and its juridical armature in particular) without losing sight of the moral psychology of communities as they straddle the domains of the religious and the secular in the public realm.

These imperatives are forcefully met in the essays that precede this afterword. Whether focusing on the callow but measured treatment of religious disputes within and between communities by the colonial government (M. Raisur Rahman), the 'codes and techniques of adjudication' that oversaw the colonial courts regulation of a disputed 'religious' site and property (Tanweer Fazal), the logics of a failed 'codification' and legal reform of Islamic personal law in a south Indian state (Abhik Majumdar, albeit echoing a pedagogical line about 'doing comparative law' within juridical/academic discourses), or the politically dismantling immediacy of competitive proclamations of 'hurt sentiments' by various groups and their 'co-constitutive' effects on the life of the rule of law in contemporary India (Malvika Maheshwari), the experiential grounds of these criss-crossing civil and political scenes press persuasively into the analysis of the politics of religion and secularism in India. This is all the more compelling and urgent in the other contributions that comprise the volume, whether it be the angularities of a court's mediation of a 'ritual death' as represented in the Jaina practice of Santhara and its attendant legal proscription (Manisha Sethi) and the connected question in 'constitutional law' terms of the impact of state power on religious practice which in effect refashions the space of the latter collapsing practice into doctrine (Mathew John), or again, lastly, but by no means skimpily, the profusely marked layering of Shari'a politics in post-colonial India as routed through the norms of a statist and norm-centred 'normativity' and the patterns of 'conviviality' in the negotiations of a broadly faith-centred laity at large (Neshat Quaiser). As we move through these settings, one is privy to an emergent heterogeneous field in which both statist and non-statist sites or arenas and their intersecting panoply of actors and agencies (and even more particularly the courts) can make and remake the experiential context of what religion is and/or what the secular could be, as indeed what the dogmatic work that the governance of religion in modern secular democracies can entail.

We also glimpse, within the ambit of the essays, less a definitional division than an overarching antinomy (if you will) between 'religion as faith' and 'religion as ideology' of the sort that the political psychologist Ashis Nandy had outlined long ago.[4] [In fact, the transformative capacity of the general genealogy that I spoke about at the start of this afterword in the context of Asad was itself premised on other antinomies of the kind drawn attention much earlier by others like Nandy, but that can pass.] Questioning a whole mode of investment on the secular idea (and ideal), Nandy had asserted that it is both possible and necessary to draw a dividing line between 'religion-as-faith' and 'religion-as-ideology', and that while the pole of 'faith' corresponds to traditions and ways of life 'definitionally nonmonolithic and operationally plural', obtaining 'outside the ideological grid of modernity', the pole of 'ideology' calls attention to an 'instrumental concept of religion' as a principle 'useful for political mobilisation and state formation'.[5] Strictly, this analysis accepts no possible mediation between 'religion-as-faith' and 'religion-as-ideology' – the latter can only distort the former – while also holding in the same breath that 'the modern state always prefers to deal with religious ideologies rather than with faiths'.[6]

3. Sounding a limit: the integuments of/for a reshaping

Surely one denouement of the essays that comprise our collection here is precisely what Nandy is getting at, thus reinforcing the division that I gestured at the very beginning of this reflection, and accordingly one's own insertion into and reiteration of that genealogy. But as I stay with and ponder across the layered histories and ethnographies on offer, I begin to wonder whether that insertion and reiteration is inevitable or even necessary; indeed of how a cognate conceptual framework might lead us to rethink this very constrained and circumscribed diagnostic genealogy and its entrenchment as the division (or antinomy) between the 'fact' of the religious and/or secular and the 'instrumental' use of religion and/or secularism. In other words, as I have denoted elsewhere off the space of Nandy[7] – and would like to think our essays on offer here as also authorizing – we must be pressing after more complex understandings of the mediations between religion, law and state. Why should the 'fact' of the religious – say, 'religion-as-faith' – be the ground on which the 'instrumental' use of religion – 'religion-as-ideology – is instituted? Or, put another way, is the analytically apt referent of 'religion-as-ideology' (the 'instrumental' use of religion) only 'religion-as-faith' (the 'fact' of the religious and/or secular)? Even more pointedly, how might a problematic of what I am terming secular moral/legal commitments touch on a revitalized analytics of secularism (and the dynamics of religion, law and state that the latter may presuppose and/or facilitate)? Hence, once again, the challenge of the papers comprising this special number, both as they present themselves and as deftly summarized by our editor here Manisha Sethi. Paradoxically, yet, there is also a diagnostic limit that I am keen to reveal of the histories and ethnographies of secularism on offer herein and elsewhere.

So let's move on. I must hasten to add that I am not thinking of the innovative and captivating thoughts anchoring the Middle East anthropologist Hussein Ali Agrama, who in postulating the 'intractability of secular power', speaks of secularism as a 'problem-space' which resists the pull of 'normative conceptions of the secular and the religious, as if they each had distinct, transhistorical essences' and opens instead to the prospect that 'the processes by which secular doctrine is implemented incessantly generate the very question that doctrine aims to answer; namely, where to draw the line between religion and politics'.[8] While I do take seriously Agrama's suggestion that 'secularism's power may lie more in the underlying question it continually provokes and obliges us to answer than in the normativity of the categories it presupposes',[9] I am also interested to think hard with 'normative secularity' – indeed, the very normativity that is the fount of secularism's power to insist on a line between religion and politics and, even more emphatically for our purposes here, binds or fortifies the singular nature of its moral/legal commitments. I will get to this presently, but let me get a further conceptual knot out of the way. After all, Agrama in his important work was drawing on Asad's inaugural explorations of secularism, while also ostensibly moving beyond the terms of that genealogy (see also our opening overture in Section 1 above).

Indeed, for this order of 'questioning secularism' – as represented for us here by Agrama – it is not enough to be accepting the 'conceptual priority of the secular' (as articulated by Asad himself, if one may); we must also be reversing the question hitherto bearing on a history and anthropology of secularism. That is to say, not quite (only) asking how the concepts, assumptions, sensibilities, and practices constitutive of the domain of the secular work to support or undermine secularism as a modern political arrangement (Asad's question, as earlier posited), but rather 'how does secularism work to support or undermine the concepts, sensibilities, assumptions, and behaviours of the secular that it draws and depends upon?'.[10] For the latter, clearly, the fact that '*secularism* and the *secular* [are] constantly drawing each other into existence .. is part of the paradoxical quality of secularism's power'; and, as a reiteration of this 'paradoxical quality', Agrama goes on to restate the questions at the centre of his work – namely, 'How then does secularism, as a form of power, work? And what work does it do upon the behaviours, attitudes, and ways of knowing that constitute our ways of life?' – which, we may note, are contextually explored 'through a consideration of state, law, politics and religion in contemporary Egypt'.[11]

Incidentally, these questions can be seen to be either bearing upon or issuing from the essays of our collection as well. But let us remain with the broad conceptual armature of the study of secularism gathered together in this mode, while skipping the specific aspects of its historical and ethnographic detailing. Again, for Agrama – as indeed for our collection here, if you will – a constitutive part of the historical frame is a genealogy implicating 'the centrality of the modern state and especially its legal power – embodied in "the rule of law" – for secularism', which is itself seen to be ordered around 'the legal concept of public order' that the state is responsible to protect as an expression of its sovereignty, and which, in turn, is the basis of 'the state's authority to decide what counts as essentially religious and what scope it should have in social life'.[12] This latter 'capacity' – what Agrama renders as 'the "active principle" of secular power' – is, for him, less a deviation from secularism than a demonstration, at once, of how secular power both 'works to entangle social life in the question of religion and politics' and 'enables the assertion of the state's sovereign capacity into broader and more intimate domains of social life'.[13]

While the force and fecundity of this demonstration need not concern us here, what must is the entailment, integral to the framework as being conceived herein, of conjoining within our understandings of secular power 'two things typically thought to be opposed: a growing space of normative critique and contestation, and the increasing assertion of state sovereignty within social life'.[14] Strictly, what this conjunction yields is a recognition that 'the very principle of state sovereignty entails that the state be properly imbricated within the sociality over which it ostensibly presides', and accordingly that state sovereignty while being 'claimed, critiqued, contested and undermined ever since its inception as a modern concept [...] has not diminished its importance as an organizing concept of contemporary life'.[15] The purpose and power of an anthropology and history of secularism is thus political and diagnostic – as a method (or genealogy) instantiating how secularism/secular power 'itself tends to make religion into an object of politics' and 'enables the assertion of the state's sovereign capacity into broader and more intimate domains of social life'.[16]

Evidently, then, for a purportedly revitalized analytics of secularism – as represented here for us by Agrama – that this order of questioning translates into, we are not far from the division/antinomy instituted by Nandy between 'religion-as-faith' and 'religion-as-ideology' (albeit a more sophisticated variant of the latter); and, strictly, does not avoid the general (scholarly?) genealogy that we alluded in Section 1 above (namely, the division between the 'fact' of the religious and/or of the secular and the 'instrumental' use of religion and/or of secularism). This takes me back to the questions that I formulated at the beginning of this Section 3 in pressing after more complex understandings of the mediations between religion, law and state. Without repeating those questions, let me condense them into a more precipitate form as a basis for the considerations to follow. How do we think about 'normative secularity' – or, on our terms, secular moral/legal commitments specifically – from within the questions that it provokes *and* the very normativity of the categories that it presupposes? Indeed, as I have formulated elsewhere, a theory of secularism in the sense of a theory about possessing the concept 'secular' is quite distinct from a theory about how the concept secular represents; and, what is more, that much of the debate on secularism in India (as also elsewhere, as our reflection herein, in these very pages, demonstrates) has been concerned to press on the latter issue.[17]

Needless to say, my answer is not going to be a full one, but the 'limits' of my response will yet bear frontally on our dynamics of revitalized *analytics* of secularism.

4. Traversing secular moral/legal commitments: a construal, and attendant complications

In getting an initial measure of what I am terming 'secular moral/legal commitments', I turn to the humanely resolute philosopher-theorist Charles Taylor whose rich corpus of writings offer a window into our theme of normative secularity. Of course, I will complicate this terrain on its own normative ground, but let us have our initial construal in all its detail. The reader, I hope, will understand my staying close to the letter and word of Taylor's explication.

Developing themes from his opus *A Secular Age*, Charles Taylor tells us that '(i)t is generally agreed that modern democracies have to be "secular"', and that '[while] a certain ethnocentricity attaches to this term ... even in the Western context it is far from limpid'.[18] He speaks quickly of 'at least two models abroad today of what constitutes a secular regime', both involving 'some kind of separation of church and state' – that 'the state can't be officially linked to some religious confession, except in a vestigial or largely symbolic sense' – but maintains that given the 'pluralism of society' secularism also requires 'some kind of neutrality, or "principled distance"'.[19] More stringently, yet, Taylor astutely posits that 'secularism involves in fact a complex requirement', in that it seeks out 'more than one good'. He singles out three 'goods', classifying them 'in the three categories of the French revolutionary trinity: liberty, equality, fraternity' which he elaborates as follows:

> (1) No one must be forced in the domain of religion, or basic belief. This is what is often defined a religious liberty, including, of course, the freedom not to believe. ... (2) There must be equality between people of different faiths or basic belief; no religious outlook or (religious or areligious) Weltanschauung can enjoy a privileged status, let alone be adopted as the official view of the state. Then, (3) all spiritual families must be heard, included in the ongoing process of determining what the society is about (its political identity), and how it is going to realize these goals (the exact regime of rights and privileges). This ... is what corresponds to "fraternity".[20]

To be sure, as Taylor also admits, these 'goals' can conflict, and 'sometimes we have to balance the goods involved here'. But – and this is important (as insisted upon by Taylor too) –

> (a) there is no such set of timeless principles which can be determined, at least in the detail they must be for a given political system, by pure reason alone; and (b) situations differ very much, and require different kinds of concrete realization of agreed general principles; so that some degree of working out is necessary in each situation. [And] it follows that (c) dictating the principles from some supposedly higher authority above the fray violates [fraternity].[21]

Of course, in committing himself to the secular moral/legal commitments of the order that he is here conceiving, it is true that Taylor is working off (if you will) 'the secular West' and its present or ongoing challenges. Need this ethnocentricity pose a debilitating constraint upon the space of our construal? I don't think so; and, besides, as I noted at the end of Section 3 above, our attempt is less about how the concept 'secular' represents than a 'theory' – some *normative* intimations, really – about *possessing* the concept secular. Taylor himself, in the article I have been quoting from as above, recognizes that the word 'secular' can 'crop up everywhere', and that there are 'subtle differences' in each iteration, 'which can bedevil cross-cultural discussion of these matters'.[22] He also admits that the 'constellation of terms, including "secular" and "religious", with all of its baggage of ambiguity and deep assumptions [in the history of the West] ... begins to travel' and can through 'creative and productive ... redefinitions ... leave the connotations of the word "secular" as they have evolved through Western history quietly to the side.'[23]

To be sure, one is certainly not denying a 'history' to secularism, but I am also saying that a characterization of secularism, even when approached in historical and/or anthropological terms, must also consider its taking on the aspects of an ideal; and *qua ideal* it can get a general formulation on the terms that we are here considering. [I realize that the politically perceptive philosopher and critic Akeel Bilgrami has in a recent work raised some very pertinent questions about such a procedure – as indeed the order of Taylor's favoured understanding of secularism – while going on to offer his own 'characterization' of secularism's 'content and context'.[24] I hope to engage with the full terms of this alternative construal elsewhere, but am flagging it all the same for the further challenges that it can pose for our normative orders of appraisal.] Let me return to the space of our construal devolving on the very normativity of secular moral/legal commitments (with Taylor as our foil, of course).

Taylor is reminding us that one needs to be wary of the 'wrong model' in dealing with the nature of our secular moral/legal commitments. He thus sharply observes: 'We think that secularism ... has to do with the relation of the state and religion; whereas in fact it has to do with the (correct) response of the democratic state to diversity ... [and, what is more, that in doing so] ... (t)here is no reason to single out religion, as against nonreligious, "secular" ... or atheist viewpoints.'[25] As he goes on to insist, all too ethnocentrically perhaps, '(i)ndeed the point of state neutrality is precisely to avoid favouring or disfavouring not just religious positions, but any basic position, religious or nonreligious. We cannot favour Christianity over Islam, nor can we favour religion over non-belief in religion, or vice versa.'[26]

Clearly, for Taylor, there is more to secularism than 'religion as the problem' – indeed that the 'idea that secularism makes a special case of religion arises from the history of its coming to be in the West',[27] but which certainly requires 'redefinition' even within the West. He also insists that we must resist 'the tendency to define secularism ... in terms of some institutional arrangement' as delivered in formulae such as 'the separation of church and state' or the 'necessity of religion from public space'[28] – what Taylor renders as a 'fetishization of the favoured institutional arrangements' – and that rather 'one should start from the goals [the three basic "goods", as detailed earlier] and derive the concrete arrangements from these.'[29] Thus, in terms of the 'revisionary polysemy' that Taylor is proposing here, as he affectingly states,

> what deserve to be called "secularist" regimes in contemporary democracy have to be conceived not primarily as bulwarks against religion but as good faith attempts to secure the three (or four) basic goals I outlined ... And this means that they attempt to shape their institutional arrangements, not to remain true to hallowed tradition, but to maximize the basic goals of liberty and equality between basic beliefs.[30]

Now it is a crucial aspect of Taylor's 'redefinition' of secularism and the reordering of our secular moral/legal commitments in this light that it places the institutional question as secondary to the ideals (or goods/goals) that can, and indeed must, animate our public avowal of these matters of normative secularity. And yet there can be difficulties here, which our public avowal of normative secularity and the attendant order of its secular moral/legal commitments (even in the way that Taylor re-characterizes it) must acknowledge and duly consider. Allow me to attend to two orders of complication bearing on our theme as reconstructed so far – one issuing from the very space of a history and anthropology of secularism that we sought to move beyond (Section 3 above) and the second consistent with the normative ground of appraisal as instantiated for us here by this ongoing section (Section 4). I am not particularly enamoured of the first order of complication, but will render it with some fullness all the same; while the second does bear on considerations that are weightier in clarifying the scope of what we are terming secular moral/legal commitments. I am also reminded of the remarkably prescient historian and early modern scholar Eric Nelson, who in a passing thought endearingly holds:

> [I]t may well be that we live, as Charles Taylor tells us, in a 'secular age', but if so, we nonetheless owe several of our most central political commitments to an age that was anything but. And it seems reasonable to suppose that we will not be able to understand the peculiar fault lines and dissonances of our contemporary political discourse until we come to terms with that basic, paradoxical fact.[31]

Be that as it may, I am still wary of the project as reconstructed by S. N. Balagandadhara and carried forward by Jakob De Roover, whose guiding premise (or, shall we say, founding rationale) is to approach the entire corpus of modern social and political thought as permeated by Christianity, and therefore as secularized versions of theological ideas.[32] The two orders of complication then.

As a way of instantiating the first order of complication, I turn to another more recent essay by Hussein Ali Agrama, who from within his history and ethnography of state, law, politics and religion in contemporary Egypt questions Taylor's 'redefinition' of normative secularity, maintaining that it (Taylor's redefinition) 'doesn't ultimately work, either as an analysis of or an ideal for secularism'.[33] He certainly finds salutary Taylor's suggestion that we must avoid the 'fetishization of the favoured institutional arrangements' which invariably singles out 'religion as the problem' and that secularism is better thought of as part of the democratic state's response to diversity; but maintains that Taylor's argument 'embeds a set of historical sensibilities and attitudes that it doesn't fully take into account and that serve to complicate and ultimately undermine it'.[34] Alluding to the 'confounding way that religious freedom is defined and implemented by a variety of contemporary states', he speaks of a 'distinctive structure of legalized suspicion' underwriting 'contemporary secularity', which while issuing from 'a distinctively liberal vigilance against power and its abuse' and 'a characteristically secular desire to draw a line between religion and material power' is 'further animated by a contradiction in the very understanding of belief … [one that] lends itself to an ever more pronounced vigilance against the potential power of religious beliefs and acts'.[35] In other words, the suggestion (through the situations explored by Agrama across different secular states, and not just limited to Egypt) 'that, under a liberal secular legal regime, suspicion of religious belief is the flip side of religious freedom; the one cannot be disentangled from the other', which ends up coercing people with respect to their basic beliefs or position and thereby opens up an 'aporia', within secularism, 'between the aspired-to freedoms and the means by which they are ideally achieved'.[36] For Agrama, therefore, 'Taylor's argument does not discern this aporia because it does not fully account for the contradictory structure of suspicion historically rooted in the secular ideal and practice of religious freedom'[37] and even 'seems to articulate' this contradictory structure '(d)espite Taylor's counselling against the singling out of religion'.[38]

To be sure, this reading of the way the contradictory structure of suspicion works in Taylor's argument about secularism is an intricate, albeit forced, one. For one, Agrama reads into Taylor's argument a construal of religion 'as essentially a species of belief', holding that such a construal 'is itself a historical outcome of the suspicion that divides it from and opposes it to knowledge' and even articulates into 'the principle that it ought to be separated from material power'[39]; and, secondly, that Taylor's insistence 'about the need to be united on a set of basic values' – even that 'such a unity is indispensable to a democratic state' – while seemingly a 'precondition for secular freedoms … is equally a characteristic manifestation of the secular state's modalities of suspicion' and, on a sociological register, has 'helped strengthen the state, increasing its sovereign sway over everyday social life'.[40] It seems to me, yet, that such a reading is constantly running against the limits of its own historical standpoint and its own unreflected context of emergence. In the context of Agrama, as we saw earlier (Section 3 above), this has to do with the fact that his order of 'questioning secularism' does not break with the general (scholarly?) genealogy we alluded at the very beginning of our interlocution (the division, namely, between the 'fact' of the religious and/or of the secular and the 'instrumental' use of religion and/or of secularism). But there is more, for, as the philosophically-minded historian Hans Blumenberg has called attention, there is also the ease with which we tend to confuse 'preconditions' (plainly, the histories of what led up to something) and 'effects' (the aggregate of the changes which that something causes or that unfold in respect to it). [Blumenberg was of course alluding to the history of science, but that also can pass!][41]

I suspect that such a conflation often underwrites Agrama – and, more generally, several histories and ethnographies on offer across terrains (as indeed in the 'discursive' content of the essays in our collection) – although it can be mentioned (in Agrama's defence, and perhaps also across our special number) that in determining what conditions are necessary about the specific workings of 'secular power', one may actually be involved in determining what is sufficient for those very conditions. It is nevertheless by no means clear, within the space of this forced, albeit intricate, construal, how the validity claim of the various diagnoses offered (including its own) should be understood. In fact, the charge that Agrama is pressing against Taylor's rendition of normative secularity – namely, that of denying the performativity of secularism (or even, on Agrama's terms, of being insufficiently attentive to the 'bind of suspicion in contemporary secularity') – could be turned against the former (that is, Agrama) as well. I am afraid demonstrating this would require one to be more exegetical than I have already been – working from within the moves internal to Agrama's questioning, while also turning (and returning) to the very terms of Taylor's redefinition of normative secularity – but that would take away from the larger point about normativity I wish to underscore here (and which will also prepare us for the second order of complication to follow). Normativity, on any register, is performative; and indeed that is the thought behind the quote from Georges Canguilhem that we placed at the head of our contribution. Canguilhem, of course, is traversing biological normativity, where the goal of every entity is to make an environment in which it *is* and can *thrive* (and therefore requiring an altering of the very grammar of subject and predicate that one may be either predisposed or inclined to posit in any given instance or stage or process).[42]

Indeed, quickly and somewhat formulaically, if one were to transpose the terms just disclosed to the terrain of our discussion, this would require us to think immanently with normative secularity and the space of its moral/legal commitments; and, given that all normativity is performative, we should probably admit and/or recognize that the various conditions and forces bearing upon normative secularity today can open a space within the latter that we can retroactively see as having always already existed. This implies, of course, seeing the space of 'normative secularity' as always phenomenologically charged and expressive, quite independently of the forces and conditions bearing upon it, while also being differentially enabled by those very conditions and force. Of course, a history and anthropology of secularism of the kind that Agrama delivers may also translate into this possibility; and certainly his characterization of 'the *problem-space* of secularism' where '(w)e remain bound to this problem space through the incessant suspicion it provokes' does encode it.[43] But, as I am maintaining, it is also premised on a forced constriction of the space of normative secularity, one tantamount to restricting the space of its performativity.

The normative force of Taylor's 'redefinition' of secularism – and the illumination of the nature and scope of secular moral/legal commitments as a whole which that prognosis affords – can still hold our attention. There is, however, a second order of complication that we must consider as part of normative secularity's immanent ground. In order to have a measure of this, let me turn to the insightful political theorist Cecile Laborde who, while admitting to Taylor's characterization of the 'secular age' as one in which 'religious belief no longer structures our social imaginary … [and instead] has become one option, one possibility, among others: one of the ways in which we give meaning to our lives', yet discerns that 'we secular moderns also give special primacy to freedom of religion, which is standardly presented as the archetypical liberal right'.[44] This, for Laborde, yields 'a paradox', which she formulates as follows: 'how (and why) do we protect freedom of religion in an age where religion is not special?'[45] Quite independent of the paradox itself, the ground traversed by Laborde is interesting; and to the extent her treatment finds its way through a specific 'translation' in law and policy terms of an aspect of Taylor's redefinition of normative secularity along the lines indicated above and which yields a theory of 'religious freedom' that calls for equal treatment of religious and secular 'conscience',[46] Laborde's discussion opens up further considerations at the heart of contemporary secularity and its own normative ground. [The discussion is also fascinating is outlining the larger overlays that attach to Taylor's examination, especially the latter's idea of 'strong evaluation' and the moral/legal ambiguities that can afflict the liberal ideal of neutrality toward the good life. The intricacies of this discussion, however, will not concern us here.]

Laborde urges us to consider, as part of an egalitarian theory of religious freedom emanating from normative secularity as configured through Taylor, the tensions that could underwrite such a theory, not quite only '(w)hat does it mean, exactly, to treat religious and nonreligious conceptions of the good alike?' but also 'Why is religious conduct worthy of protection in the first place?'.[47] She offers an important clarification impinging on the very nature and scope of secular moral/legal commitments when, with particular acuity and deference to Taylor's ideas about 'negative freedoms' in general, she alludes to 'a key feature of freedom of religion – one that is strangely neglected by contemporary liberals', namely (and I shall quote Laborde at some length here, for reasons that will become clear soon enough)

> *Freedom of religion, in contrast to more generic freedoms of thought, belief, and association, relies on a moralized distinction between valuable and nonvaluable activities and serves to protect a subset of the former.* It is a freedom to pursue a specific end and activity: it refers to the pursuit of a conception of the good with a specific shape, content, and form rather than the means through which any conception of the good can be pursued. *Furthermore, in the case of exemptions and accommodations ... freedom of religion generates demands of positive assistance in pursuing those activities. This means that, when adjudicating such claims, it must be decided which claim correctly expresses the values underpinning the general principle.*[48]

Mark the emphasis underscoring the lines that I have italicized above. What they entail are (as Laborde also acknowledges) 'openly perfectionist evaluations, setting "trivial" against "central" commitments and "mere preferences" against "core convictions"'; and, what is more, that *'(s)uch perfectionist discriminations ... are inherent in any serious reflection about the value of freedom of religion'*.[49] The point has a direct bearing on most of the papers of our collection – specifically those by Matthew John, Manisha Sethi, Neshat Quaiser and perhaps also Malvika Maheshwari – in that even as these 'perfectionist discriminations' are alluded in the course of their treatment, the prognosis on offer seems to be quite dismissive of such propensities as part of a general genealogical thrust (along the lines we have disclosed in our foregoing sections). Of course, one is not denying that such 'perfectionist discriminations' can also end up (as Laborde observes) 'giv[ing] the state the authority arbitrarily to discriminate between better and worse ways to exercise one's freedoms'[50] – and clearly this is what our contributors here are arraigning against – but this does not of itself restrict (or even constrict) the space of normative secularity. If indeed, as we disclosed above in this very section, normativity on any register is performative, then the performativity of normative secularity has also to do with its moral/legal commitments becoming normative not quite only in the sense disclosed by our contributors here, but also along the lines that we have been formulating. I realize that this affirmation does not take care of all the problems inherent to normative secularity and the nature and scope of its moral/legal commitments. In perspective are forms of 'truth-speaking' – or 'truth-seeking' – inherent to (modern) law and the state, which while presupposing a given organization of subject, referent and world can also be productive of its normative refashioning.

Laborde, to be sure, is inflecting the 'paradox' underlying contemporary secularity in a way that is redemptive of its promise of equal treatment of religious and secular conscience. And yet, as she perceptively remarks, there can be problems in 'collapsing religion into conscience and implicitly assuming that the latter category is more inclusive than the former'.[51] More emphatically, for Laborde, 'the redescription of freedom of religion as freedom of conscience' can have the effect of 'perversely encourag[ing] the most fundamentalist and rigid interpretations of religious dogma', while also driving a 'normative wedge between two kinds of meaning-giving commitments, those that are inflexible and conscientious and those that are habitual and embodied' and in the process 'singling out individual conscience – as opposed to cultural or community membership – as especially worthy of protection'.[52] Of course, this latter effect may be important for securing further the nature of secular moral/legal commitments. But the upshot may be that, as Laborde attentively reminds, 'a self-proclaimed inclusive theory of freedom of religion actually excludes what most religious believers would take to be freedom of religion to be about'.[53]

Surely the orders of this construal is premised on religion 'as a matter of private conviction rather than of public performance', but (as Laborde helpfully prompts) one 'could add that, even when freedom of religion relates to actual performances and practices ... it still draws its moral force from its presumed connection with individual conscience'.[54] In fact, for Laborde, the redescription of freedom of religion as freedom of conscience, while consistent with the individualization and subjectification of religious experience in contemporary societies, 'tends to favour a Protestant understanding of what a religion is'[55] Likewise, with reference to the problematic category of conscience, it can translate into a 'proliferation of claims', which leads to the further problem of distinguishing, within freedom of conscience, 'trivial from morally significant beliefs', as well as getting a measure of 'what conscience really requires of us'.[56] In addition then, I think, collapsing the distinction between religious and secular conscience can translate into obscuring the reasons why religious conscience needs strong protection and, at the same time, ignoring some of the strongest justifications for protecting secular convictions.

To be sure, conflicts between the demands of religious conscience and the commands of the state involve more than conflicts involving secular conscience. The complications thus opened up would certainly require us to revisit ideas of normative secularity and redraw the nature of secular moral/legal commitments. But, as Laborde also clearly states, the problems alluded to 'are not so much fatal flaws as unavoidable tensions within the politicolegal philosophy of religious exemptions',[57] accentuated of course by the modern ideal of neutrality towards the good life. I think this latter point needs underscoring, particularly since some of our contributors here in this special number are concerned to deliver directly on the problematic character of the 'essential practice' test as determined by and within Indian courts. At stake, I reiterate here all over again, is the very ground and horizon of our secular moral/legal commitments.

5. Toward a revitalized analytics of secularism?

I realize that my 'afterword' has exceeded its brief, but that is the lure of this special number. In succumbing to it, and perhaps also taking it forward, I join my fellow contributors in advancing the claims of this collection, as part and as whole. A few final remarks all the same. Considering that these are rounding thoughts, I will have to be phlegmatic and conclusive.

How might this juxtaposing of the claims of an anthropology and history of secularism with the demands of a normative order of construal given over to securing secularism change the way in which we approach the very nature and scope of secular moral/legal commitments? For one, the general (scholarly?) genealogy implicating the study of these themes – including the essays that comprise this special number – both reinforcing and reinforced by, as it were, the division between the 'fact' of the religious and/or of the secular and the 'instrumental' use of religion and/or of secularism, would have to be transcended. The 'moral psychology' of religion (as indeed of the secular) would no longer be the phenomenological (or lived) reality against which the politics of secularism is configured and/or staged. Second, even if one wishes to stay with this diagnostic genealogy, we need to consider, in the course of pressing after more complex understandings of the mediations between religion, law and state, the ground and horizon of 'normative secularity' from within the questions that it provokes *and* the very normativity of the categories that it presupposes. And finally, normative secularity can and must emerge wholly as a discursive register in its own right, whose immanent performativity can set off in ways not entirely contingent upon an anthropology and history of secularism a complex series of questions about the very nature and scope of 'secular moral/legal commitments' specifically.

After all, as we affirmed above, normativity is performative *tout court*. A problematic of secular moral/legal commitments might yet have to break with the pluralizing universalism of our times, even as it remains wary of a 'triumphalist history of the secular'.

Notes

1. Canguilhem, *The Normal and the Pathological*, 126–27.
2. See Asad, *Formations of the Secular*.
3. Ibid., 16.
4. See Nandy, 'The Politics of Secularism and the Recovery of Religious Tolerance'.
5. Ibid., 70–91.
6. Ibid., 70.
7. Hegde, 'Always Already Secular? Afterthoughts on the Secular-Communal Question', 327–28.
8. Agrama, *Questioning Secularism*, 23–31.
9. Ibid., 29.
10. Ibid., 2.
11. Ibid.
12. Ibid., 30.
13. Ibid., 30–31.
14. Ibid., 31.
15. Ibid.
16. Ibid., 30–31.
17. See Hegde, 'Always Already Secular? Afterthoughts on the Secular-Communal Question'.
18. Taylor, 'What Does Secularism Mean?', 309. Also, Taylor, *A Secular Age*.
19. Taylor, 'What Does Secularism Mean?'. The term 'principled distance' is, as Taylor acknowledges, drawn from Bhargava, 'What Is Secularism For?'.
20. Ibid., 309.
21. Ibid., 310.
22. Ibid., 303.
23. Ibid., 308; see also Taylor, 'Can Secularism Travel?'.
24. See Bilgrami, 'Secularism: Its Content and Context'.
25. Taylor, 'What Does Secularism Mean?', 311.
26. Ibid.
27. Ibid., 311.
28. Ibid.
29. Ibid., 314.
30. Ibid., 325.
31. Nelson, *The Hebrew Republic*, 5.
32. See Balagandadhara, *The Heathen in His Blindness ..*, as also his *Reconceptualizing India Studies*. For De Roover, see his *Europe, India, and the Limits of Secularism*.
33. Agrama, 'Religious Freedom and the Bind of Suspicion in Contemporary Secularity', 301.
34. Ibid., 302.
35. Ibid., 302, 306–07.
36. Ibid., 307.
37. Ibid.
38. Ibid., 309.
39. Ibid., 307.
40. Ibid., 308.
41. See Blumenberg, *The Genesis of the Copernican World*, 127.
42. See Canguilhem, *The Normal and the Pathological*.
43. Agrama, 'Religious Freedom and the Bind of Suspicion in Contemporary Secularity', 311; see also his *Questioning Secularism*, 23–31.
44. Laborde, 'Protecting Freedom of Religion in the Secular Age', 269.
45. Ibid.
46. See, in particular, Maclure and Taylor, *Secularism and Freedom of Conscience*.
47. Laborde, 'Protecting Freedom of Religion in the Secular Age', 270–71.
48. Ibid., 273, emphasis added.
49. Ibid., emphasis added.
50. Ibid., 274.
51. Ibid.
52. Ibid., 274–76.
53. Ibid., 276.
54. Ibid.
55. Ibid., 278.
56. Ibid., 277–78.

57. Ibid., 278.

Disclosure statement

No potential conflict of interest was reported by the author.

Bibliography

Agrama, H. A. *Questioning Secularism: Islam, Sovereignty, and the Rule of Law in Modern Egypt*. Chicago: University of Chicago Press, 2012.

Agrama, H. A. "Religious Freedom and the Bind of Suspicion in Contemporary Secularity." In *Politics of Religious Freedom*, edited by W. F. Sullivan, E. S. Hurd, S. Mahmood, and P. G. Danchin, 301–312. Chicago: University of Chicago Press, 2015.

Asad, T. *Formations of the Secular: Christianity, Islam, Modernity*. Stanford, CA: Stanford University Press, 2003.

Balagangadhara, S. N. *'The Heathen in His Blindness ...': Asia, the West and the Dynamic of Religion*. Leiden: E. J. Brill, 1994.

Balagangadhara, S. N. *Reconceptualizing India Studies*. Delhi: Oxford University Press, 2012.

Bhargava, R. "What Is Secularism For?" In *Secularism and Its Critics*, edited by R. Bhargava, 486–542. Delhi: Oxford University Press, 1998.

Bilgrami, A. *Secularism, Identity and Enchantment*. Cambridge, MA: Harvard University Press, 2014.

Blumenberg, H. *The Genesis of the Copernican World*. Cambridge, MA: MIT Press, 1987.

Canguilhem, G. *The Normal and the Pathological*. New York: Zone Books, 1991.

De Roover, J. *Europe, India, and the Limits of Secularism*. Delhi: Oxford University Press, 2015.

Hegde, S. "Always Already Secular? Afterthoughts on the Secular-Communal Question." *Economic and Political Weekly* 40, no. 4 (2005): 322–334.

Laborde, C. "Protecting Freedom of Religion in the Secular Age." In *Politics of Religious Freedom*, edited by W. F. Sullivan, E. S. Hurd, S. Mahmood, and P. G. Danchin, 269–279. Chicago: University of Chicago Press, 2015.

Maclure, J., and C. Taylor. *Secularism and Freedom of Conscience*. Cambridge, MA: Harvard University Press, 2011.

Nandy, A. "The Politics of Secularism and the Recovery of Religious Tolerance." In *Mirrors of Violence: Communities, Riots and Survivors in South Asia*, edited by V. Das, 69–93. Delhi: Oxford University Press, 1990.

Nelson, E. *The Hebrew Republic: Jewish Sources and the Transformation of European Political Thought*. Cambridge, MA: Harvard University Press, 2010.

Taylor, C. *A Secular Age*. Cambridge, MA: Harvard University Press, 2007.

Taylor, C. *Dilemmas and Connections: Selected Essays*. Cambridge, MA: Harvard University Press, 2011.

Taylor, C. "Can Secularism Travel?" In *Beyond the Secular West*, edited by A. Bilgrami, 1–27. New York: Columbia University Press, 2016.

Index

Note: Page numbers followed by 'n' denote endnotes.

Taylor & Francis Group
an informa business

Taylor & Francis eBooks

www.taylorfrancis.com

A single destination for eBooks from Taylor & Francis with increased functionality and an improved user experience to meet the needs of our customers.

90,000+ eBooks of award-winning academic content in Humanities, Social Science, Science, Technology, Engineering, and Medical written by a global network of editors and authors.

TAYLOR & FRANCIS EBOOKS OFFERS:

- A streamlined experience for our library customers
- A single point of discovery for all of our eBook content
- Improved search and discovery of content at both book and chapter level

REQUEST A FREE TRIAL

support@taylorfrancis.com

Routledge
Taylor & Francis Group

CRC Press
Taylor & Francis Group